**North Carolina Planters and
Their Children, 1800–1860**

NORTH CAROLINA PLANTERS AND THEIR CHILDREN

1800–1860

JANE TURNER CENSER

Louisiana State University Press
Baton Rouge and London

Copyright © 1984 by Louisiana State University Press
All rights reserved
Manufactured in the United States of America
Designer: Albert Crochet
Typeface: Linotron Trump Mediaeval
Typesetter: Moran Colorgraphic Incorporated
Printer & Binder: Vail-Ballou Press

Publication of this book has been assisted by
a grant from the Andrew W. Mellon Foundation.

LIBRARY OF CONGRESS CATALOGING IN PUBLICATION DATA

Censer, Jane Turner, 1951–
  North Carolina planters and their children, 1800–1860.

  Bibliography: p.
  Includes index.
    1. Family—North Carolina—History—19th century.   2. Plantation owners—North
Carolina—History—19th century.   3. Plantation life—North Carolina—History—19th
century.   4. North Carolina—Social life and customs.   I. Title.
HQ535.C38   1984   305.5′232′09756   83-19966
ISBN 0-8071-1135-X

*To my father
and the memory of my mother*

Contents

Maps and Tables

Preface

Although southern planters have long evoked general interest, until recently little scholarly research focused upon that elite. To be sure, biographical and political studies have examined individual planters. But analyses of them as a group generally appeared only incidentally to examinations of plantation slavery, agriculture, or politics.[1] Relatively little was done to ascertain social ideology or behavior.

In the last several years, research on the planters as a social group has begun to flower. At least two developments in the discipline of history have contributed to this upsurge of interest. A large—and still growing—corpus of excellent studies of antebellum black life and slave culture has made scholars realize that similar areas in the lives of southern white folks have not been explored.[2] Another influence,

1. Such works include: Weymouth T. Jordan, *Hugh Davis and His Alabama Plantation* (University, Ala., 1948); William K. Scarborough, *The Overseer: Plantation Management in the Old South* (Baton Rouge, 1966); Edward M. Steel, Jr., *T. Butler King of Georgia* (Athens, Ga., 1964). Earlier studies of planters are: Rosser H. Taylor, "The Gentry of Antebellum South Carolina," *North Carolina Historical Review*, XVII (1940), 114–31; Chalmers G. Davidson, *The Last Foray: The South Carolina Planters of 1860* (Columbia, S.C., 1971).

2. See, for example, James L. Roark, *Masters Without Slaves: Southern Planters in the Civil War and Reconstruction* (New York, 1977); Russell L . Blake, "Ties of Intimacy: Social Values and Personal Relationships of Ante-bellum Slaveholders" (Ph.D. dissertation, University of Michigan, 1978); Daniel Blake Smith, *Inside the Great House: Planter Family Life in Eighteenth-Century Chesapeake Society* (Ithaca, N.Y., 1980); George M. Fredrickson, "Masters and Mudsills: The Role of Race in the Planter Ideology of South Carolina," in Jack R. Censer and N. Steven Steinert (eds.), *South Atlantic Urban Studies*, II (1978), 34–48. Among the most influential books of the last decade on slave life are Lawrencë W. Levine, *Black Culture and Black Consciousness: Afro-American Folk Thought from Slavery to Freedom* (New York, 1977); Herbert G. Gutman, *The Black Family in Slavery and Freedom, 1750–1925* (New York, 1976); Eugene D. Genovese, *Roll, Jordan, Roll: The World the Slaves Made* (New York, 1974); Leon F. Litwack, *Been in the Storm So Long: The Aftermath of Slavery* (New York, 1979).

no doubt, has been the "new social history" with its emphasis upon close scrutiny of social and occupational groupings.

The growing interest in planters has thus far sparked increased controversy about their outlook and behavior, since the newest assessments vary widely. On the one hand, historians following the lead of Eugene D. Genovese have tended to view the large slaveholders as seigneurs who presided rather grandly and autocratically over plantations filled with black and white dependents. On the other hand, dissenters have pointed out more capitalist "bourgeois" aspects of the planters' attitudes and actions.[3]

A new approach to these questions is taken here through the systematic study of the family, a major area of planters' lives. I have chosen to focus upon home and family as a way to penetrate the planters' social and cultural world. Scholars generally agree that in the functioning of a family the transmission of values from one generation to the next can be discerned. An examination of the elite's family relations also has value in itself, since historians have only recently begun such explorations.[4]

Thus, to till these fertile areas, I decided to set up a case study of the planter family in one southern state, North Carolina. That appeared fruitful, in part, because those socioeconomic leaders have been little examined and the only studies of them have focused upon a sin-

3. Eugene D. Genovese, *The Political Economy of Slavery: Studies in the Economy and Society of the Slave South* (New York, 1965), and *Roll, Jordan, Roll*; Michael P. Johnson, "Planters and Patriarchy: Charleston, 1800–1860," *Journal of Southern History*, XLVI (1980), 45–72; Bertram Wyatt-Brown, "The Ideal Typology and Antebellum Southern History: A Testing of a New Approach," *Societas*, V (1975), 16–20; Dorothy Ann Gay, "The Tangled Skein of Romanticism and Violence in the Old South: The Southern Response to Abolitionism and Feminism" (Ph.D. dissertation, University of North Carolina, 1975). For opposing points of view, see Blake, "Ties of Intimacy," 211–14; Robert W. Fogel and Stanley L. Engerman, *Time on the Cross: The Economics of American Negro Slavery* (Boston, 1974), 73, 103–106; James Oakes, *The Ruling Race: A History of American Slaveholders* (New York, 1982), 153–91.

4. Lawrence Stone, *The Family, Sex and Marriage in England, 1500–1800* (New York, 1977), 3–4; Philippe Ariès, *Centuries of Childhood: A Social History of Family Life*, trans. Robert Baldick (New York, 1962), 9–11. On the planter family, see Wyatt-Brown, "The Ideal Typology"; M. P. Johnson, "Planters and Patriarchy"; Anne Firor Scott, *The Southern Lady: From Pedestal to Politics, 1830–1930* (Chicago, 1970); Ann Williams Boucher, "Wealthy Planter Families in Nineteenth-Century Alabama" (Ph.D. dissertation, University of Connecticut, 1978); Steven Mac Stowe, "All the Relations of Life: A Study in Sexuality, Family, and Social Values in the Southern Planter Class" (Ph.D. dissertation, State University of New York at Stony Brook, 1979).

gle prominent family.[5] An investigation of North Carolina planters should also provide insights into the lives of planters Southwide. Most likely the Carolinians did not differ significantly from those of similar economic standing elsewhere in the South. Social interactions show no distinctions; Tar Heel planters in areas bordering Virginia and South Carolina freely visited and socialized with their wealthy out-of-state neighbors. In marriage, an area deemed important for showing equality between groups, planters from other states showed no reluctance to become allied to North Carolina's elite.

North Carolina planters, moreover, were thoroughly integrated into the staple crop cultivation that other southern planters followed. Cotton, tobacco, and rice, important elsewhere in the South, were principal crops in the Old North State as well. In short, socially and economically, North Carolina large slaveholders appear to have resembled their counterparts in other southern states. Although it is possible that much higher concentrations of slaves in the lower South produced a planter society intrinsically different from the upper South's, two recent studies of planters Southwide lend no weight to such a supposition. James L. Roark's and Russell L. Blake's investigations of the slaveholding elite's attitudes do not indicate any differences between North Carolina and other southern planters—whether upper or lower South.[6]

An investigation of all planter families, even in North Carolina alone, would be impracticable because of the large number involved. This project surveys a more manageable group, all those owning seventy or more slaves in 1830. Seventy necessarily is a somewhat arbitrary number. Gavin Wright has characterized the distribution of slaveholding sizes as "remarkably smooth," thus indicating that no "natural" cut-off point exists. Seventy slaves was a large holding on a rice, tobacco, or cotton plantation. Since little reason exists for be-

5. For instance, Charles Richard Sanders, *The Cameron Plantation in Central North Carolina (1776–1973) and Its Founder, Richard Bennehan* (Durham, N.C., 1974); J. Carlyle Sitterson, "Lewis Thompson, a Carolinian and His Louisiana Plantation, 1848–1888: A Study in Absentee Ownership," in Fletcher M. Green (ed.), *Essays in Southern History* (Chapel Hill, 1949), 16–27; Edward W. Phifer, Jr., "Saga of a Burke County Family," *North Carolina Historical Review*, XXXIX (1962), 1–17, 140–47, 305–339.

6. Lewis Cecil Gray, *History of Agriculture in the Southern United States to 1860* (Washington, D.C., 1933), I, 119–20, 349, 438–40, 444–45, II, 909–910; Roark, *Masters Without Slaves*; Blake, "Ties of Intimacy."

lieving these slaveowners radically differed from those with forty or fifty slaves, a study of them should also illuminate the familial life of other wealthy planters. My sample will be called great planters, the planter elite, wealthy North Carolinians, or, more simply, planters; and unless specifically noted, those terms apply to both men and women.[7]

I have also found it useful to narrow my focus in other ways. Rather than describing the entire range of kinship, I concentrate upon the conjugal unit of parents and children. Relationships within that smaller group were most significant to planters, and that unit constituted the most common household. Although I touch upon all aspects of the conjugal family, the generational exchange between parents and children is central. Subjects such as the relations between husbands and wives and among siblings deserve closer examination, but treating them more fully here would distract without appreciably altering the tenor or conclusions of my study.[8]

This analysis of the conjugal family explores what are often held to be its most significant areas. Family composition and demographic characteristics form a basic backdrop. Since I agree with those scholars who believe the family to be a process rather than a fixed, unchanging entity, I attempt to capture the planter household at its important tasks: the socialization and education of children, the creation of new families through courtship and marriage, and the intergenerational transfer of property in portioning and inheritance.[9]

Although the years 1800 through 1860 are considered, most closely detailed is the period after 1830 representing the apogee of the plan-

7. Generally scholars have defined a planter as the owner of twenty slaves and have called the owner of fifty or more slaves a large planter or planter-aristocrat. Even the group holding fifty slaves in North Carolina in 1830 included over four hundred individuals, too large an aggregation for the intensive examination here undertaken. See Kenneth M. Stampp, *The Peculiar Institution: Slavery in the Antebellum South* (New York, 1956), 30. Gavin Wright, *The Political Economy of the Cotton South: Households, Markets, and Wealth in the Nineteenth Century* (New York, 1978), 32.

8. When I conducted the research for this project, I intended to treat all kin relations. The discovery, however, that planters' family lives revolved around the conjugal family led me to focus upon it. Such scrutiny does not mean to deny the existence of strong bonds to other kin; it simply asserts the primacy of what nineteenth-century people called the "family circle."

9. For example, see Tamara K. Hareven, "Cycles, Courses and Cohorts: Reflections on Theoretical and Methodological Approaches to the Historical Study of Family Development," *Journal of Social History*, XII (1978), 97–109.

tation system based upon slave labor. The tale ends at 1861, but not because the Civil War deposed the North Carolina great planters or stripped them of their wealth. In fact, many families appear to have weathered the crisis and to have retained much nonslave property.[10] But dislocations and exigencies of war disrupted family life at least temporarily, and that story is both complex and worth telling separately.

By studying specific members of a social group over a relatively limited time, I hope to bring them into sharp focus. I have also sought to place North Carolina planters in a broader context by frequent reference to the growing body of literature in family history. The family practices of other American and western European groups—especially those of similar high economic standing—should provide a perspective for better understanding of the planters and their society. My study should in turn contribute to family history, since relatively little attention has been paid nineteenth-century people who were not urban, immigrant, or a part of the emerging industrial order. Examining the planters can tell us about a wealthy rural group's attitudes and actions.

Indeed, North Carolina planters were strongly influenced by the sentimentalization of family life and children that swept like a tidal wave over the wealthy—and perhaps others—in western European and American societies during the eighteenth and nineteenth centuries. The causes and emergence of the "modern" child-centered planter family will not be examined here, for that institution was well established in North Carolina by 1800. Most likely, large slaveholders there, like their counterparts in the Chesapeake studied by Daniel Blake Smith and the wealthy in English society examined by Randolph Trumbach and Lawrence Stone, moved toward this orientation sometime in the mid- to late eighteenth century.[11]

10. Dwight B. Billings, Jr., *Planters and the Making of a "New South": Class, Politics, and Development in North Carolina, 1865–1900* (Chapel Hill, 1979), 47–65, 71–82.

11. D. B. Smith, *Inside the Great House;* Randolph Trumbach, *The Rise of the Egalitarian Family: Aristocratic Kinship and Domestic Relations in Eighteenth-Century England* (New York, 1978); Stone, *The Family, Sex and Marriage.* See also Carl N. Degler, *At Odds: Women and the Family in America from the Revolution to the Present* (New York, 1980), 3–9.

Not only did North Carolina planters share in the fascination with family life so common among the privileged in nineteenth-century America, they also held high expectations for their numerous progeny. Parental affection interacted in various ways with this desire for successful, self-motivated offspring. In the areas of education, career, and mate choice, a growing respect for the younger generation's opinions and wishes characterized parental action. And an examination of the second generation's later economic position shows that the elders had cause for pride as well as affection. Although many children could not rival the parental level of wealth, most quite successfully maintained high economic position.

The planters' relations with their slaves form a stark contrast to this picture of domesticity. A scrutiny of black-white interaction reveals the emotional gap between the two. Few wealthy whites bridged the chasm that their racism, fear, and view of blacks as property had created between them and their slaves. An irony of planters' lives lay in the bifurcation of their beliefs and behavior regarding their own families and those regarding blacks.

In the research and writing of this book, I have received much help and encouragement from numerous people. The capable staffs of the North Carolina Division of Archives and History, the North Carolina State Library and its Genealogical Section, the North Carolina Collection at the University of North Carolina, and the Manuscript Department of Perkins Library at Duke University were invariably helpful and informative. Carolyn Wallace and her associates made research in the Southern Historical Collection at the University of North Carolina a pleasure. I am grateful for their efforts to make microfilmed copies of several collections available to me through interlibrary loan. Ron Vestal, Lori Overington, Ed Morris, and Joe Mobley helped to make my time at the Archives enjoyable as well as useful. Michelle Lawing was kind enough to check several references that I had misplaced. Stephen Kraft prepared the maps with his usual skill.

I wish to thank Willie Lee Rose especially. While overseeing this study's inception, she greatly aided its conceptualization, research, and writing. Her indirect contribution to it through her tutelage in the study of history has been even larger. I value the kind, careful, and tolerant guidance that has characterized her as a teacher. William W. Freehling and Ronald G. Walters conscientiously waded through many drafts, and their comments forced me to evaluate and sharpen many of my arguments. At an early stage Joel Williamson graciously helped me to sort through my questions and formulate precise answers. Lenard Berlanstein read several drafts and offered suggestions from his own wealth of knowledge about European and American social and family history. James C. Turner's painstakingly thorough analysis of this work led to important improvements. Among the others who gave me helpful criticism and advice were J. William Harris, Laurence Glasco, James T. Currie, and James Klotter. My colleagues at the Frederick Law Olmsted Papers, Charles C. McLaughlin and Charles E. Beveridge, have been very supportive of my interest in and work on this non-Olmstedian topic.

My husband Jack R. Censer has contributed in a multiplicity of ways to this study. From its very beginning, he has given generously of his time to discuss and help me resolve problems ranging from methodology to interpretation. He has also read and criticized the many drafts the manuscript passed through, and practically every page is better written and thought-out because of his labor. I am grateful for his willingness to read and think far more about North Carolina planters than he ever dreamed possible. He also knows my appreciation for helping me cope with the many ups and downs that accompany a project such as this.

Note on Sources and Methodology

The specific group of people studied here was selected and traced in the following way. All slaveholdings of seventy or more slaves in a single county—181 in all—formed the group abstracted from the 1830 federal manuscript census. One hundred seventy-six people in forty-one counties owned these parcels. Other sources indicated that 5 of this original group were overseers so these men were dropped from consideration.[1] Unfortunately I was unable to ascertain their employers. I also removed another 3 men whose large slaveholdings appeared to be the property of cooperative business ventures.[2] One hundred sixty-eight planters including 2 who jointly owned one holding formed the population studied. Twenty-two of them (totaling 21 holdings) had no legitimate offspring, and another 22 moved their permanent residence to another state. The remaining 124 planters, who lived in North Carolina and left direct descendants, receive closest scrutiny for their family practices and attitudes.

Because the population schedule of the federal census of 1830 forms the source for the group studied, some evaluation of its merits appears necessary. As the only statewide indicator of wealth, it is indispensable. Still some unavoidable shortcomings of the document should also be mentioned. First, its only measurement of wealth (before 1850) is the number of slaves owned. Second, the census does not

1. These five men were Michael Hollands of Hyde County and Thomas Hall, Henry Hall, John R. Chestnut, and Jobe Smith of Jones County.
2. These men were George Blaney of Brunswick County and William H. Williams and Thomas J. Robards of Burke County. Blaney was a captain in the U.S. Army Corps of Engineers, and the slaves listed as belonging to him had probably been hired out for a federal project near Wilmington. The two Burke County holdings probably belonged to cooperative gold mining operations.

consistently indicate the slaves' owner when they were hired out or rented—a failing that tax lists usually share. Third, censuses sometimes list the steward or overseer on absentee plantations as the slaveowner, a mistake that is relatively easy to discover.

Other drawbacks are more indirectly linked to the census' shortcomings. This study examines only those planters who owned seventy or more slaves in a single holding within one county. Obviously some slaveowners may have possessed that number but in two or more holdings in the same or differing counties or even outside the state. I deemed the problems of finding and combining such holdings too great to attempt. Therefore, some elite planters may have been omitted. Since the group surveyed still included many planters with holdings that crossed county lines and with more distant properties, such omissions should not affect the sample's reliability. In general, the large number of wealthy slaveholders studied would suggest that any omitted would be similar to those scrutinized.[3]

To penetrate the lives of great planters, I linked various public and private records. Tracing the rural wealthy does not pose the same problems that occur with other social groups. The county was a smaller unit in population than contemporary cities, the setting for most groups that other historians have studied through record linkage. My search was further aided by the distinctive surnames many planters possessed, and many had middle names as well. The other public records such as tax lists, deeds, and inventories further confirmed their high economic standing.[4]

To learn more about planters' social and family lives, I consulted a variety of sources. I determined religious affiliation by church histories, membership rolls, gift deeds or bequests to churches, family letters, and local and county histories. Given the strength of individual preference in such areas, I was extremely wary of attributing religious inclinations of one family member to another. The planters' kinship ties and socioeconomic background were also evident in such

3. For discussions of the census as a tool for measuring wealth, see Hyman Alterman, *Counting People: The Census in History* (New York, 1969), 202–221; Jonathan M. Wiener, *Social Origins of the New South: Alabama, 1860–1885* (Baton Rouge, 1978), 235–46.

4. See Ian Winchester, "The Linkage of Historical Records by Man and Computer: Techniques and Problems," *Journal of Interdisciplinary History*, I (1970), 107–124.

local histories, published genealogical works, and compiled unpublished genealogies held by the North Carolina Division of Archives and History, as well as in wills and inventories of both the planters and their parents. Newspaper announcements of marriages, county marriage bonds, genealogies, and family records revealed the number of marriages and marriage partners of 134 of the 168 planters.

Much of my effort focused upon a reconstitution of the planters' conjugal families. Although I was not able to pinpoint the number of marriages among some childless planters and even a few of the planters with children, I was able to learn the identity of most children in 122 of the 124 families remaining in North Carolina. Although wills and documents settling the estate usually identified children alive at the planter's death, I supplemented this list with family Bible records, tombstone records prepared by the WPA (both held by the North Carolina Division of Archives and History), newspaper death notices as well as genealogical and church records. Such supplementary materials almost always boosted the total number of children found. Since no systematic state or local recording of births or deaths existed, some babies born dead or dying in infancy were not discovered or even discoverable. Thus I was able to obtain only very crude indicators of family size and of child mortality.

My information upon the education of planters' children came from a number of publications and unpublished sources such as manuscript collections. Documentary editions such as that compiled by Charles L. Coon on North Carolina academies, alumni directories, and institutional histories provided information on the training of numerous children. Newspaper notices as well as alumni directories and the census' listing of occcupation contributed to my tally of the number of planters' sons pursuing professional or nonagricultural careers.

As I began to chart the marriages of the younger generation in North Carolina, marriage bonds and newspaper announcements formed my major sources. Since marriage bonds were taken out in the county where the bride lived, they sometimes proved difficult to locate for planters' sons who married outside their home county. A microfiche name index to all extant marriage bonds recently prepared by the North Carolina Division of Archives and History should make such searching considerably easier. A more serious flaw is the paucity of evidence provided by the marriage bond: merely the names of the couple planning to wed and of their bondsmen and witnesses and the date when the bond was obtained. Only through newspaper announcements can the name of the bride's father and possibly his residence and that of the groom be ascertained; there is no general way to determine the name of the groom's father. Such sketchy information meant that a thorough economic analysis could not be attempted. It also reduced the number of cases in which I was able to calculate age at first marriage and place of residence for bride and groom. Similarly my analysis of cousin marriage was limited to families for which I could construct kinship networks stretching back several generations, and I undoubtedly overlooked some unions between cousins.

Tracing the transfer of property between the generations, especially through formal deeds of gift, presented difficult problems, many of which stemmed from different practices of registration. Generally deeds to slaves were recorded in the county where the buyer or grantee lived; deeds to land, in the county where the tract was located. North Carolina planters, however, often owned land outside their home county, and their children frequently lived in other counties or states and sometimes moved several times. Variations in the quality of indexing by county clerks and the destruction or loss of records further added to the difficulties and ensured that my reconstruction of gift giving could only be partial and incomplete.

The final disposition of planters' property appeared in their wills, generally easy to discover, or in the settlement of their estates. The North Carolina Division of Archives and History has generally arranged both wills and estates papers alphabetically within the records of the county of origin. I do supply volume numbers whenever relevant. By necessity my characterizations of how wills divided property are rough estimates of the level of equality. Only with those planters who explicitly called for equality of inheritance could one be sure how one child's actual share compared with another's. I did attempt to take into account property that had earlier been given formally or informally. I did not include in my reckoning small legacies given to grandchildren or body servants, keepsakes, or extra payment for services performed by children.

In wills and earlier property transfers, I discovered that the nine women of the group—all widows—posed some special problems. Tracing all property transfers by these women and the planters' widows revealed that, almost without exception, women gained control of property only by their husbands' deaths and that even then their holdings were actually much smaller than the estate usually had been. Thus, I decided not to group deeds of gift or wills by women planters with those of the other planters but instead substituted the property arrangements drawn up by their deceased husbands. That the disposal of property by women also seemed to follow a different pattern from the males' further confirmed my decision to treat them separately.

Tracing these planters' families over time in the seventh manuscript census gave me a chance to measure the second generation's economic position and geographical mobility. For my discussion of children's prosperity, I elected to include only offspring over twenty-one years of age and living in North Carolina. I omitted the descendants of any deceased offspring and also any unmarried (either single or widowed) women over twenty-one (unless property was recorded for them). Census takers, influenced by the biases of the day, were apt either to overlook women's property or to include it with that owned by a male in the same household. I included the husbands of planters' deceased daughters—even those husbands who had remarried—because they usually received and retained their late wives' estates and legacies. Since widows by law received only a small part of their deceased husbands' estates, I assumed that the property of remarried widows of planters' sons did not accurately reflect the sons' wealth, and I omitted those women and their new husbands.

Several other decisions made regarding the calculation of wealth are also noteworthy. To determine the number of large slaveholdings in each county in 1850 and 1860, I used my own tally of slaveholdings from the manuscript slave schedules of the seventh and eighth federal censuses; my figures varied slightly from the published totals. Also my survey of the younger generation's wealth holding is not strictly analogous to most surveys of wealth, since I included off-spring who were not heads of a household (the usual measuring unit). I also counted a few people twice—in cases in which one planter's son had married another's daughter or in which a man had married women from two elite families, since these people represented more than one family.

My examination of the second generation's patterns of geographical mobility encountered some methodological problems. Moves within a county are not usually detectable through the census, and even moves across county lines can escape discovery. Thus, I described only long-distance migration, and even then, I dealt with the total of children migrating rather than rates per decade. Since most students of historical migration have measured population turnovers within a city or town over a limited time, a comparison of their and my populations is not really possible.[5] Also, while my discussion of migrant children's property holdings relies heavily on evidence from manuscript collections and lists of wealthy slaveholders, a random sampling of other migrant children from the seventh federal manu-script census convinced me that those children discovered were not atypical of migrants as a whole.

Although this variety of source materials allowed me to identify and trace North Carolina planters and their children and to describe their characteristics and actions, much of my analysis of their atti-tudes and behavior is based upon the personal documents found in manuscript collections. Such collections existed for 55 of 124 fami-lies. While it is possible that families writing and preserving such materials might be atypical of their peers, the large percentage of my group leaving such records builds confidence in their typicality. That letters and diaries in the collections also frequently described the be-havior of other families in my sample which had not themselves left such personal documents further adds to this source's reliability. Oc-casionally I have drawn my examples and illustrations from the let-ters and diaries of the planter elite's offspring. Since there was such a wide span of ages (from twenty-one to over eighty) among the plant-ers, the generational lines were already tangled. For example, Wil-

5. For example, consult Peter W. Knights, *The Plain People of Boston, 1830–1860: A Study in City Growth* (New York, 1971).

liam Polk was great planter Philemon Hawkins' son-in-law but was also the father of great planter Thomas G. Polk. Alexander Gaston's second wife was the granddaughter of James Murphy. When using the comments of offspring to illustrate planters' attitudes, however, I limited myself to those owning at least twenty slaves, and, in most cases, over fifty.

Some of my information is presented in tabular form. The number and variety of materials used to compile the data in these tables are so large that it would be unwieldy to list specifically these sources. Furthermore, some of the percentages in the tables add to more or less than 100 percent because of rounding.

**North Carolina Planters and
Their Children, 1800–1860**

ONE

An Introduction to the Planter Elite

One important question about any social group concerns what holds members together. A group of planters might, in theory, have no common characteristic except ownership of many slaves. But the North Carolina planter elite consisted of a series of local groups with many similarities. Common traits, beliefs, and shared institutional affiliations all contributed to uniformity. Even in their emphasis upon local ties and loyalties, North Carolina planters were alike.

One obvious characteristic of this group of great planters was geographical dispersion. Scattered from Camden County in the east to Burke County in the west, they occupied the richest areas in eastern and piedmont North Carolina. In this large area, however, staple production divided along geographic lines; and several concentrations of great planters are evident. The rich Roanoke River valley near the Virginia border contained the largest number of wealthy planters (see Map 1). Lush river and creek bottomland in Warren, Halifax, Northampton, Bertie, and parts of Edgecombe, Martin, and Granville counties nourished a thriving staple agriculture (see Map 2). Tobacco in the eighteenth century provided a cornerstone upon which wealthy and ambitious Virginia emigrants built their fortunes. This section remained part of North Carolina's tobacco belt during the nineteenth century; but cotton also flourished there, and many enterprising planters switched to it.[1]

Although planters along the Roanoke River were the most prosperous and were growing in numbers and riches in 1830, the lower Cape Fear and Albemarle regions contained older elites. South Car-

1. C. O. Cathey, *Agricultural Developments in North Carolina, 1783–1860* (Chapel Hill, 1956), 119–24.

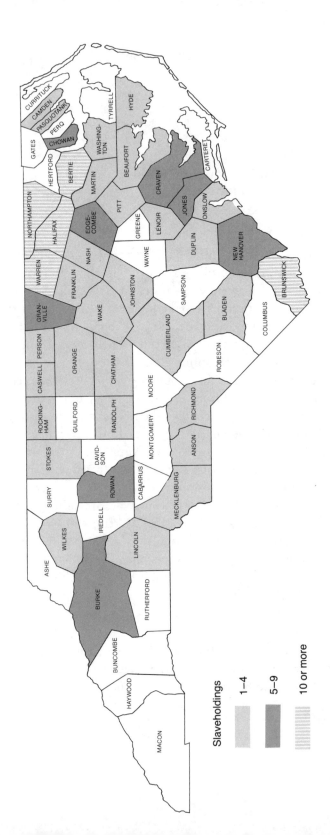

Map 1. County Distribution in 1830 of Slaveholdings of Seventy or More Slaves

Slaveholdings

1–4

5–9

10 or more

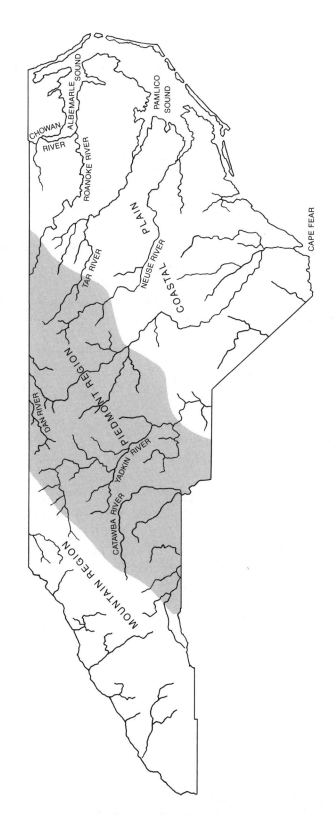

Map 2. Principal Rivers and Regions of North Carolina

olinians wended their way northward in the 1720s, took up huge grants of land in Brunswick and New Hanover counties, and worked them with slave labor. Rice growers there constituted North Carolina's principal plantation society in the eighteenth century, and their mansions, on the banks of the Cape Fear River and its tributaries, testified to their wealth. North Carolina rice planters were never able to rival South Carolinians in quality or quantity of rice produced, but that crop, though increasingly restricted to Brunswick County, remained an important antebellum North Carolina staple.[2]

The northeastern Albemarle, colonized in the late seventeenth century by Virginians, was North Carolina's oldest settlement. Planters there had first raised tobacco, but wheat, corn, and cotton had replaced that crop in importance by the early nineteeth century. Chowan County and neighboring areas possessed a self-assured elite with colonial origins but also with generally more modest fortunes than Cape Fear planters.[3]

Other North Carolina large slaveholders lived in the coastal plain and the piedmont regions. Wealthy agriculturists in coastal-plain counties such as Craven, Duplin, and Onslow tended by 1830 to concentrate upon cotton; the piedmont also supported cotton, mainly in the tier of counties—Richmond, Anson, Mecklenburg—bordering South Carolina. Other piedmont planters cultivated tobacco and grains. In the western piedmont, diversified farming predominated, with some large planters heavily involved in raising beef cattle.[4]

Even though growing different staple crops, great planters from east and west were not particularly dissimilar. Western piedmont planters differed slightly from wealthy eastern North Carolinians in ethnic background, but varied far more from their own poorer neighbors. Scotch-Irish and Scottish descent tended to be more common among western than eastern elites, whose origins more often were English. In contrast, Moravian settlements at Salem combined with individual migrations to form a considerable German-speaking population

2. *Ibid.*, 140; Lawrence Lee, *The Lower Cape Fear in Colonial Days* (Chapel Hill, 1965), 102, 147, 187–91.

3. Cathey, *Agricultural Developments*, 50–51, 116, 140; Rosser H. Taylor, *Slaveholding in North Carolina: An Economic View* (Chapel Hill, 1926), 30–33.

4. R. H. Taylor, *Slaveholding*, 6, 30–33; Cathey, *Agricultural Developments*, 119–24, 134–38, 145, 170.

in the piedmont. Thus, in language and some other aspects of culture, wealthy western Carolinians showed greater similarity to easterners of British origin than to many of their own neighbors.[5]

Basic similarities in religious beliefs existed despite some diversity in affiliation that tended to be related to geographical location (see Table 1). Episcopalians were scattered throughout the coastal plain and the piedmont but were especially numerous in the lower Cape Fear, where most planters belonged to that denomination. Methodists, though prominent in the piedmont, tended to cluster in the Roanoke River valley, where they and Episcopalians formed the major sects among the well-to-do. Baptists were most prevalent in inland coastal-plain counties such as Nash, Edgecombe, and Bertie, while Presbyterian strongholds lay in Granville County on the Virginia border and in the western piedmont.

Differences in religious affiliation not only were related to geographical origin but also sprang from personal convictions. Many in elite families thought religion very important, and some found that their parents' church did not meet their own spiritual or social needs. A restive churchgoer might transfer from a more evangelical to a more ritualistic church—from the Baptist or Methodist, for example, to the Episcopal church. James S. Battle was a devout member of the Primitive Baptist church, but some of his children, like those of his fellow

Table 1. Religious Affiliations
of North Carolina Great Planters

Denomination	Number of Planters	Percentage of Planters
Episcopalian	42	57.5
Baptist	12	16.4
Methodist	8	11.0
Presbyterian	9	12.3
Roman Catholic	2	2.7
TOTAL	73	99.9

5. Harry R. Merrens, *Colonial North Carolina in the Eighteenth Century: A Study in Historical Geography* (Chapel Hill, 1964), 65–69; William Herman Gehrke, "The German Element in Rowan and Cabarrus Counties, North Carolina" (M.A. thesis, University of North Carolina, 1934).

churchman Francis L. Dancy, helped add to the revitalization of the Episcopal church in Edgecombe County. Probably a majority of conversions in wealthy planter families matched a new, more prestigious religious sect membership to the individual's high socioeconomic status, but changes of the opposite nature also occurred. Ella R. Eaton, a very wealthy young woman in search of spiritual peace, left the Episcopal church of her distinguished forebears and, after several years as a Roman Catholic, joined the Baptist church.[6]

Despite some diversity in affiliation, planters were much alike in religion. The great majority were Episcopalian—no other denomination comprehended more than 17 percent. The Protestantism of the planter elite, moreover, shared some characteristics. Successive waves of religious revivalism had swept across North Carolina in the late eighteenth and early nineteenth centuries and had affected all churches. As Donald G. Mathews has pointed out, even the Episcopal church, usually seen as most ritualistic and least emotional, was not immune to the growth of evangelical piety. Baptist, Methodist, Presbyterian, and Episcopalian planters might disagree on many matters of religious doctrine and practice but their outlook was similar. They believed in a close personal God who held them strictly accountable. He was a jealous taskmaster who demanded intense commitment and who directly intervened in human affairs to aid, reward, or chastise. As Methodist Henry G. Williams saw God's hand in his family's good health during an epidemic, Presbyterian Isaac T. Avery similarly attributed his mother's rescue from a fire to Divine Providence. Planters also saw deaths of spouses, beloved friends, and relatives as ordained by God.[7]

This group of widely separated planters also shared a pervasive lo-

6. William F. Dancy *et al.* to Russell Chapman *et al.*, 1857, in Edgecombe County Deeds, Vol. 27, pp. 820–22, North Carolina Division of Archives and History, Raleigh (hereafter cited as NCDAH); Joseph K. Turner and J. L. Bridgers, *History of Edgecombe County* (Raleigh, 1920), 451; Perceval Reniers, *The Springs of Virginia: Life, Love, and Death at the Waters, 1775–1900* (Chapel Hill, 1941), 181; E. C. Montague to the Baptist church, December 1, 1866, in William Eaton Papers, Southern Historical Collection, Library of the University of North Carolina at Chapel Hill (hereafter cited as SHC).

7. Donald G. Mathews, *Religion in the Old South* (Chicago, 1977), xvi–xvii, 121–22, 129–31; Henry G. Williams to "Esteemed Friend," November 20, 1811, in Henry G. Williams Papers, SHC; Isaac T. Avery to Thomas Lenoir, July 7, 1824, in Lenoir Family Papers, SHC.

calism illustrated by kinship. Such ties, especially the closest ones, clustered the elite into small, local groups. A minimum of eighty planters—almost one-half of the group—held a relationship of cousinhood or closer kinship with another in the group. At least fifty-nine planters—one-third of the total—shared a primary relationship, that of parent-child or between siblings. Almost all of these kinfolks—twenty-nine of thirty-one groups—lived in the same or adjoining counties. In a typical case, James Hilliard of Nash and Colonel Jeremiah Perry of neighboring Franklin County had married sisters from the wealthy Boddie family of Nash County, and their brother-in-law George Boddie also lived in the ancestral home there.[8]

Other ties of blood and marriage similarly showed local attachment. At least fifty of the great planters possessed more distant ties of affinity and consanguinity, and this number is undoubtedly an underestimation. Most of these relatives—fourteen of twenty-one groups—also lived in the same or neighboring counties. All these relationships, like religious affiliation and geographical location, tended to create a network of small groups of planters who were much alike.

Planters' daily routines and social pursuits further reveal a primarily localistic focus. Their activities show a firm attachment to their home plantations and counties. Men occasionally left their superintendence of farm affairs to transact business such as the purchase of supplies in town. Attendance at the court sessions provided invaluable information for the planter who was also a creditor by indicating if any of his debtors were encountering financial difficulties. Meetings of the county court, an administrative body that made decisions about county roads, jails, poorhouses, and other local matters, proved deeds and bills of sale, and probated wills, also demanded some planters' attendance. Membership on that elite governing body conferred intimate knowledge about the community and much power within it.[9]

Although much of men's time was spent within the county, their wives' horizons were usually still more limited. Women had busy

8. John Thomas Boddie and John Bennett Boddie, *Boddie and Allied Families* (Chicago[?], 1918), 23.
9. Guion G. Johnson, *Ante-bellum North Carolina: A Social History* (Chapel Hill, 1937), 613–44.

households to oversee and a routine offering fewer excuses for trips to town. Some weeks they never left the plantation.[10]

Social life revolved around neighborhood and county. Relatives, fellow church members, and other genteel local people were friends. Short visits, parties, weddings, and church attendance provided diversions. Difficulties in transportation meant that visits from distant friends or relatives often lasted for weeks or even months.[11]

These strong local ties were, however, supplemented by some activities which introduced planters to others of their class. Men with a second occupation or legislative experience—one-half of the planter elite—encountered a wider circle of genteel people. These lawyers, judges, politicians, merchants, and ministers, all of whose occupations required travel, often formed numerous acquaintances outside their home county. Planters serving in the state legislature met prominent men and others of their "own kind" from throughout the state.[12]

Religious and recreational institutions and activities provided additions to regular social life. Annual statewide church conventions were opportunities to visit with like-minded well-to-do people from other sections. One Wilmington lady pronounced an Episcopalian gathering most pleasant since "the houses of all Episcopalians were thrown open and dinner parties every day." Such meetings also gave planters an occasional chance to renew existing dormant relationships. Joseph B. Skinner urged his old friends, Duncan Cameron and Thomas Bennehan of Orange County, to stay at his home during an upcoming Episcopal convention in Edenton.[13]

Planters' summering habits also varied their routine. North Carolinians, like their northern and southern contemporaries, often spent part of that season away from their homes in what were seen as more

10. *Ibid.*, 232–47; Rebecca Cameron to Duncan Cameron, April 17, 1830, in Cameron Family Papers, SHC.

11. Paton Yoder, "Private Hospitality in the South, 1775–1850," *Mississippi Valley Historical Review*, XLVII (1960), 419–33.

12. Eighty-three of the great planters (49.4 percent) and sixty-three of the nonmigrants with direct descendants (50.8 percent) either possessed a second occupation or served in the state legislature.

13. Eliza DeRosset to Kate Meares, May 19, 1858, in DeRosset Family Papers, SHC; Joseph B. Skinner to Duncan Cameron, February 27, 1843, in Cameron Family Papers. See also Mary S. Henderson Diary, June 3, 1857, in John S. Henderson Papers, SHC.

healthful locations. Seaside cottages at Nag's Head or near Wilmington could form a refreshing change from "miasmatic" plantations. Other wealthy lowlanders moved inland to the higher ground of the pine barrens or the upcountry. Some Cape Fear planters regularly summered in Pittsboro; others from the coastal plain visited Hillsborough.[14]

The mineral springs in New York, Virginia, and North Carolina also served the same purposes for many elite Carolinians. Spas functioned both as social centers and as health clinics and retreats. Planter families visiting the springs often used the potential or actual ill health of family members as a reason for attendance. They hoped that the waters would cure illnesses such as tuberculosis and arthritis as well as relieve more general debility. Still, healthy family members who could enjoy the social whirl often accompanied infirm relatives.

Newport and Saratoga Springs were early resorts for those fleeing North Carolina summers. George Pollok and the Devereuxes often traveled to northern cities or spas, and other elite entourages occasionally journeyed there. By the early nineteenth century, however, various western Virginia springs became alternatives for those who for reasons of money, ideology, or convenience did not wish to travel to the North. These spas attracted a varied but generally southern clientele. North Carolina springs such as Shocco in Warren and Catawba in Lincoln County possessed a more local following but still would acquaint visitors with other genteel Carolinians.[15]

Planters' reading also augmented their everyday fare of local gossip. Newspapers, with their announcements, advertisements, sentimental poems and stories as well as political propaganda and business news, formed a source of amusement and knowledge. Those journals published in Raleigh, the state capital, had statewide circu-

14. Lawrence Fay Brewster, *Summer Migrations and Resorts of South Carolina Low Country Planters* (Durham, N.C., 1947); Mary B. Biddle to James O. K. Williams, September 4, 1838, in Samuel Simpson Biddle Papers, Manuscript Department, Duke University Library, Durham (hereafter cited as Duke); Sophia Capehart to Robert Martin, August 16, 1857, in Robert C. Martin Papers, SHC; W. B. Grove to William Gaston, June 30, 1807, in William Gaston Papers, SHC.

15. See Barnes A. Lathrop (ed.), "A Southern Girl at Saratoga Springs, 1834," *North Carolina Historical Review*, XV (1938), 159–60; James S. Green to Gaston Meares, September 11, 1849, in DeRosset Family Papers; John W. Brodnax to Mary Brodnax, August 23, 1860, in John G. Brodnax Papers, SHC; Chalmers G. Davidson, "Catawba Springs—Carolina's Spa," *North Carolina Historical Review*, XXVIII (1951), 414–20.

lation and printed obituary and marriage notices of virtually all the wealthiest planter families. Even though elite North Carolinians might not be personally acquainted, they well might "know of" each other.

Of all social groups in early-nineteenth-century North Carolina, the planter elite was the most cohesive statewide. Planters' activities had so long brought them into contact with one another that the midcentury advances in transportation likely affected them far less than other, middling sorts. The railroads facilitated communication, but the links that bound planters together had been forged earlier.

Social activities helped to prevent the isolation of planters but did not break down or supplant their basic local affiliations. Their highest allegiance remained to their area. Still such pursuits provided communication among similar though geographically separated people.

In addition to sharing an attachment to their localities, wealthy North Carolinians showed similarities in social origins and in attitudes toward business enterprises. Almost all came from comfortable, privileged backgrounds. Although many older men had built moderate slave- and landholdings into splendid fortunes, few "rags to riches" stories can be discovered. Cape Fear residents considered Ezekiel Lane a self-made man after his purchase of several large plantations in New Hanover County. William Dula, an illiterate western planter, probably had humble beginnings. Patrick Hamilton, a Scottish immigrant, combined mercantile concerns with marriage to a well-to-do young woman to launch his fortune. Approximately 5 to 10 percent of the great planters probably began poor and ended rich.[16]

16. James Sprunt, *Chronicles of the Cape Fear River* (Raleigh, 1914), 64–68; Patrick H. Baskervill, *The Hamiltons of Burnside, North Carolina and Their Ancestors and Descendants* (Richmond, 1916), 98–106; Will of William Dula, in Wilkes County Wills, NCDAH. All wills, estates, deeds, etc., are held by NCDAH unless otherwise noted.

Eight men—Lane, Hamilton, Dula, Thomas Cowan, Alexander Cuningham, Alexander Gray, Luke Huggins, and Edward Ward—possibly came from humble origins. Eight others—Francis L. Dancy, John Brodie, Peter R. and Stephen Davis, John Devereux, Horace Ely, William Watts Jones, and John E. Wood—may have made their fortunes, but were privileged in their educations and training. Origins of fourteen others—John Atkinson, John C. Baker, Thomas Cox, Littlebury Wilcox, Peter Hairston, Hugh Telfair, James Murphy, G. L. Huie, Willie McPherson, William Moody, Ralph Outlaw, John Perry, Jeremiah (Fork) Perry, and John Sanders—were not determined.

Most great planters were among at least the second generation of their family in wealthy or genteel circumstances. For example, Samuel Simpson's father had, by mid-eighteenth century, obtained large holdings in eastern North Carolina. Western planters similarly had ancestors among their local elite. William Hogan's father was a Revolutionary soldier and one of the donors of the University of North Carolina's site. Isaac T. Avery's father, Waightstill, had migrated to North Carolina, served as state attorney general, and successfully built a large plantation in Burke County. The planter elite of 1830 also included old colonial families. James C. Johnston, Robert A. Jones, and George Pollok belonged to families long possessed of political prestige as well as wealth. Both Pollok and Johnston numbered colonial governors among their distinguished forebears.[17]

Wealthy North Carolina planters derived their fortunes from agriculture, land speculation, or mercantile enterprises. Much like the eighteenth-century planter-merchants of the northern Chesapeake, some Carolinians combined two or even all three avenues to riches. Instructive is the pattern of the Collins family. In the eighteenth century, the first Josiah Collins used profits from his trading house to purchase thousands of acres of land and equip that plantation with part of a shipload of slaves personally imported from Africa. Philemon Hawkins the elder, whose life spanned most of the eighteenth century, and his wealthy descendants combined agriculture along the creeks of the Roanoke River valley with land grabs of thousands of acres in state grants. Other families, such as the Hamiltons and Eatons, also had successfully mixed agriculture with trade or speculation.[18]

17. Simpson and Bryan Family Papers, North Carolina Collection, University of North Carolina Library, Chapel Hill (hereafter cited as NCC); Kemp P. Battle, *History of the University of North Carolina* . . . (2 vols.; Raleigh, 1907–1912), I, 27; Phifer, "Saga of a Burke County Family," 8–12; Blackwell P. Robinson, "Willie Jones of Halifax," *North Carolina Historical Review*, XVIII (1941), 1–26; *Cyclopedia of Eminent and Representative Men of the Carolinas of the Nineteenth Century* (2 vols.; Madison, 1892), II, 12.

18. Aubrey C. Land, "Economic Base and Social Structure: The Northern Chesapeake in the Eighteenth Century," in Gary B. Nash (ed.), *Class and Society in Early America* (Englewood Cliffs, N.J., 1970), 117–33; Bennett H. Wall, "The Founding of the Pettigrew Plantations," *North Carolina Historical Review*, XXVII (1950), 395–418; Hawkins Family Papers, SHC; Baskervill, *The Hamiltons of Burnside*, 98, 101, 103, 106; Estate of John R. Eaton, in Granville County Estates; John R. Eaton Papers, SHC.

Yet no matter how family fortunes had been acquired, great planters, not surprisingly, were primarily farmers. Only one-fourth of the group had another profession, and some of them did not practice it after early life. Many elite planters depended not only upon their staple crop but also upon activities mainly connected to the plantation economy to bring in money. As agricultural businessmen, not simple agrarians, they were inextricably tied to a market economy. Both Camden County great planters produced large quantities of shingles. Other eastern planters used their work forces to process turpentine. Most Albemarle Sound and several Roanoke River great planters operated fisheries and sold their catches to commission merchants.[19]

Wealthy Carolinians also profited from providing their neighborhoods with a variety of goods and services. Some sold surpluses of pork or corn to neighbors with insufficient supplies. They also owned saw- and gristmills, cotton gins, blacksmith, wheelwright, and carpentry tools and workers, tanneries, brandy stills, and ferries. Few great planters provided most of these services, many supplied one or more. For example, John D. Hawkins ran both saw- and gristmills and a tannery and also had a profit-splitting agreement with a man who manufactured plows.[20]

Just as they used plantations to increase income, planters utilized other assets for moneymaking. Gold mining, a more speculative venture, engaged some wealthy agriculturists' land- and slaveholdings. When North Carolina's gold rush began in the 1820s, some invested in land and used part of their slave force as miners. Isaac T. Avery and William Davidson were the principal gold mining great planters, but even easterners such as Cullen Capehart, William Watts Jones, and William Williams also attempted to gain money in the mines.[21]

19. Thirty-eight planters (22.6 percent) and thirty-one of the nonmigrants with direct descendants possessed a second occupation; the group included fourteen lawyers, thirteen merchants, eight doctors, two manufacturers, and one minister. Estate of Samuel Proctor, in Camden County Estates; Estate of Ralph Outlaw, in Bertie County Estates; Will of Thomas Benbury, in Chowan County Wills; Thomas Barrow to William R. Smith, Sr., December 1, 1840, in Peter E. Smith Papers, SHC.

20. See Hawkins Family Papers; Sarah and Sarah R. Cowan to Thomas Cowan, 1848, in New Hanover County Deeds, Vol. FF, pp. 573–74; Estate of John Brodie, in Warren County Estates; Eugene D. Genovese, "Yeomen Farmers in a Slaveholders' Democracy," *Agricultural History*, XLIX (1975), 331–43.

21. List of Taxables, 1830, Burke County, in NCDAH; William Davidson to Joseph Curtis *et al.*, 1834, in Mecklenburg County Deeds, Vol. 23, pp. 122–27; Phifer, "Saga

Elite planters further attempted to augment their wealth by banking or moneylending. Lawyer-planter Duncan Cameron long served as president of the State Bank of North Carolina. In Burke County the Erwin family and its affinal relations filled many positions of the state bank branch office for over thirty years. At least sixteen planters—one-tenth of the total group—held bank stock, but the majority, like other southern planters, lent money at interest. Although they advanced cash to relatives, close friends, and neighbors, this activity was not primarily altruistic or status enhancing. Most transactions included interest charges. Planters' caution and commercial orientation were revealed in their requirement of security, usually a mortgage on land or slaves, for large loans or from less dependable borrowers. An 1830s equity case in Bertie County, in which a deceased planter's son and daughter sued the estate of their former guardian (and great-uncle) to recover money he had loaned to several men who subsequently became bankrupt, reveals the attitudes of the elite about credit and the lending of money. All took the practice for granted. Thomas Speller testified that he knew one debtor to be harassed by creditors and added, "I would not have credited him myself for any considerable amount without good security for a few years back." To be sure, some could show forbearance in their collections when a debtor was, as William Pugh characterized one of his, a "relation [and] a gentlemanly man." But even though they were primarily farmers, planters were interested in, rather than averse to, letting their money make money for them.[22]

Consistent with their role as commercial farmers and their interest in moneymaking, most wealthy planters favored internal improvements likely to benefit their area. Although the 1840s and 1850s were the great period of railroad building in North Carolina and al-

of a Burke County Family," 339; Thomas H. Kean and John D. Hawkins *et al.*, Agreement, November 8, 1837, in Hawkins Family Papers. On gold mining in North Carolina, consult Edward W. Phifer, Jr., "Champagne at Brindletown: The Story of the Burke County Gold Rush, 1829–1833," *North Carolina Historical Review*, XL (1963), 489–500; Robert S. Starobin, *Industrial Slavery in the Old South* (New York, 1970), 23.

22. *Cyclopedia of Eminent Men*, II, 93–95; Edward W. Phifer, Jr., "Money, Banking, and Burke County in the Ante-bellum Era," *North Carolina Historical Review*, XXXVII (1960), 22–37; Testimony in Equity Case, *Noah and William A. Thompson* v. *Thomas Thompson's Executors*, Estate of William T. Thompson, in Bertie County Estates; Julia Floyd Smith, *Slavery and Plantation Growth in Ante-bellum Florida, 1821–1860* (Gainesville, Fla., 1973), 158–65.

most one-third of this sample of planters was dead by 1840, at least nineteen of the nonmigrants owned stock in an internal improvements company. Some such as state senator Bartlett Yancey of Caswell County advocated a better statewide system of transportation. Harold J. Counihan in his study of North Carolina politics has chronicled how Yancey as speaker of the state legislature controlled committee appointments and consistently chose advocates of internal improvements for that committee. Among his appointments were wealthy planters Durant Hatch, John Owen, Duncan Cameron, Edward T. Brodnax, Joseph J. Williams, and Daniel Forney, son of Peter Forney. Others took a more parochial view and supported only railroad and canal companies and legislative measures that would aid their own areas. Although political party lines customarily revealed Democrats opposed and Whigs in favor of public works measures, some Democrats such as Isaac T. Avery and John D. Hawkins were heavily involved in railroad building. In general, elite planters, regardless of political affiliation, tended to back proposals bettering their own access to markets.[23]

As well as similar economic backgrounds and attitudes, planters also shared similar moral attitudes. Related to their religious and businesslike stance was an ideal of prudent leisure that condemned "dissipation" but condoned mild amusements that did not include any excesses. Hunting was a most respectable sport, and planters expressed only admiration for skill in it. A family tradition held that young John Devereux, on a visit to his great planter grandfather, bragged that he could shoot one hundred squirrels in a single day. Successful, "he hastened gaily home and with pride emptied his bag before his delighted old grandfather." In that case, hunting had been transformed into a manly accomplishment. Many planters owned hunting dogs and enjoyed a day's chase in the woods. Hunting held several benefits and no liabilities for the Carolinians. As well as furnishing recreation, it provided game for the table and eliminated an-

23. Harold J. Counihan, "North Carolina, 1815–1836: State and Local Perspectives on the Age of Jackson" (Ph.D. dissertation, University of North Carolina, 1971), 78–79; Clarence C. Norton, *The Democratic Party in Ante-bellum North Carolina, 1835–1861* (Chapel Hill, 1930), 124–29; Harry L. Watson, "Squire Oldway and His Friends: Opposition to Internal Improvements in Ante-bellum North Carolina," *North Carolina Historical Review,* LIV (1977), 105–119.

imals preying upon stock or gardens. Since it involved only the expense of maintaining dogs, planters did not view the pastime as a luxury. In recreation, they endorsed the notion that amusements could be enjoyed so long as there were few expenses and no injury to character.[24]

With somewhat less fidelity to these principles, the planter elite also tended to accept an interest in fine horses and horse racing. Appreciation was particularly widespread among planters in the Roanoke River valley. They often matched their horses at William Eaton's racetrack in Warrenton or at tracks in Southside Virginia. Almost all the wealthy planters of Northampton County bred horses and put them into competition. But even among those interested in racing, the admiration of fine horseflesh seems to have attracted more attention than betting.[25]

Purses at horse races were acceptable, but other forms of gambling seemed disreputable or, at least, dangerous. Settled family men saw gambling as a harbinger of ruin for their families and sought to discourage it among impressionable youths. Appropriately enough, the great planter most closely associated with gambling, Peter R. Davis, who owned an "open gaming house" near the county courthouse, was a bachelor.[26]

The rather straitlaced values of most planters distinguished them from rowdier elements in the countryside. In particular, the genteel objected to such popular local vices as cockfighting and heavy drinking. Many years later, W. B. Grove still remembered the admonitions he and Alexander Gaston had received from Gaston's father. "I often

24. Margaret Devereux, *Plantation Sketches* (Cambridge, Mass., 1946), 11–14; Roger G. Shingleton, "The Utility of Leisure: Game as a Source of Food in the Old South," *Mississippi Quarterly*, XXV (1972), 429–45; Dickson D. Bruce, Jr., "Hunting: Dimensions of Antebellum Southern Culture," *Mississippi Quarterly*, XXX (1977), 259–81; George W. Capehart to William R. Capehart, November 1, 1848, in William R. Capehart Papers, SHC; Peter W. Hairston Diary, December 25, n.d., in Peter W. Hairston Papers, SHC.

25. Henry W. Lewis, "Horses and Horsemen in Northampton Before 1900," *North Carolina Historical Review*, LI (1974), 126–48; Rules Governing Horseracing ... at Tarborough, in Simpson and Bryan Family Papers; Estate of William Eaton, in Warren County Estates; G. G. Johnson, *Ante-bellum North Carolina*, 181–83.

26. Lizzie W. Montgomery, *Sketches of Old Warrenton, North Carolina* (Raleigh, 1924), 41; G. G. Johnson, *Ante-bellum North Carolina*, 186–87; Hugh Waddell to James K. Polk, May 22, 1847, in Elizabeth G. McPherson (ed.), "Unpublished Letters from North Carolinians to Polk," *North Carolina Historical Review*, XVII (1940), 160.

think of the lecture you once gave him and I," Grove reminisced to the elder Gaston, "for *cockfighting* in the suburbs of Raleigh." Many wealthy Carolinians tolerated the use of alcohol in moderation but strongly censured drunkenness. David Outlaw criticized a fellow congressman: "It is bad enough for a man of his station and age to drink too much at all, but outrageous he should expose and disgrace himself and his constituents in the Halls of legislation." Others were even less tolerant of drinking. Some of the more reform-minded like Lewis Bond, a devout Baptist, belonged to temperance societies. Mary B. Polk described her venerable old grandfather Philemon Hawkins as "all his life *being very averse to liquer*." Heavy drinking by itself would not place a planter outside the pale of "respectable society," but increasingly as the nineteenth century progressed, the group ethic did not encourage overindulgence.[27]

Obviously not all planters lived up to such ideals. Wild fun, careless abandon, and carousing at brothels, gambling parlors, or taverns still existed in the nineteenth-century South. But the elite did not approve of raffish activities and promulgated a model of the respectable, moderate Christian gentleman.

Also common among wealthy Carolinians was a tendency toward sentimentality. Although difficult to define, sentimentality is usually considered an excess of emotion expressed in a stereotyped manner. Like middle- and upper-class northerners, genteel North Carolinians interpreted their experiences in highly emotional phrases. During their friends' or families' encounters with death, the planter elite constantly resorted to sentimental modes of expression. A typical description of death recalled the last minutes of Augusta Lane Hardin, whose "character through life was so beautifully depicted in her last moments, giving herself up to die with so much sweetness and firmness." Others used similar characterizations. E. Jones Erwin exaltedly told his son: "Never in my life has it been my Lot to wit-

27. W. B. Grove to William Gaston, July 20, 1836, in Gaston Papers; B. W. C. Roberts, "Cockfighting: An Early Entertainment in North Carolina," *North Carolina Historical Review*, XLII (1965), 306–374; David Outlaw to Emily Outlaw, September 3, 1850, in David Outlaw Papers, SHC; G. G. Johnson, *Ante-bellum North Carolina*, 97; Lewis Bond Obituary, in Raleigh *Register*, July 19, 1851; Mary B. Polk to Lucius J. Polk, June 3, 1826, in Polk, Badger, and McGehee Family Papers, SHC. See also Sarah A. Tarry to Edward Tarry, October 29, 1840, in William Tarry Papers, Duke; Kenneth M. Clark to Lewis Thompson, January 22, 1854, in Lewis Thompson Papers, SHC.

ness so calm & peaceful & happy a death[.] she drew her last breath[,] she was seen to close her eyes & mouth & it was sometime before anyone knew or was sensible that her immortal spirit had winged it[s] flight to heaven."[28]

Not only did they stylize and sentimentalize the victim's passing, they described their own mourning in emotion-laden terminology. Sarah Biddle Norcott told friends that she regretted "that I could not before parting mingle my tears with theirs and weep over the great loss they had sustained, in the death of their much loved brother." Robert T. Paine lamented the death of a close friend's young daughter: "Alas! it is too true, our fair friend, yes the friend of all & loved one of friends has gone to her God." In his will, Joseph B. Skinner described his deceased wife, "my ever lamented Maria Louisa," as "one who has ever lived in the heart of her Husband and whose memory . . . will be cherished to his latest breath."[29]

This sentimental view embraced valued companions as well as the dead and dying. Friendship to wealthy Carolinians meant an expression of affection and harmony of minds. Tristrim L. Skinner expected "confidence and candour" to "arise from nothing less than warm friendship." To an intimate female friend, Elizabeth Johnson sighed that she had lived through the summer hoping they could spend much of the winter together, but feared that was unlikely. Elizabeth then confided her marriage plans, expecting only agreement from "a friend an[d] such a one as I believe you to be." Robert Brodnax's illness led Paul C. Cameron to muse that his friend was "truly one of the excellent of the earth—a true nobleman . . . for whom I shall ever feel the most devoted affection."[30]

28. Lewis O. Saum, "Death in the Popular Mind of Pre–Civil War America," *American Quarterly*, XXVI (1974), 477–95; M. H. Walker to Walter W. Lane, June 28, 1856, in Levin Lane Papers, SHC; E. Jones Erwin to George Phifer Erwin, June 2, 1859, in George Phifer Erwin Papers, SHC. See also Thomas W. Harriss to Archibald D. Alston, September 24, 1848, in Archibald D. Alston Papers, SHC; Nannie Johnson to Mary T. Granberry, February 13, 1844, in John L. Bailey Papers, SHC.

29. Sarah F. Norcott to Rebecca Hodge, January 15, 1844, in Simpson and Bryan Family Papers; Robert T. Paine to Lavinia Paine, November 7, 1847, in Robert T. Paine Papers, SHC; Will of Joseph B. Skinner, in Chowan County Wills.

30. Tristrim L. Skinner to Eliza Harwood, February 25, 1846, in Skinner Family Papers, SHC; Elizabeth E. Johnson to Sarah A. B. Granberry, November 10, 1832, in Bailey Papers; Paul C. Cameron to Margaret and Mildred Cameron, n.d., in Cameron Family Papers.

Nature, too, received sentimentalized treatment. Willie P. Mangum sketched his surroundings: "I am now in the pleasant little village of Lincolnton.— Spring is rapidly clothing in her rich & verdant robes the lovely landscape.— The weather is soft, and delightful, and nought but my anxiety to get home disturbs the sweet serenity of the scene." On her visit to the mountains, Catherine Erwin declared, "'tis indeed impossible to conceive the grandeur of the scenery." Often nature provided a backdrop reflecting human preoccupations. "When I look at the fresh flowers and trees," brooded Rebecca Cameron, "how it brings to mind our beloved sister who is gone." A young man's parting view of the woman he loved suggested harmony between her and nature: "I left her leaning out the window and a holy sadness seemed to rest on her countenance, as she looked at Nature silently resigning herself, as it was, to the gentle embraces of Night." [31]

Among men who were successful and interested in increasing their wealth, sentimentality held potential conflicts with their entrepreneurial urges. In practice, however, men divided their world so that such emotions received expression almost exclusively in their private lives consisting of friends, home, and family where they could more easily be kept from compromising the drive toward success.[32] Probably most planters successfully juggled their commitments and never realized the possible contradictions.

Before the analysis of parent-child relations among elite North Carolinians, some speculations about the relationship between family practices and the social and economic milieu are pertinent. One cannot show that the Carolinians' family arrangements directly stemmed from their socioeconomic position. Their attitudes and actions toward their children show many similarities to those of people from different occupational backgrounds. Indeed, planter family practices

31. Willie P. Mangum to Charity Mangum, April 25, 1820, in Henry T. Shanks (ed.), *The Papers of Willie Person Mangum* (5 vols.; Raleigh, 1952–56), I, 25; Catherine Erwin to Mira Lenoir, September 9, 1826, in Lenoir Family Papers; Rebecca Cameron to Duncan Cameron, April 12, 1838, in Cameron Family Papers; R. S. Smith to Peter E. Smith, August 13, 1850, in P. E. Smith Papers. See also Meeta Armistead to Sophia Armistead, July 30, 1857, in Meeta A. Capehart Papers, SHC.

32. But see Ann Douglas, *The Feminization of American Culture* (New York, 1977), 8–49, who speaks of nineteenth-century sentimentality as the product of northern middle-class women and their ministers.

closely resembled those of genteel urban northerners. Wealthy North Carolinians, in family matters, were closer to their contemporaries than to prosperous agriculturists of other times and areas, who had ordered their domestic lives quite differently.

Even though the planters' milieu cannot be said to have brought about their family practices, links may be drawn between such practices and their general attitudes. These family arrangements were clearly consistent with planters' other beliefs. Their relationships with sons and daughters illustrated their prudery, sentimentality, and concern over economic matters. In fact, these interactions even showed their localism.

The North Carolina elite sought to rear children who would seize the world's opportunities. From youngsters' early years, parents urged the pursuit of achievement and success, quests that could be and were translated into material terms. Planters also expected sons and daughters to choose mates from the wealthy or at least the well-to-do.

Consistent with their prudery, genteel North Carolinians wished the younger generation to avoid pitfalls and temptations. Parental advice emphasized self-restraint and self-discipline, virtues which should inform children's work habits as well as recreation. Parents similarly assumed that their offspring would select spouses whose behavior conformed to conventional moral standards. Here their localism surfaced in distrust of suitors from other areas.

Planters' sentimentality infused every stage of their progeny's lives and development. From their first excited comments about newborn infants to their thoughtful gifts and letters to adult offspring, parents cared deeply for their children and sought to evoke a similar emotion in response. Even as the elders demanded achievement they also expressed deep sorrow over parting with children who were going away to school. Wealthy North Carolinians' general views and family practices were much in accord with each other.

TWO

Heaven's Best Gifts: Young Children
and Family Life

Among the many things they shared, North Carolina planter families held a common vision of the conjugal family as father, mother, and their children bound together by ties of affection. They struggled to maintain those warm family relations despite the ravages of mortality—that is, demographic conditions that historians have considered not conducive to this goal.

Several interacting factors produced broken or patched together families. Almost two-thirds of the planter households lost at least one parent before the youngest child reached age twenty-one. Nineteenth-century mortality cut down many young adults, especially females during the childbearing years. Planters such as George Boddie, Simmons J. Baker, and John Sanders lost youthful wives at childbirth or from its complications. Fertility patterns also contributed to incomplete or patched-up families. As elsewhere in America before the end of the nineteenth century, women in marriages unbroken by early death often had active childbearing spans of over twenty years. B. H. J. Maria Kearney's fifteen children arrived over a period of twenty-nine years (1811–1840), and Elizabeth Frink's twelve children were spaced over twenty-two years (1808–1830).[1]

Children born to middle-aged women whose husbands were older might well lose one or both parents. Planter parents were well aware of that possibility. Musing upon the birth of one of his youngest chil-

---

1. Boddie Family Bible, Sanders Family Records, both in Compiled Genealogies, NCDAH; Baker Genealogy, in Benbury and Haywood Family Papers, SHC; Robert V. Wells, "Demographic Change and the Life Cycle of American Families," *Journal of Interdisciplinary History*, II (1971), 273–82; Joseph A. Groves, *The Alstons and Allstons of North and South Carolina . . .* (Atlanta, 1901), 495–505; B. Otis Prince, *Southern Frinks* (N.p., n.d.), 23–24, 28–29.

dren, Isaac T. Avery declared that he had always been gladdened by such events, "but in the present instance when I reflected that in a few days I should be 50 years old; that if we were both spared, I might train his childhood; but in the course of nature, the direction of his early manhood, would devolve on others, melancholy feelings would obtrude themselves on me although I am sensible that duty enjoins gratitude for present good, and resignation as to the future." Avery miscalculated his age span and lived to be almost eighty years old, but his wife died before some of their children reached adulthood.[2]

Patterns of marriage further increased the possibility of children becoming orphaned. Much like the men of colonial New England, widowers—even some who were quite elderly—tended to marry again. Almost 60 percent of these men remarried, and if one excludes those widowed at age sixty-five or older, the rate approaches 70 percent. Desires for companionship and love, together with the need for someone to run the household and care for children, encouraged remarriage. Planters often chose as second wives young women still in their fertile years. David Sills, who died at age sixty, left a youthful second wife and three young children ranging down to age four. A thirty-year-old second wife and three children under age ten survived sixty-nine-year-old Micajah T. Hawkins.[3]

Consequently, in planter households the person filling the role of mother or father was not necessarily the actual procreator. Many children grew up with stepparents and sometimes stepsiblings and half brothers and sisters. Historians such as Lawrence Stone and Micheline Baulant have posited that ties within fractured or reconstituted families became tenuous. To Baulant, a reconstituted family was "by its nature extremely unstable." In such a view, biological ties are thought necessary for the family unit to cohere.[4]

2. Isaac T. Avery to Selina L. Lenoir, September 14, 1835, in Lenoir Family Papers.
3. John Demos, *A Little Commonwealth: Family Life in Plymouth Colony* (New York, 1970), 67; Philip J. Greven, Jr., *Four Generations: Population, Land, and Family in Colonial Massachusetts* (Ithaca, N.Y., 1970), 29; MS Census of 1850, North Carolina, Warren County, Schedule I, p. 10, and Franklin County, Schedule I, p. 369.
4. Micheline Baulant, "The Scattered Family: Another Aspect of Seventeenth Century Demography," in Robert Forster and Orest Ranum (eds.), *Family and Society: Selections from the Annales, Economies, Sociétés, Civilisations*, trans. Elborg Forster and Patricia Ranum (Baltimore, 1976), 104–116; Stone, *The Family, Sex and Marriage*, 56–58, 81, 103.

In reconstituted planter families, relationships could and some-times did become strained but were not necessarily fragile. In fact, wealthy North Carolinians sought to smooth over distinctions be-tween step- and biological parents by not recognizing any difference. Stepparents and their spouses tried to integrate family members into a single unit. They usually addressed stepchildren as "my dear daughter" or "my dear child," and the offspring invariably called a stepmother "Mother," a stepfather "Father," or a popular variant of those terms.[5]

Such families often achieved cohesion and even affection. Al-though studies of modern stepparents suggest that the majority of them do not receive the same level of affection as the real parent, many children in nineteenth-century North Carolina families thoroughly appreciated—and even loved—their stepparents. Stark Armistead, Jr., illustrated his affection for his stepmother by a generous legacy of three thousand dollars and lifetime use of his town real estate. Susan Gaston wrote tenderly of her stepmother, and Laura Saunders named her only daughter for the stepmother who had reared her from age five. And such warmth ran in both directions. Celia Outlaw gave valuable property to a favorite stepdaughter.[6]

Other stepparents were tolerated, even when not loved. In cases in which these parents became disliked, offspring almost always at-tempted to cloak rancor with the forms of family amity. Susan Hines detested her stepmother but believed she must treat that lady as a close relative: "I do not and I can not love her as a Mother, but I hope that I have too much respect for myself and my Fathers memory to treat her otherwise than with the greatest deference and respect that her relation to me demands." In fact, Susan seriously contemplated

---

5. Examples are Joseph John Norcott to Sarah F. Norcott, July 16, 1847, in Mary N. Bryan Scrapbook, SHC; J. W. Biddle to Mary E. V. Biddle, November 23, 1859, in Biddle Papers; Delia Badger to Melissa Williams, July 9, 1836, in Badger Family Papers, SHC.

6. Charles E. Bowerman and Donald P. Irish, "Some Relationships of Stepchildren to Their Parents," in Ruth S. Cavan (ed.), *Marriage and Family in the Modern World: A Book of Readings* (3rd ed.; New York, 1969), 556–80; Will of Stark Armistead, Jr., in Warren County Wills; "A Genealogical Table . . . for the Use of Joseph H. Saun-ders," in Joseph H. Saunders Papers, SHC; Susan Gaston to William Gaston, February 14, 1822, in Gaston Papers; Celia Outlaw to Jane E. Cherry, 1842, in Bertie County Deeds, Vol. FF, pp. 462–64.

continuing to reside with her widowed stepmother and gave financial rather than personal reasons for her decision to live separately. In this and other cases, the presence of half siblings helped to bind together a household containing a stepparent and stepchildren. Even those who disliked a stepparent usually liked their half siblings. Thomas P. Devereux's daughters tried to be polite to their heartily disliked stepmother, not only to please their father, but also to avoid wounding a beloved half sister. Away at boarding school, Melissa Williams sent presents back to her young half sister and half brother.[7]

Even one-parent families attempted to approximate the conjugal family. In female-headed households, a male relative often played a quasi-paternal role. If the children were young, the male relative might be the widow's father or brother. Simmons J. Baker financially aided his widowed daughter Laura Saunders and frequently visited, wrote, and advised her children. In families with adult offspring, older brothers and half brothers counseled the youngsters and administered their affairs. James N. McPherson consulted with his stepmother about his half sisters' educations and wrote encouraging and lovingly admonitory letters to the girls. Grandparents, aunts, uncles, or older siblings often provided homes or care for children who had lost their mothers. John W. Brodnax fondly recalled his sister's care of his children: "to my children she has been nearer a mother than any other person would have been[,] always sacrificing her own feelings and inclinations for their comfort or gratification."[8]

Despite biological onslaughts against the conjugal family, planters obviously tried to pattern fractured or disparate families after the ideal and often successfully rebuilt the "two-parent" family. Even on occasions when reconstituted families could not attain the desired affection, planters retained the forms and usages of kinship. Their ef-

7. Susan Hines to Peter Evans, February 14, 1852, in P. E. Smith Papers; Josiah Turner, Jr., to Sophia Devereux, January 20, [1856], in Josiah Turner Papers, SHC; Delia Badger to Melissa Williams, July 9, 1836, in Badger Family Papers.

8. Simmons J. Baker to William L. Saunders, October 7, 1852, in William L. Saunders Papers, Duke; James N. McPherson to Elizabeth McPherson, December 22, 1836, March 26, 1837, both in Ferebee, Gregory, and McPherson Family Papers, SHC; John W. Brodnax to Robert Brodnax, August 5, 1852, in J. G. Brodnax Papers, SHC. See also Isabella Baskerville to Charles E. Hamilton, October 6, 1850, in John Bullock and Charles E. Hamilton Papers, SHC.

forts to re-create this conjugal unit highlight its importance. Not surprisingly, those with "normal" households echoed this dedication to and admiration of the conjugal family.

Another similarity linking North Carolina planter families was a child-centeredness that existed despite demographic structures that many historians would deem unpromising. The growth of the child-centered family has often been associated with the declines in fertility and child mortality rates. Scholars have suggested that unrestricted fertility and high mortality produced families indifferent to infants and youngsters since parents could not afford to become emotionally involved with young children who might never live to grow up. With a lowering of child mortality, so the argument runs, parents were able to restrict the number of their offspring (yet still ensure lineal continuity) and to pay more attention to each child. As couples came to value their progeny more highly, they wished for fewer. Thus the child-centered family emerged in the eighteenth and nineteenth centuries.[9]

North Carolina planters were indeed child-centered, but their patterns of fertility and child mortality do not conform to this model. Wealthy North Carolina families—most of whom began their childbearing period at the end of the eighteenth or beginning of the nineteenth century—had many children. Great planters with legitimate offspring averaged seven. Given the poor quality of data available on births, this number undoubtedly underestimates the total number of children born. Some men with over ten children could account for that large number by more than one marriage; for example, George Boddie owed his seventeen children to two wives. If, however, one surveys only those planters producing children by one marriage, the average number of children per family remains at seven.[10] A majority of

9. Louise A. Tilly and Joan W. Scott, *Women, Work, and Family* (New York, 1978), 58–59; François Le Brun, *La Vie conjugale sous l'Ancien Régime* (Paris, 1975), 144–45, 169–75; Stone, *The Family, Sex and Marriage*, 81–82, 410–21, 477, 651–57; Ivy Pinchbeck and Margaret Hewitt, *Children in English Society* (2 vols.; London, 1969–73), I, 4.

10. Among helpful historical studies of American fertility are John Modell, "Family and Fertility on the Indiana Frontier, 1820," *American Quarterly*, XXIII (1971), 615–34; Yasukichi Yasuba, *Birth Rates of the White Population in the United States, 1800–1860* (Baltimore, 1961); Richard A. Easterlin, George Alter, and Gretchen A. Condran, "Farms and Farm Families in Old and New Areas: The Northern States in 1860,"

planter marriages producing fewer than four children were "incomplete" marriages, terminated by a spouse's death before the end of the wife's childbearing period. For example, James Coffield's wife Lavinia, who bore only one child, died at age twenty-one during the fourth year of their marriage. William T. Thompson died while his young wife was pregnant with their second child.[11]

Most likely these planters did not try to limit family size. The large number of births alone would suggest unrestrained fertility. Furthermore, the planters themselves sometimes voiced an appreciation of large families. Philemon Hawkins, who had sired a brood of thirteen, congratulated his son in 1825 on the latest arrival and urged his daughter-in-law to continue her good work: "tell her that I give you and her Joy with him [the infant] and that she is doing well bringing such fine children for this world and there is no doubt but you and she will be rewarded for it in the next world, and it is my opinion the more she brings the greater will be the reward." Certainly for Philemon Hawkins the biblical injunction to be fruitful and multiply was a divine commandment still in force for himself, his children, and— his daughter-in-law. Other planters expressed a more secular admiration for numerous progeny. John Waddell, whose elder children were almost all males, proudly announced a birth in his family to his friend Duncan Cameron: "Altho' I can't boast of being rich in money I may with propriety say I am so in sons, you must know my wife brought me a sixth son the very day she reached this place."[12]

Women too recorded appreciation and joy over the birth of children, even when such events became frequent. A young matron, grieving over deceased children, fondly recollected that her seventh child's "birth was hailed with so much joy, but how fleeting are all earthly pleasures." Temperance Williams (then the mother of six but

in Tamara K. Hareven and Maris A. Vinovskis (eds.), *Family and Population in Nineteenth-Century America* (Princeton, 1978), 22–73.

11. Chowan County Marriage Bonds; Lavinia Coffield Tombstone Record, in WPA Pre-1914 Grave Index, NCDAH; Will of William T. Thompson, in Bertie County Wills. At least eleven of the nineteen families producing three or fewer children were the result of incomplete marriages.

12. Philemon Hawkins to John D. Hawkins, January 26, 1825, in Hawkins Family Papers; John Waddell to Duncan Cameron, December 22, 1806, in Cameron Family Papers. See also Isaac T. Avery to Selina L. Lenoir, September 14, 1835, in Lenoir Family Papers.

eventually of nine) summed up the attitudes of many women when she thanked her sister-in-law for leaving her youngsters with the Williams family during an absence: "I thank you and Brother E— much, for the confidence you have shown us—I know well with whom we confide *our greatest treasures*—and our children are Heavens best gifts."[13]

To be sure, this pleasure was not unalloyed. Pregnancy had its inconveniences and discomforts for women. My health is good, pregnant Missouri Alston assured her mother, "but I always do my share of complaining in my present condition." More important, women and men alike had fears—all too often justified—about the dangers of childbearing. Mary Henderson, despite an intense desire for children, was struck by trepidations during her pregnancies. In 1858 she penned in her diary, "I dread my travail but try not to think of it[.] the time is rapidly approaching & I am not ready." Two and one-half years earlier, with the birth of her eighth child imminent, Mary had resolved to put her affairs in order for she feared that "my days are numbered." These forebodings led her to have her best clothes washed and starched "for they may be needed"—for her funeral. Men also voiced such concerns. Isaac T. Avery told his sister that his pregnant wife was not very well "but as her disease is one she is having, perhaps for the 12th time[,] it neither excites as much sympathy or apprehension, as it ought."[14]

A general disregard of family planning probably continued among North Carolina planter families through much of the mid-nineteenth century. A survey of the number of children ever born to the fifty-six planters' daughters and daughters-in-law who were alive and aged forty to sixty in 1850 reveals an average of 6.02 children. And if incomplete marriages, broken during the wife's childbearing years, are excepted, the mean number of offspring rises to 6.36. So these women, who usually had begun childbearing between 1810 and 1835,

13. M. S. Henderson Diary, December 21, 1854, in Henderson Papers; Temperance Williams to Rebecca Hilliard, August 3, 1853, in John Buxton Williams Papers, Duke; MS Census of 1850, N.C., Warren County, Sch. I, p. 49. See also Charity Mangum to Willie P. Mangum, January 7, 1826, in Shanks (ed.), *The Papers of Willie Person Mangum*, I, 225.

14. Missouri F. Alston to Sarah M. Alston, January 19, 1849, in Alston Papers; M. S. Henderson Diary, January 14, 1858, July 12, August 11, 1855, in Henderson Papers; Isaac T. Avery to Selina L. Lenoir, February 18, 1835, in Lenoir Family Papers.

had only slightly reduced fertility compared with their mothers' levels.

Family limitation also appears to have received little vocal support among the younger generation. Frances Miller, presenting her younger sister with a gift for the new baby, wished that the latter might have at least six children. Also typical was another young woman who informed her sister that their cousin was "in the situation that ladies wish to be who love their lords." To be sure, an occasional veiled remark suggested that some preferred a small family. When wealthy William Plummer "had the blues" after the birth of his seventh child, he told a friend that "he must not believe the birth of the child caused them." But Plummer's anxiety to dispel any linkage between his depression and the newborn's birth only made his sister, herself the mother of a large family, more certain that the two were in fact related: "as he seemed so suspicious that he would be accused of it, we have come to the conclusion that it was the fact." And possibly some of the younger generation consciously limited the size of their families. After Robert T. Paine's only child begged her uncle to send one of his children to live with her family because she had no siblings, Paine chided his wife: "See now in what a lovely situation you have left our daughter, are you not sorry for it." But whether he was referring to her deliberate decision to limit births or simply was reproaching her for an inability to bear other children is unfathomable.[15]

The extent to which North Carolina planter families' fertility was typical, either of the upper class or of women nationwide, is extremely difficult to determine. Wealthy Carolinians may have lagged somewhat behind in the general decline in American family size that occurred from the late eighteenth century through the nineteenth century. Ann Williams Boucher in her study of wealthy Alabama planter families has argued that the number of children born to elite Alabama women at midcentury—approximately 5.5—was considerably higher than that born to wealthy Boston matrons because of the latter's older age at first marriage. In North Carolina young women

15. Frances Miller to Sophia Turner, November 20, 1856, in Turner Papers; Mary B. Badger to Mary Polk, October 13, 1832, in Polk, Badger, and McGehee Family Papers; Lucy M. Battle to William H. Battle, May 5, 1841, in Battle Family Papers, SHC; Robert T. Paine to Lavinia Paine, June 18, 1850, in Paine Papers.

married younger, and the proportion of spinsters, although increasing over time, remained smaller than in the North. But these factors probably cannot explain all the difference since Daniel Scott Smith has convincingly held that one-half to three-fourths of the nationwide drop was attributable to efforts at family limitation. James C. Mohr and Carl N. Degler have also argued that deliberate limitation of fertility—whether through abortion-inducing drugs, contraceptive methods or devices, or sexual abstinence—increased during the course of the nineteenth century. Little evidence, however, exists to indicate that elite North Carolinians took similar steps to control family size.[16]

These planter families not only gave birth to many children but also lost many. An accurate measurement of child mortality among these North Carolina families is not possible, but a rough survey of the nine families with what appear to be complete birth and death records suggests a rate of 230 per 1,000—at least one child in four did not reach its fifth birthday. Impressionistic evidence suggesting that these families were much healthier than average means this very crude figure should be interpreted as a minimum rather than a maximum. Very likely Maris Vinovskis' reckoning that mortality during the first year of life alone hovered between 115 and 313 per 1,000 births for the antebellum period in America also held true for the Carolinians. While child mortality in America never attained the heights prevailing in early modern Europe, it also showed little decrease before the late nineteenth century.[17] The death of children remained a scourge of family life in North Carolina.

Despite their large numbers of children and considerable child mortality, elite Carolinians recorded an appreciation of children as intense as other nineteenth-century well-to-do Americans. The most

16. Boucher, "Wealthy Planter Families," 138–43; Daniel Scott Smith, "Family Limitation, Sexual Control, and Domestic Feminism in Victorian America," *Feminist Studies*, I (1973), 40–57; Ansley J. Coale and Melvin Zelnik, *New Estimates of Fertility and Population in the United States: A Study of Annual White Births . . .* (Princeton, 1963), 31–41; Yasuba, *Birth Rates*, 49–101; James C. Mohr, *Abortion in America: The Origins and Evolution of National Policy, 1800–1900* (New York, 1978), 46–102; Degler, *At Odds*, 178–248.

17. Maris A. Vinovskis, "Angels' Heads and Weeping Willows: Death in Early America," in Tamara K. Hareven (ed.), *Themes in the History of the Family* (Worcester, Mass., 1978), 25–44; Jacques Gélis, Mireille Laget, and Marie-France Morel, *Entrer dans la vie: Naissances et enfances dans la France traditionelle* (Paris, 1978), 185–93.

poignant illustration of the high value that planters placed upon their progeny was their reaction to youngsters' and infants' deaths. Parents never bore death well despite elaborate preparations to steel themselves. Some attempted to keep an infant's or child's possible demise in mind. Leonidas Polk typified this attitude when describing his two-week-old son: "Thus far his promise has been all we could wish, but we know that the tenure of life at such an age is extremely feeble and our brightest hopes may at any moment be nipped in the bud. This I endeavor constantly to realize." Planters' consciousness of mortality was not, however, limited to extremely young infants but extended to older children and even adults. Throughout the antebellum period, parents added such phrases as "if she should live" or "should he survive" to discussions of their offspring, like charms to ward off complacency and remind themselves of the menace of death. Whether ritual incantation against death or simply *memento mori*, planters' fatalism could not remove their sorrow.[18]

Most commonly, parents grieved deeply over deceased children. James L. G. Baker attempted to comfort his bereaved brother-in-law: "I know my dear Brother how to appreciate your feelings. I too have lost fond and affectionate children endeared to me by a thousand infantile ties known to no one but a parent." Susan B. Capehart ended a distressed letter about the death of her toddler daughter, "I thought the loss of my Sister was the greatest trial I ever met with but it was a small one in comparison with the loss of my child."[19]

Although Lawrence Stone has shown that children younger than two years were little mourned in some large early modern European families, wealthy North Carolinians lamented such deaths. Some parents, however, recognized a difference in the quality of grief for children and for infants. Mary Henderson believed her deceased six- and two-year-old sons were "more missed" than her "precious babes," but she obviously mourned the wee ones also. Probably other par-

18. Leonidas Polk to his brother, February 10, 1831, in Leonidas Polk Papers, SHC. Consult Isaac T. Avery to W. B. Lenoir, January 11, 1824, in Lenoir Family Papers; Moorhead Wright to Isaac Wright, August 7, 1847, in Gillespie and Wright Family Papers, SHC; Charles E. Johnson to Charles E. Johnson, Jr., December 18, 1849, in Charles Earl Johnson Papers, Duke.

19. James L. G. Baker to William R. Smith, December 10, 1845, in P. E. Smith Papers; Susan B. Capehart to Peter Martin, August 24, 1836, in Scotch Hall Papers, SHC.

ents' reaction to the loss of infants paralleled that of Harriet and Isaac T. Avery. He described the baby and their emotions over the loss: "she was turned of nine months old, and had never been sick an hour in her life, had been the heartiest child we ever raised. I feel this dispensation as a Parent and I endeavor to bear it as a man, but to a Mother, to have a promising Child at that interesting age where it is Just beginning to discover the first gleams of intelligence[,] the loss is almost insupportable, may you never as a Parent experience such a trial." Such sorrow also extended to newborn infants. Moorhead Wright sadly noted that his premature child died approximately six hours after birth: "[My wife] had been very carefull [sic], and much we both regret [it] for if there is anyone that have a fondness for children I am that individual." [20]

Bereavements disheartened men like Wright and Avery, but their wives were more likely to sink into depression. Norms of conduct, though not condoning inordinate grief, allowed women more leeway to express sorrow. Their husbands had to try to "bear it as men." Religious beliefs strongly influenced expressions of grief and probably muted such utterances. Planters, Episcopalian as well as those of more Calvinist inclination, believed in a jealous God, the Old Testament Jehovah, who would brook no competitors. This creed, positing an active, omnipotent deity, demanded that love for family and mourning of the deceased be restrained. Like earlier Puritans, religious planters feared too great worldly attachments. But that fear arose only from the possible consequences of too much love; such idolatry tempted their God to chastise the offender by removing the object. Pious Mary Bethell revealingly reminisced about her deceased daughter: "Sometimes her remarks were so sweet and sensible, I was lead [sic] to exclaim, we must not love her too much, the Lord might take her." Agony over the deaths of five children and anxiety about her remaining offspring filled Mary Henderson's diary. She found her God a hard taskmaster, "but God doeth all things well. He gave and he surely had the right to take. . . . I feel so unhappy about the two

20. Stone, *The Family, Sex and Marriage*, 81, 420; M. S. Henderson Diary, August 20, 1855, in Henderson Papers; Isaac T. Avery to W. B. Lenoir, July 14, 1825, in Lenoir Family Papers; Moorhead Wright to Isaac Wright, August 10, 1850, in Gillespie and Wright Family Papers. See Anne Cameron to Paul C. Cameron, n.d., in Cameron Family Papers.

remaining ones[,] thinking it may be God's good pleasure to recall them and shuddering at the bare idea." [21]

The death of a child—unless severely deformed or otherwise handicapped—was believed a calamity by its parents. Still religious beliefs combined with attitudes toward decorum to produce a model of parental mourning that suppressed long or excessively emotional grief. Fathers and mothers who did not conform risked criticism. A wealthy young matron commented unfavorably upon a great planter's wife who "is still very dejected owing to the loss of her infant— I should judge her to be a woman of little fortitude." Even this disparaging comment about mourning demeanor reveals that the death of a child was regarded as a trial demanding fortitude. Such lamentations and grief closely resembled those of other well-to-do parents in eighteenth- and nineteenth-century France, England, and America.[22] Among these other groups, such attitudes have often been linked to family limitation and greatly reduced child mortality; among the planters, affection existed despite large families and the frequent loss of children.

Just as planters' grief demonstrated attachment to and a high esteem for children, their other parental attitudes marked an early recognition of each child's individuality. Carefully surveying their infants, mothers and fathers found the distinctive in each. His newborn son was unusually large with intensely blue eyes, M. M. Harrison noted, and the infant "takes decidedly after his mother." Parents also chronicled activities and abilities of young infants. Rebecca Cameron's six-week-old baby could crow and laugh. Isaac T. Avery proudly described his four-month-old son: "Thomas Lenoir Avery, a young gentleman . . . can sit alone, laugh out loud and cut other smart capers for a fellow of his age and is the handsomest of all [our] . . . children." [23]

21. Edmund S. Morgan, *The Puritan Family: Religion and Domestic Relations in Seventeenth Century New England* (New York, 1966), 48–51, 76–79; Mary Jeffreys Bethell Diary, April 3, 1849, in SHC; M. S. Henderson Diary, July 1, 1855, in Henderson Papers.

22. Mary B. Badger to Sarah Polk, October 27, 1827, in Polk, Badger, and McGehee Family Papers; Philip J. Greven, Jr., *The Protestant Temperament: Patterns of Child-Rearing, Religious Experience, and the Self in Early America* (New York, 1977), 156–59; Gélis, Laget, and Morel, *Entrer dans la vie*, 194–98.

23. M. M. Harrison to Alexander Cuningham, September 9, 1845, in Alexander

Like Avery, other parents were interested in the appearance of their infants—even newborn babies. Most preferred large, fat babies since size was equated with well-being. Nurslings who were plump and bigger than average inspired bragging. Paul C. Cameron exultingly called his newborn son "a 'buster' of prodigious size—weighing 12 pounds." Parents who remarked on the smallness or thinness of infants were troubled by fears. Isaac T. Avery noted: "the little Babe is small; but thus far appears healthy." Mary Henderson described her newborn son: "he is very small and poor and has turned very yellow, but appears healthy, he sucks as strong as any child—I trust he will be spared to us."[24]

This belief in the child's individuality was not compromised by planters' naming practices, which reflected a variety of concerns. One recent study of Charleston, South Carolina, planters has suggested that their naming practices indicated the group's "glorification of the father" as part of a general patriarchal orientation. But an examination of naming practices among wealthy North Carolinians suggests an alternative explanation: the crucial roles played by kinship—especially bilateral descent—and affection. Generally planter families, like English villagers or twentieth-century American families not usually considered patriarchal, used their own parents and other close relatives as principal sources for names. In fact, in the sixty-seven families for which fairly complete information can be compiled, at least one child bore a grandparent's name. For example, Joseph John Alston and his wife Martha named two children after her parents and one after him or his father. William and Rachel Herring named their first two daughters after their own mothers and a son after Rachel's father. Occasionally parents explicitly noted that their children were named after the grandparents. Archibald Glenn, not on particularly good terms with his parents-in-law and living away from their area, reminded his father-in-law Alexander Cuningham of the children:

Cuningham Papers, Duke; Rebecca Cameron to Duncan Cameron, September 11, 1806, in Cameron Family Papers; Isaac T. Avery to Thomas Lenoir, July 23, 1821, in Lenoir Family Papers.

24. Paul C. Cameron to Duncan Cameron, November 23, 1850, in Cameron Family Papers; Isaac T. Avery to Selina L. Lenoir, January 4, 1829, in Lenoir Family Papers; Mary S. Henderson to Archibald Henderson, January 12, 1846, in Henderson Papers. See also M. W. Leach to Charity Mangum, February 27, 1859, in Shanks (ed.), *The Papers of Willie Person Mangum*, V, 359.

"Martha called you recollect after your wife—James A. after my Father, and Alexander C. after yourself."[25]

Even the way that parents arrived at names suggests that one should not overemphasize any patriarchal aspects. The naming of children did not fall solely to men who then sometimes chose to honor the more worthy representatives of their wives' lineage. Instead both husband and wife played a role. Sometimes they agreed upon a mutually acceptable name or each contributed a part, but more often the two took turns, each usually naming a child after a beloved member of his or her own family of origin. Thus it was Ann Hawkins Little who made the decision to name her newborn after her father Philemon Hawkins. Mary S. Henderson voluntarily relinquished her role in naming at one point because "I have been so unfortunate in the naming of our children, have not the heart to do it again." All the children she had named—each with a name drawn from her own family—had died. Thus her husband chose the name, calling the infant after Mary herself.[26]

As these practices indicate, naming could strengthen ties among family members—even the somewhat tenuous ties binding Archibald Glenn's family and the Cuninghams—by the esteem it signified. Children by their names could also carry memories of the past into the future. But more important for the family's child-centeredness, naming practices firmly placed the infant in the conjugal family by identifying it with an important relative from a parent's family of origin.

A special category of passing along family names was giving the newborn infant the name of its deceased older sibling. Some historians of the family have linked such necronymic naming to a callousness toward children or a lack of concern with their individuality, but this interpretation takes too narrow a view. Planter families occasionally used necronymic naming as a way of perpetuating the

---

25. M. P. Johnson, "Planters and Patriarchy," 48–50; William M. Williams, *The Sociology of an English Village: Gosforth* (London, 1956), 79–82; Alice S. Rossi, "Naming Children in Middle Class Families," *American Sociological Review*, XXX (1965), 499–513; Groves, *The Alstons and Allstons*, 126–27; Herring Family Records, in Compiled Genealogies, NCDAH; Archibald Glenn to Alexander Cuningham, n.d. [ca. 1843], in Cuningham Papers.

26. Sarah Polk to Mary B. Polk, July 8, 1823, in Polk, Badger, and McGehee Family Papers; M. S. Henderson Diary, February 15, 1858, in Henderson Papers.

memory of very dear relatives. Simmons J. Baker's high regard for his father probably inspired him to give two sons that name. Simmons cannot be called an indifferent father; his letters show much affection and a keen interest in his children, even the youngest. Some wealthy North Carolinians were aware of and troubled by some of the implications of passing along a deceased child's name to a later-born one. Although they may, as Jacques Gélis has suggested for other groups, have used necronymic naming to commemorate the dead child, the practice threatened that the dead child would be replaced and the memory of it submerged. Paul C. Cameron told his father Duncan: "The little boy is looking in fine health—is no beauty—I think he will take the name of 'Bennehan'—I wish to give him your name—but my wife is too much troubled with former associations to know any other 'Duncan' than the dear little one gone before us to the grave." Despite these misgivings and their obvious affection for their children, Paul and Anne Cameron named their new baby Duncan. Necronymic naming then identified the infant with an especially valued relative and may possibly have enhanced the newborn's position in the household.[27]

So fond of their babies were North Carolina elite parents that they were unwilling to send them away to wet nurses as families in eighteenth-century France and England had. Nor did they often install wet nurses in their own households as had some eighteenth-century American elites. North Carolina ladies, like their counterparts Southwide studied by Sally McMillen, generally breast-fed their own infants. Modern experts on child development have postulated that the act of suckling an infant encourages close mother-child relations, and ties of affection do seem often to have arisen.[28] Although nursing

27. Edward Shorter, *The Making of the Modern Family* (New York, 1975), 168–72; Stone, *The Family, Sex and Marriage*, 70; Degler, *At Odds*, 71; Baker Genealogy, in Benbury and Haywood Family Papers; "Recollections of Family of Dr. Simmons J. Baker," in Simmons J. Baker Papers, NCDAH; Simmons J. Baker to Emily Baker, August 2, 1811, in W. L. Saunders Papers, Duke; Gélis, Laget, and Morel, *Entrer dans la vie*, 194; Paul C. Cameron to Duncan Cameron, March 13, 1851, in Cameron Family Papers.

28. Randolph Trumbach, "The Aristocratic Family in England, 1690–1780: Studies in Childhood and Kinship" (Ph.D. dissertation, Johns Hopkins University, 1972), 57–68; Claire E. Fox, "Pregnancy, Childbirth, and Early Infancy in Anglo-American Culture, 1675–1830" (Ph.D. dissertation, University of Pennsylvania, 1966), 233–34; Stone, *The Family, Sex and Marriage*, 529–32; Sally McMillen, "Mother or Mammy?

a child could be exhausting and physically debilitating, some mothers wrote contented, happy letters with a baby at the breast.

Planter families showed much concern for nurslings. Nursing mothers frequently worried about their supply of milk. Jane Hamilton's sister, congratulating her upon the new baby, included a wish often exchanged among mothers: "I hope you are well and will have plenty of nourishment for your child." In fact, some mothers attempted to nurse children when such activity was extremely painful. Anne Cameron, while reassuring her husband that her health had improved, revealed that she had continued to suckle their infant despite great discomfort: "I had suffered with great soreness of the muscles between the arm and the breast and the operation of nursing dear little Mary drew tears almost every time."[29]

Only ill health or an insufficient supply of milk appears to have prevented wealthy North Carolina matrons, like those elsewhere in the South, from suckling their own children. When mothers were physically incapable of nursing, they used a wet nurse at home rather than sending the infant away from the household. Most wet nurses were slave women who either had lost an infant or had an ample supply of milk, and the feeding took place under maternal supervision. That elite Carolinian women who resorted to a wet nurse for one infant usually breast-fed others suggests that temporary health problems rather than any aversion to nursing guided their actions. Although lactation by inhibiting ovulation could serve as a natural— though not foolproof—method of birth control, planter women left no evidence that they consciously used or even thought of using it to that end.[30]

Concerned mothers found weaning children, usually between the ages of eight and eighteen months, a difficult though necessary task. Generally a diminishing supply of milk, the child's growing ability

Infant Feeding in the Antebellum South" (paper, Duke University, 1981); Therese Benedek, "Psychological Aspects of Mothering," *Journal of Orthopsychiatry*, XXVI (1956), 272–78; Theodore Lidz, *The Person: His or Her Development Throughout the Life Cycle* (2nd ed.; New York, 1976), 116, 133–36.

29. S. E. Chalmers to Jane Hamilton, February 23, 1847, in Bullock and Hamilton Papers; Anne Cameron to Paul C. Cameron, December 26, 1844, in Cameron Family Papers.

30. McMillen, "Mother or Mammy?," 11–16; M. S. Henderson Diary, October 18, 1855, January 8, February 23, 1856, July 11, October 27, 1858, in Henderson Papers.

to eat semisolid foods, and the continuing tax on their own strength led mothers to wean children. At least one woman weaned her one-year-old when she discovered that she was again pregnant. Tristrim L. Skinner, alarmed by his wife's steady loss of weight, urged her to wean their eight-month-old son: "His 6 teeth ought certainly to enable him to draw 2/3rds of his nourishment from bread and meat, and I think it your duty to yourself to accustom him and not by slow degrees, to get on without you."[31]

The ill effects—both physical and emotional—that sometimes stemmed from weaning made the process difficult for mothers. Mary Bethell was distraught when her efforts to wean her eight-month-old daughter went awry: "It went very hard with her, feeding her on solid food did not agree with her, she became sick and weak." Bethell's stepmother aided her by feeding cow's milk to the baby until it recovered. The anger and irritability children sometimes displayed during weaning dismayed and worried other mothers. "She is very fretful and sometimes cries a great deal," wrote Jane Hamilton about her one-year-old daughter; "her appetite is very good indeed, I have to allowance her constantly. She tries very hard to suck, when she first began to want to eat, and would scream and cry very much when I would not let her have the breast, particularly at night. Poor little thing I felt sorry for her."[32]

Planter parents, especially mothers, also showed an ongoing interest in their young children's activities despite their use of nursemaids and other child tenders. The question of nurses' importance in children's lives has long interested historians of the South and of the family. According to Eugene D. Genovese, the nursemaid or mammy, a middle-aged or older woman of authority, petted, cared for, corrected, and advised the children. Mammy then allegedly became a principal source of authority in young children's lives. Although Philip J. Greven, Jr., could find little information about nurses in genteel northern and southern families, he concluded that nurses' "sig-

31. Tristrim L. Skinner to Eliza Skinner, August 15, 1850, in Skinner Family Papers.
32. Bethell Diary, p. 6; Jane Hamilton to Charles E. Hamilton, December 17, 1844, in Bullock and Hamilton Papers. See also Rebecca Cameron to Duncan Cameron, November 5, 1805, in Cameron Family Papers.

nificance for the functioning of the household was immense." According to Greven, nursemaids allowed parents to become distant, awe-inspiring figures involved with children in formal relationships.[33] Many North Carolina planter families rarely mentioned their nursemaids or mammies; and even when they did, the nurse's importance often was questionable. It is unlikely that many supplanted mothers in either affection or authority.

Far from being women of authority, some nurses were little more than children themselves. The nurse of Mary Bethell's children was only thirteen years old, and Mary Henderson and Anne Cameron also used young girls as child tenders. Like their middle-class counterparts in nineteenth-century England, some southern ladies gave part of the drudgery of child care to young, inexperienced women. It seems likely that these slave girls functioned more as modern baby-sitters than as full mother surrogates. Nurses also sometimes proved incompetent. Mary Henderson, after many years, still fulminated bitterly about the unconcern of a slave woman who had cared for one of her children. Anne Cameron could not find a reliable child tender after the loss of her usual nurse.[34]

Black nurses and mammies may have played a larger role for children whose mother had died. The care of widowed Joseph B. Skinner's children is suggestive. Their first nurse was the slave Barbara, whom Skinner believed devoted to her charges. Later Annie, the most important slave in the Skinner household, became the children's nurse. Their relationship with her appears to have been close and affectionate. But even though Skinner appears to have had few female relatives, he still provided a white surrogate mother in addition to these black ones. During his frequent visits to Hillsborough he left the youngsters under the care of a professional colleague, Frederick Nash, and his wife. Aunt Nash, as the children Penelope and Tris-

33. Genovese, *Roll, Jordan, Roll*, 353–61; Greven, *The Protestant Temperament*, 274–76.

34. Bethell Diary, November 3, 1856; M. S. Henderson Diary, February 23, 1856, in Henderson Papers; Theresa McBride, " 'As the Twig Is Bent': The Victorian Nanny," in Anthony S. Wohl (ed.), *The Victorian Family: Structure and Stresses* (New York, 1978), 44–58; M. S. Henderson Diary, July 8, 1855, in Henderson Papers; Anne Cameron to Margaret Cameron, February 24, 1844, in Cameron Family Papers.

trim called her, integrated them into her household. Years later, when Penelope, married less than a year and pregnant, left Chowan County for her health, she stayed in Hillsborough where Aunt Nash could advise her.[35]

Even nursemaids believed reliable probably had rather limited autonomy and influence over children. Despite Annie's favored position of long standing with the Skinner family, Tristrim L. Skinner cautioned his wife to inspect carefully any food that Annie, as his own baby's nurse, might give it. Parents like Tristrim may have been influenced by the popular child-rearing manuals of the day—including one published in North Carolina—which urged the curbing of servants' role. In this view, nurses should be used only for the heavier and more fatiguing aspects of child care, and mothers should vigilantly supervise the routine.[36]

More important, however, was the care that many mothers lavished upon children who had competent nursemaids. During the years women such as Anne Cameron, Margaret Devereux, and Mary Henderson had nurses they considered trustworthy, they spent much time with their children; their letters reveal constant preoccupation. Margaret Devereux thought her eldest daughter "the smartest little thing I ever saw in my life and twenty times a day I wish someone else was here to hear her." Ann Williams Boucher in her study of Alabama planter families has recorded a similar maternal focus on children's activities. Modern studies of kibbutzim and group care have pointed out that children in those settings identify more strongly with their mothers than their caretakers.[37] Given the close attention planter mothers gave to children, probably few allowed nurses to assume major importance. Imbued with the notion of personal responsibility to rear their children, planter parents were willing to delegate some

35. Will of Joseph B. Skinner, in Chowan County Wills; Joseph B. Skinner to Joshua Skinner, June 26, 1826, Frederick Nash to Joseph B. Skinner, May 2, 1827, Penelope Skinner Warren to Thomas D. Warren, August 28, 1840, all in Skinner Family Papers.

36. Tristrim L. Skinner to Eliza Skinner, August 15, 1850, in Skinner Family Papers; James W. Milden, "The Sacred Sanctuary: Family Life in Nineteenth Century America" (Ph.D. dissertation, University of Maryland, 1974), 145–48; G. G. Johnson, *Ante-bellum North Carolina*, 235–36.

37. Margaret Devereux to Ellen Mordecai, November 7, 1846, in Margaret M. Devereux Papers, SHC; Boucher, "Wealthy Planter Families," 149–51; Jerome Kagan, "The Child in the Family," in Alice S. Rossi, Jerome Kagan, and Tamara K. Hareven (eds.), *The Family* (New York, 1978), 36–37.

authority to able nurses, but were unwilling to yield their favored position.

Fathers as well as mothers often took great interest in their children's activities. A young man admiringly chronicled how his toddler daughter "takes great delight in looking at her little colors and is frequently feeding the little chickens." To be sure, the daily overseeing of preschoolers fell to women, but males too recorded perceptions of domestic bliss and children's romps. One planter, shut in at his absentee plantation by a snowstorm, invidiously contrasted his day there to how he would have spent it at his own house: "At home I should have given the day to Wife and little ones—here to books." Like the genteel eighteenth-century northerners and southerners studied by Greven and by Daniel Blake Smith, North Carolinians pampered young children and frequently gave them gifts. Children missed their father during any extended absences, but even very young ones learned that their father's return usually included presents. Part of the fun of talking about the reunion lay in speculating about the gifts. In 1812, Jane Wright told her husband that the children asked about him and when he would return to bring them "pocket handkerchiefs, knives, books, cakes, and ect. [sic]." One little daughter, Catherine, aged only three, expected a pair of kid shoes.[38]

Like many well-to-do European and American families of the day, elite North Carolinians were much concerned with their children's health. They sought both to prevent illness and to cure disease. Rebecca Cameron carefully had her young children inoculated against smallpox. When her five-month-old daughter became ill with a fever, Rebecca also sent for the doctor although she "did not apprehend any danger." Popular belief held fruit responsible for many complaints common among youngsters, and mothers like Mary Biddle watched their children closely to prevent them from eating it. John Waddell, whose one-year-old son was ill, decided to move into a new, partly

38. Franklin L. Smith to Mary Smith, May 21, 1837, in Rufus Reid Papers, SHC; Paul C. Cameron to Thomas Ruffin, February 1, 1858, in J. G. de Roulhac Hamilton (ed.), *The Papers of Thomas Ruffin* (4 vols.; Raleigh, 1918), II, 583; Greven, *The Protestant Temperament*, 268–74, 276–78; D. B. Smith, *Inside the Great House*, 40–53; Jane Wright to Isaac Wright, December 8, 1812, in Gillespie and Wright Family Papers. Also consult Josiah Collins, Jr., to Josiah Collins, December 29, 1818, in Josiah Collins Papers, NCDAH; Simmons J. Baker to Emily Baker, August 2, 1811, in W. L. Saunders Papers, Duke.

unfinished house rather than spend any time twenty-seven miles from medical assistance.[39]

These early years did not pass without lessons in socialization and discipline although both, in keeping with the planters' fondness for their progeny, were mild. Parents, even while admiring a bit of sauciness and spirit, wanted their offspring to be well behaved. A certain amount of good manners and "proper behavior" was required even of very young children. Important were politeness and respect toward older relatives (even though such respect was to be tempered by affection). Jane Hamilton illustrated such concerns when she wrote about her four-year-old son: "I try to make him *behave* himself at the table, and be polite to every body, but particularly his Grandfather." [40]

Like late-eighteenth-century Chesapeake planters, wealthy North Carolinians showed no interest in "breaking children's wills" and compelling strict subordination—in fact, they never mentioned such a possibility. Although desirous of obedient sons and daughters, these parents did not demand complete submissiveness. Eliza Gaston, a young mother, admitted she had not yet learned the "art of managing little people." She believed that she must begin using "some little authority" with her toddler daughter who said "no no" to every command.[41]

Elite Carolinians did not completely eschew physical punishments but, as was the case among their middle-class northern counterparts, did not much like them. Generally spankings appear to have been the usual correction for truculent youngsters. Some planter families relied on slightly different means. Sophia Devereux later re-

39. Ariès, *Centuries of Childhood*, 400–401; Rebecca Cameron to Duncan Cameron, July 14, 1811, May 22, 1804, both in Cameron Family Papers; Mary E. V. Biddle to Samuel S. Biddle, July 10, 1847, in Biddle Papers; John Waddell to Duncan Cameron, November 10, 1805, in Cameron Family Papers. See also Franklin L. Smith to Mary Smith, May 21, 1837, in Reid Papers; Isaac T. Avery to Thomas Lenoir, July 23, 1821, in Lenoir Family Papers.

40. Jane Hamilton to Charles E. Hamilton, October 15, 1844, in Bullock and Hamilton Papers. Consult Susan B. Capehart to William R. Capehart, January 23, 1849, in W. R. Capehart Papers.

41. Greven, *The Protestant Temperament*, 277–81; D. B. Smith, *Inside the Great House*, 40–53; Eliza Gaston to William Gaston, December 9, 1818, in Gaston Papers. See M. S. Henderson Diary, July 2, 1855, in Henderson Papers; Tristrim L. Skinner to Eliza Skinner, June 15, 1859, in Skinner Family Papers.

called that her father would chastise an erring child by thumping his thumb against the offender's head. She disliked the punishment but did not consider it particularly painful or cruel. Temperance Hilliard registered her disapproval of unseemly conduct with pointed scowls, which her son later described as *"withering in the extreme."*[42]

Despite their many children and the toll taken by child mortality, North Carolina planter families closely resembled the sentimental units that owed their existence, some historians have implied, to reductions in fertility and child mortality. Indeed, although lowered rates in these two areas may contribute to child-centered families, the structure of these elite families suggests that they were not necessary preconditions. Planters' attitudes toward their children were similar to those of other contemporary well-to-do families in America, England, and France that were limiting their family size. Like these other parents, wealthy North Carolinians were grief-stricken at the loss of even young infants. They, too, early recognized the child as an important part of the household and were unwilling to send it out to a wet nurse. Planters, like other privileged families in nineteenth-century Western societies, both cosseted children and attempted to safeguard their health. Overshadowing other aspects of the relationship was the Carolinians' fascination with and affection for their progeny. That love remained, but as children grew older, parental expectations changed and became more demanding.

42. Sophia Devereux to Josiah Turner, Jr., n.d. [*ca.* November, 1855], in Turner Papers; Elijah B. Hilliard to Mary E. V. Biddle, November 24, 1846, in Biddle Papers; Robert Sunley, "Early Nineteenth Century American Literature on Child Rearing," in Margaret Mead and Martha Wolfenstein (eds.), *Childhood in Contemporary Cultures* (Chicago, 1955), 159–62. Compare to the discipline described in William G. McLoughlin, "Evangelical Childrearing in the Age of Jackson: Francis Wayland's Views on When and How to Subdue the Willfulness of Children," *Journal of Social History*, IX (1975), 20–43.

THREE

A Parent's Fond yet Watchful Eye
Youth and Education

As children in North Carolina elite families reached school age, parents became more demanding. Planters, with help from the schools, sought to inculcate sons and daughters with knowledge and virtue but at the same time wished to have warm relations with them. Combined affection and high expectations similarly characterized interactions with older youth, whose maturing led to a changing pattern of parental authority.

To North Carolina planters, the years of youth demanded close attention to formal education and to the building of character traits helpful in later life. And this was an attitude they often explicitly expressed to their children, as Margaret Collet did in her admonition to her eldest daughter: "I hope my dear child that you will begin to feel the value and importance of education and will embrace the present opportunity of acquiring all useful knowledge." Certainly none among this elite defended ignorance, at least in their own kind. As Willie P. Mangum told his twelve-year-old daughter, "Ignorance in grown people is a great misfortune; and in those who had opportunity to be otherwise, it is a great sin."[1]

Rebecca and Duncan Cameron's efforts illustrate parental determination that their children be educated. When their eldest son Thomas showed problems in learning, they enrolled him in a New Jersey boarding school, where he received individualized instruction. Upon the thirteen-year-old's departure, Rebecca queried her husband about whether Thomas still appeared "content to leave his paternal

---

1. Margaret Collet to Eliza Murphy, August 17, 1834, in Thomas G. Walton Papers, SHC; Willie P. Mangum to Sally A. Mangum, April 7, 1836, in Shanks (ed.), *The Papers of Willie Person Mangum*, II, 421. Compare to Wyatt-Brown, "The Ideal Typology," 6.

roof and dear relatives and to go among strangers? a truly painful reflection to a fond Mother, and but for the hope it may ultimately prove beneficial to our dear child, I could not consent to it." Despite his slow progress, the Camerons retained Thomas in that school for three years and then sent the docile backward boy to a military academy (also attended by his brother and a cousin) for three additional years. Even Thomas' attendance at this second school appears to have sprung from the desire that he receive as nearly as possible (with some indulgence shown his handicaps) the same training as his more talented brother. His case highlights the resolution planters could show toward education.[2]

Boys and girls, who as young children had been allowed to play in fairly similar ways, found their paths diverging during schooling. Like other nineteenth-century Americans, Carolinians expected the sexes to learn different curricula as well as different behavior. Planters wished, however, both their sons and their daughters to be well educated and well prepared for later life. Boys received preparatory instruction for the classical studies most would pursue in college. Few formal barriers separated secondary and college level training, and sufficiently skilled young men entered college at an early age. A rough survey of approximately 150 sons suggests that most began college between ages fifteen and nineteen and graduated between ages nineteen and twenty-two. Over two-thirds of the great planters sent a son to college, and at least one-third gave two or more sons collegiate experience.[3] Although classical in orientation, male education was practical in its results, since it fitted young men for a variety of positions. It provided them with the necessary literacy for local administration and the oratorical skills for state and national politics. A

2. Rebecca Cameron to Duncan Cameron, May 3, 1820, J. C. Rudd to Duncan Cameron, March 15, 1822, E. B. Williston to Duncan Cameron, May 14, 1824, Paul C. Cameron to Duncan Cameron, September 3, 1826, all in Cameron Family Papers.

3. Thomas Woody, *A History of Women's Education in the United States* (2 vols.; New York, 1966). At least 77 (68 percent) of 113 planters with sons sent at least one son to college, and at least 37 of that number sent two or more sons (11 sent an only son). Eight other planters had sons in professions who probably attended college. College entry ages, curricula, and activities are covered in Joseph F. Kett, *Rites of Passage: Adolescence in America, 1790 to the Present* (New York, 1977), 21–35; William E. Drake, *Higher Education in North Carolina Before 1860* (New York, 1964); Battle, *History of the University of North Carolina*; E. Merton Coulter, *College Life in the Old South* (Athens, Ga., 1951).

higher education also served as preliminary training for law, medicine, and the ministry. Although contemporary standards did not require a college degree to study or to practice, many doctors and lawyers—especially the most respected and successful—had at least some college training. Thus education could help to secure continued high positions in society for planters' sons.[4]

Although girls studied a different curriculum that usually did not include Greek or Latin, parents also took great interest in their daughters' tutelage. Elite North Carolinians, like the wealthy northern millowners studied by Anthony F. C. Wallace, highly valued a good, thorough education for their daughters. The schooling of females was more than just an indication of high social status; planters looked upon education as a necessary preparation for the young woman's future position as a capable wife and mother. They, like other well-to-do Americans, firmly believed in educating women to develop their allegedly more sensitive, spiritual natures and their general intellect. No northern mid-Victorian could have better expressed such views than elite Carolinian John D. Hawkins, who in an address to a female academy emphasized the twofold practical importance of female education: "It is doubly important that women should be well educated; in the first place to do their duty in managing, raising and instructing their children; and in the second place they should be educated in self-defense." By self-defense Hawkins meant the ability to preserve their virtue. He avowed that education more successfully elevated women's than men's character.[5]

To planters, useful knowledge for females fell into the two major categories that Hawkins indicated. A young lady should study subjects that not only would fit her for her future role as mother and household manager but also would nurture her character and lift it to a lofty level. Like other genteel Americans, planters admired and em-

4. Antoine Prost, *Histoire de l'enseignement en France, 1800–1967* (Paris, 1968), 54–55; Daniel Walker Howe, *The Unitarian Conscience: Harvard Moral Philosophy, 1805–1861* (Cambridge, Mass., 1970), 255–64.
5. Anthony F. C. Wallace, *Rockdale: The Growth of an American Village in the Early Industrial Revolution . . .* (New York, 1978), 23; Woody, *A History of Women's Education*, I, 397–407, 526; Anne L. Kuhn, *The Mother's Role in Childhood Education: New England Concepts, 1830–1860* (New Haven, 1947), 33–41; John D. Hawkins, "Address to a Young Ladies Academy," May 28, 1852, in Hawkins Family Papers.

phasized the spiritual and emotional nature of women, an idealization that in its more extreme forms has been dubbed the "cult of true womanhood." Thus the Tar Heelers considered the two categories as partly overlapping—character traits developed by proper studies would also be necessary to produce a good wife and mother.[6]

Wealthy North Carolinians selected specific courses of study for their daughters which were compatible with this philosophy of education. William Polk cautioned that chemistry, philosophy, and astronomy would be an "idle waste of time" for his daughter and that she should concentrate upon grammar, geography, mathematics, history, belles-lettres, and French. William Cain recommended a similar course of study to his sixteen-year-old daughter: "Those arts and sciences which are peculiar to certain professions need not be known by ladies, as for instance law, politics, physic, &c. But History, Geography[,] Biography &c both ancient and modern should be attended to by you— This, I confess, is a pretty large circle of knowledge, attended with some difficulties and requiring some trouble; which however, an active and industrious mind will overcome and be amply repaid." Polk's and Cain's prescriptions included some intrinsically useful subjects such as arithmetic and grammar; others, such as history and belles-lettres, were practical because they built character. Parents also sometimes endorsed such womanly arts as plain needlework. Still, their notions of education had risen far beyond mere training for housewifery—with only rudimentary reading and writing—which had constituted many eighteenth-century genteel young ladies' instruction.[7]

Although young women's education differed from their brothers', southern historians have probably overemphasized the "ornamen-

6. Barbara Welter, "The Cult of True Womanhood, 1820–1860," *American Quarterly*, XVIII (1966), 151–74.

7. Kuhn, *The Mother's Role*, 33–41; Woody, *A History of Women's Education*, I, 411–16, 144–232; Christie Farnum Pope, "Preparation for Pedestals: North Carolina Ante-bellum Female Seminaries" (Ph.D. dissertation, University of Chicago, 1977), 145–71; Madeline May Allen, "A Historical Study of Moravian Education in North Carolina: The Evolution and Practice of the Moravian Concept of Education as It Applied to Women" (Ph.D. dissertation, Florida State University, 1971), 99–103; William Polk to Mary B. Polk, July 1, 1823, in Polk, Badger, and McGehee Family Papers; William Cain to Minerva Cain, February 22, 1837, in Tod R. Caldwell Papers, SHC; Edmund S. Morgan, *Virginians at Home: Family Life in the Eighteenth Century* (Williamsburg, Va., 1952), 10–19.

tal" aspects of female instruction. No North Carolina planters were found to lay more stress on voice lessons and china painting than on academic subjects. To be sure, Carolinians, like wealthy northerners, did not repudiate or ignore such peculiarly "feminine" accomplishments. They wished their daughters to learn the graceful arts necessary for polite society—to dance well, to sing, and to play an instrument—but designated them a lesser aim of education. William Polk reminded his daughter Mary, "I have on a former occasion stated that I would not have you neglect your studies or exercises on the Piano and Harp and in French; but I hold these as a secondary accomplishment, tho' highly to be appreciated." Even more skeptical of ornamental learning, Margaret Collet informed her daughters' headmistress, "I do not particularly desire that the girls should learn Musick or Painting, but leave it to their choice, and your judgement of their tallents for those branches." Ornamental subjects held a distinctly secondary place in planters' notions of female education; at most such endeavors formed the frosting upon a cake of "useful education." [8]

Wealthy Carolinians' concern about their daughters' educations, guided as it was by visions of young women as future wives and mothers, demanded schooling lasting only into the middle teen years. Most planters' daughters left female academies between ages fifteen and eighteen, not to be married as at least one historian has suggested, but because their educations were considered complete. A few women went almost directly from school to marriage, but most returned home for a season or more of courtship. [9]

As well as teaching academic subjects, the schools should, in the view of the planter elite, impose discipline and cultivate important character traits. Female academies, as Christie Farnum Pope has documented, spent much time socializing girls into the properly self-abnegatory behavior but sought to impose their controls gently. Pope

8. William Polk to Mary B. Polk, July 25, 1823, in Polk, Badger, and McGehee Family Papers; Margaret Collet to Miss Jones, April 1, 1834, in Walton Papers; Wallace, *Rockdale*, 23. Compare to Clement Eaton, *The Growth of Southern Civilization, 1790–1860* (New York, 1961), 116–17; and A. F. Scott, *The Southern Lady*, 67–77.

9. Lucy L. Wenhold, "The Salem Boarding School Between 1802 and 1822," *North Carolina Historical Review*, XXVII (1950), 32–45. Compare to my discussion of age at first marriage (Chapter Four herein).

has pointed out that North Carolina female seminaries and their northern counterparts emphasized self-reporting of infractions of rules and eschewed physical punishments. The schools adhered to a passive, pious ideal of female behavior, tried to build strong consciences in the young ladies, and closely oversaw their activities. Robert T. Paine summed up both parental attitudes and the schools' regimens when he praised St. Mary's school in Raleigh: "It is in fact one great and entire family & the girls are managed exactly as they should be by kind yet careful & anxious parents." [10]

These parents also wanted schools to discipline sons firmly but reasonably. "You must know that a Teacher must be a governor or his qualities as a Teacher will be of an inferior order," John D. Hawkins lectured a young tutor, but "a Governor who governs with too much severity must rely on despotism rather than enlightened policy to get along." Boys attending school away from home usually boarded with an approved family or at the school. Discipline then stemmed from a family or a setting modeled after the family. The Episcopal School for boys in Raleigh, like others of its day, depicted its headmaster as a "firm but generous father figure." Although American male academies were generally not harsh or cruel, they sought to produce well-ordered youth through numerous regulations and occasional corporal punishment. [11]

Problems arose for planters when their sons appealed to them to be exempted from the institutional regulations. To yield to requests might undermine school authority; to uphold regulations against their own judgment might lessen the boys' affection for them. Paul C. Cameron repeatedly asked his father to circumvent the academy's ordinance forbidding money from home and persuasively climaxed his appeal on the eve of a trip to Washington, D.C.: "I would be will-

10. Pope, "Preparation for Pedestals," 118–37, 224–35; Woody, *A History of Women's Education*, I, 485; Robert T. Paine to Lavinia Paine, December 22, 1844, in Paine Papers.

11. John D. Hawkins to ABC, August 31, 1828, in Hawkins Family Papers; as quoted in Michael T. Malone, "The Episcopal School of North Carolina, 1832–1842," *North Carolina Historical Review*, XLIX (1972), 183; James McLachlan, *American Boarding Schools: A Historical Study* (New York, 1970), 32–47, 86–88, 114–23; Kett, *Rites of Passage*, 45–51. See also Isaac T. Avery to Thomas Lenoir, May 9, 1825, in Lenoir Family Papers; William H. Haywood to John D. Hawkins, January 30, 1832, in Hawkins Family Papers.

ing to say that every cadet that goes . . . to Washington City will be furnished by their parents. I do not see what injury it can do me as I know that I have as good a mind and as sound a judgment as any of them and yet I have to do [sic] along wanting a great many articles for comfort and pleasure." Duncan Cameron's replies consistently skirted the subject of money, and he silently supported the school's position. Other fathers, like William Polk and William Gaston, also chose noninterference. They believed that youths for their future well-being must learn to accept rules and punishments that did not seem fair and, in Willie McPherson's advice to his disgruntled son, "bare the common tryals of human nature." [12]

Parents did not leave instruction and guidance solely to schools. Keeping close watch over their offspring's education, planters also sought to transmit habits and character traits. The older generation, through admonitions and urgings, sought to mold the younger into self-reliant, self-controlled individuals. Wealthy North Carolinians especially desired industrious children. Like middle-class American and English parents, planters lauded the value of hard work; and none defended idleness as their class's prerogative. Mary S. Henderson confided to her diary that her eldest son's disinclination for his studies and his tendency toward idleness "grieved" her, and her letters to him stressed the importance of effort and work. Isaac T. Avery admonished his twelve-year-old son, then on a visit to Tennessee, to write home more frequently and added that the family wished to hear "that you were well; and also that you were doing well, that you were spending some time every day in studying, reading, writing or trying to learn something—going to school with your cousins, if there is a school in the neighborhood." [13]

Girls received the same advice. An old family friend, John Dever-

12. Paul C. Cameron to Duncan Cameron, June 14, September 3, November 11, 1826, all in Cameron Family Papers; Willie McPherson to Joshua McPherson, May 4, 1822, in Ferebee, Gregory, and McPherson Family Papers; Leonidas Polk to William Polk, December 4, 1825, in Leonidas Polk Papers; William Gaston to Susan Gaston, November 5, 1820, in Gaston Papers.

13. M. S. Henderson Diary, March 27, 1855, and Mary S. Henderson to Leonard Henderson, March 1, April 11, 1857, all in Henderson Papers; Isaac T. Avery to Waightstill W. Avery, February 28, 1828, in Waightstill Avery Papers, SHC; David Roberts, "The Paterfamilias of the Victorian Governing Classes," in Wohl (ed.), *The Victorian Family*, 68–70, 77. See David N. Sills to Gray and Louisa M. Sills, January 21, 1851, in Louisa M. (Jelks) Sills Papers, Duke.

eux, told Emily Baker how much her parents' happiness depended upon her success in school, and he counseled wise use of her time. William Cain reminded his daughter that habits of industry should serve her well then and throughout life: "I have so often (in conversation) recommended to you and my other children attention, industry and application to whatever you see[,] hear and are about doing, that I do not mention them now as duties merely; but I point them out to you again and again, as conducive, nay as absolutely necessary to your pleasures, your happiness and your respectability." Like their middle-class northern counterparts who worried about spending their time properly and studying hard enough, some young Carolinians realized that parents wished habits of diligence to extend outside the classroom. During her vacation, thirteen-year-old Penelope Skinner read Gilly's "interesting and instructive" history of ancient Greece; and she proudly summed up her achievements: "I have also grown very industrious always having something to do." Her comments would have pleased most planter parents.[14]

Elite Carolinians desired that girls away at school cultivate habits of thrift and the wise use of money. Young ladies sometimes selected their own clothing under the guidance of their school's headmistress. Planters expected them to choose high-quality garments befitting their social standing but not to buy foolishly or extravagantly. Frances Devereux advised thirteen-year-old Emily Baker about fabrics and emphasized the importance of prudent expenditure and careful selection: "I . . . leave you to follow your own fancy both in respect to the shawl and that your Parents wish you to dress as genteely as your associates, but you will bear in mind, that they have a large family to educate— This is merely to induce you to restrain unnecessary expenses but in making purchases remember the *cheapest* is sometimes the Dearest in the end— Do not buy a mean Shawl but be careful of it when you get a good one." James S. Battle gently reminded his motherless daughter to be prudent but not to deny herself necessary items. "I have been trying some time to empress upon you all

14. John Devereux to Emily Baker, October 10, 1810, in Devereux Family Papers, Duke; William Cain to Minerva Cain, February 22, 1837, in Caldwell Papers, SHC; John R. Frisch, "Youth Culture in America, 1790–1865" (Ph.D. dissertation, University of Missouri, 1970), 304–311; Penelope Skinner to Joseph B. Skinner, January 9, 1833, in Skinner Family Papers.

economy," he continued. "I do not wish you, dear Pattie to spend unnecessarily, but whatever you need as long *as I am able*, I hope I shall always willingly grant." Wealthy parents believed that daughters should learn to choose the approved middle course between reckless expenditure that would reduce the family fortune and an unnecessary parsimony that would also drive poor bargains and expose them to scornful remarks. Martha Cuningham struck both chords of parental concern when she assured her father that although she wished to dress like the other girls in her Philadelphia school, she would not be extravagant. Mothers and fathers cautioned forethought as well as restraint in spending. "A habit of unnecessary expense, of inattention to cost, of useless ornament will prove most pernicious," William Gaston warned his daughter. He did not believe that educational costs or expenses "enjoined by a decent respect for the usages of society" could be avoided, but "all that go beyond these—which can only gratify vanity or which result from thoughtlessness—are to be anxiously shunned."[15]

Planters similarly admonished boys about thrift. "My dear son spend no money foolishly or extravagantly," urged Joseph B. Skinner. William P. Biddle asked his eldest son to counsel the two younger in college: "I wish you to advise Franklin in the distribution of money to pay first what should be first paid. He and Hervey seem not sufficiently saving of money, tell them how you used to do." Although sons sometimes requested money matter-of-factly, they on occasion stressed their frugality to cost-conscious parents. Paul C. Cameron discussed his wardrobe at length to illustrate his need for purchases and justification for them: "I hope you have more confidence in me than to suppose I would spend money foolishly in dress." James W. Downey requested thirty dollars to meet bills and fix his watch: "father you have more than you will at present put in actual use[.] why not let me have some[?] I will not throw it away[.] I hope I am trustworthy."[16]

15. Frances Devereux to Emily Baker, November 5, 1810, in Devereux Family Papers; Margaret Collet to Lauretta and Eliza Murphy, n.d. [ca. 1835], in Walton Papers; James S. Battle to Martha Battle, May 8, 1849, in Battle Family Papers; Martha Cuningham to Alexander Cuningham, April 17, 1840, in Cuningham Papers; William Gaston to Susan Gaston, March 10, 1823, in Gaston Papers. See also Sarah Polk to Mary B. Polk, March 17, 1823, in Polk, Badger, and McGehee Family Papers.

16. Joseph B. Skinner to Tristrim L. Skinner, May 30, 1838, in Skinner Family Pa-

Although both girls and boys received lectures about the wise use of money, a slightly different emphasis can be discerned in these parental admonitions. Planters pushed daughters, perhaps because their future role would be that of household manager, to learn prudent purchasing. To sons, parents stressed an avoidance of squandering money upon frivolities rather than expert comparison shopping. Part of this concern stemmed from the kind of extravagance and self-indulgence the young of each sex could fall victim to.

The North Carolina elite urged self-control as well as thrift and industriousness upon its offspring. By college age, sons were exhorted to provide their own discipline—a self-control that would bar such expensive and dangerous pastimes as gambling, heavy drinking, and the frequenting of prostitutes. Some mothers and fathers explicitly wished that hard work would prevent dissipation and self-indulgence. Joseph B. Skinner, gratified that his son Tristrim found the College of William and Mary's course work demanding, believed that studying might restrain the lad from "dissipation, idle and extravagant habits." Joseph cautioned his son to avoid bad company and "its snares of vice, dissipation, extravagance and idleness, the sure road to disgrace, ruin and destruction."[17]

Since college life with its throngs of young, often unruly males was believed a breeding ground of dissipation, some collegians—who also likely sensed their parents' and relatives' concern—assured them of a similar disapproval and distaste. Philemon Hawkins told his father that two relatives had been dismissed from college because of a holiday drinking spree: "The Messrs Polk are very much dejected indeed, I well know that they cannot help feeling and that deeply and sensibly too, the disgraceful act which they have committed. Their parents will be mortified in the extreme." James Hamilton avowed himself "tired of" the College of William and Mary and observed, "The

---

pers; William P. Biddle to Samuel S. Biddle, August 19, 1851, in Biddle Papers; Paul C. Cameron to Duncan Cameron, n.d., in Cameron Family Papers; James W. Downey to Samuel S. Downey, March 27, 1842, in Samuel Smith Downey Papers, Duke. See also Alexander Cuningham, Jr., to Alexander Cuningham, March 31, 1847, in Cuningham Papers; John D. Hawkins, Jr., to John D. Hawkins, February 22, 1841, in Hawkins Family Papers; Levin Lane to Walter W. Lane, May 14, 1856, in Lane Papers.

17. Joseph B. Skinner to Tristrim L. Skinner, December 4, 1838, in Skinner Family Papers.

students are very dissipated[,] I have no inclination to indulge in it."[18]

While hoping that their sons would not "sow wild oats," wealthy planters, like other genteel Americans, expected daughters to develop a greater and more rigorous self-control. Christie Farnum Pope in her study of North Carolina female academies has noted how the curricula, clubs, and teachers all emphasized ladylike behavior and its passive, restrained nature. Some young women sensed the purposes for which their education molded them. One fifteen-year-old described a romp so invigorating that "I thought I was a young thing of some six or seven years and could do as I pleased without being noticed." In yet a more pensive vein, she continued: "Oh do you not regret that as you grow up into womanhood, the world expects more from you and you have to renounce your childish pleasures, and amusements, and finally settle down into a sedate old maid, or else have a lord to rule over you and whose will you are obliged to obey, sometimes to receive his smiles, and then again when something provokes him bear his frown. Oh that I could be a girl forever." Planters applauded the girls' transition to dignity and self-control and further advocated a reserve in dealing with the world. Young women learned mild dissimulation, the ability to hide emotions or uncertainty under a calm exterior, and parents counseled when such deception would be necessary. Margaret Collet, after admitting uncertainty about whether her daughter would return to the same academy, told the girl that it would be proper "for you to leave that place as though you will not return . . . tho I think it highly probable you will return again." Samuel S. Biddle advised his daughter upon her departure from a school: "you must act to everybody as though you expected to return as I think you probably will, but I do not know." In both cases the recommended behavior was the same: a firm, polite stance masking indecision.[19]

18. Philemon B. Hawkins to John D. Hawkins, February 26, 1841, in Hawkins Family Papers; James Hamilton to Charles E. Hamilton, May 4, 1850, in Bullock and Hamilton Papers; Drake, *Higher Education*, 227.

19. Pope, "Preparation for Pedestals," 157–62, 171–73; Barbara Welter, "Coming of Age in America: The American Girl in the Nineteenth Century," in *Dimity Convictions: The American Woman in the Nineteenth Century* (Athens, Ohio, 1976), 3–6; A. to Mary W. Brodnax, n.d., in J. G. Brodnax Papers, SHC; Margaret Collet to Eliza

Not only did parents try to underscore the traits they considered most desirable for their maturing offspring, they also touted success in school as an important goal. Willie McPherson urged his daughters, Elizabeth and Courtney, on to achievement: "we should be Glad to here [sic] from you and at the time have some information on your progress in your studies, your examination is coming on and I hope you will remember the advantages it will be to you to acquit yourselves with credit[.] It will be a satisfaction to your preceptors and a pleasure to all your acquaintance."[20] This emphasis upon success held greater ironies for daughters, whose competitiveness had to be held in check lest it become unladylike and whose academic training held less relevance for later life. Indeed, this push to achievement, unwittingly nurtured by parents, may be almost as important as the actual inequalities in education in explaining the frustrations some elite southern young women felt about their training. But parents rarely considered such a possibility; caught up in their admiration for education and success, they encouraged and complimented both sexes on accomplishments.

Some planters particularly wished their children to excel in competition. George W. Capehart prodded his son William: "I am in hopes you are improving in all your studies. You must try and keep ahead of all the little boy[s]." Other parents' exultation in their youngsters' achievements similarly included this competitive element: their child had bested his schoolmates.[21]

The Carolina elite fully backed a "useful" education for its children, instructing them in necessary learning for their future roles in society. Wishing to rear sober, virtuous offspring, great planters did not leave that task to the schools. Instead, through advice and guidance, they sought to mold youngsters into conscientious adults. Parents' exhortations to hard work, frugality, self-control, and success do not at all resemble the ideals of leisure and conspicuous con-

and Lauretta Murphy, November 18, 1834, in Walton Papers; Samuel S. Biddle to Mary S. Biddle, November 28, 1853, in Biddle Papers.

20. Willie McPherson to Courtney and Elizabeth McPherson, May 30, 1835, in Ferebee, Gregory, and McPherson Family Papers. See also Delia Badger to Melissa Williams, July 9, 1836, in Badger Family Papers.

21. George W. Capehart to William R. Capehart, November 1, 1848, in W. R. Capehart Papers; William Gaston to Eliza Gaston, July 20, 1842, in Gaston Papers; Josiah Collins, Jr., to Josiah Collins, December 29, 1818, in Collins Papers, NCDAH.

sumption that Genovese believes southern planters firmly espoused. Nor do wealthy North Carolinians' wishes appear similar to the "finishing school" education of few restrictions that Greven believes genteel families North and South gave their offspring. Instead, North Carolina planters voiced concerns similar to those held by middle-class American and English parents. The Carolinians' interest in education, their emphasis upon the wise use of time as well as their ambitions for their children all are aspects of the "future orientation" that Daniel Walker Howe has found so characteristic of American Victorians.[22]

Warm affection usually accompanied and blended with planters' high standards for and close supervision of children. A wish not only for their progeny's good performance but also for their well-being and happiness can be discerned among planter families. They manifested love for youngsters in several different ways.

Parents usually sent children away to school, but this separation did not arise, as historians studying other groups utilizing boarding schools have suggested, from lack of affection. Most planters lived in isolated rural areas where children would have to leave home to attend any school beyond the primary level. A concern for education and the child's future welfare prompted parents to enroll children in academies.[23]

Planters' education of their young children indicated a fondness that kept the youngsters close to home even if this somewhat impaired the quality of their schooling. Formal education very often began at home with the mother as instructor. Some women such as Hannah Gaston developed a set routine: her six-year-old son recited "six or seven lessons" each day. In cases in which the mother was burdened

22. Eugene D. Genovese, *The World the Slaveholders Made: Two Essays in Interpretation* (New York, 1969); Genovese, *The Political Economy of Slavery*, 18; Greven, *The Protestant Temperament*, 174–91, 209–216, 285–90, 312–18; Roberts "The Paterfamilias," 68–71, 77; Walter E. Houghton, *The Victorian Frame of Mind, 1830–1870* (New Haven, 1957), 183–91, 233–34, 243–62; Daniel Walker Howe, "Victorian Culture in America," in Howe (ed.), *Victorian America* (Philadelphia, 1976), 15–19.

23. At least fifty-two of the nonmigrant great planters sent either sons or daughters away to secondary schools or academies. Compare John F. Walzer, "A Period of Ambivalence: Eighteenth Century American Childhood," in Lloyd de Mause (ed.), *The History of Childhood* (New York, 1975), 355, 368–74; Ariès, *Centuries of Childhood*, 281–85, 374–75.

with numerous children and a multiplicity of plantation chores, instruction probably became more haphazard. Isaac T. and Harriet Avery's third son, aged only three, learned the alphabet at home, but busy Harriet Avery likely did not have a usual period for teaching. Other parents sent their young children to nearby schools, usually for short periods at first. For example, Joseph B. Skinner's five-year-old daughter began to attend classes on a part-time basis, as he described: "I have the last two days sent Penelope to school for two hours, but she has not yet been prevailed upon to say a single letter— I am in hopes to succeed today, altho' it hurts me very much to see her depressed or mortified." For young children school attendance might not be particularly demanding. Mary S. Henderson's five-year-old learned relatively little, she observed, "because his teacher took no pains to instruct him."[24]

Many children among North Carolina's elite families attended small "subscription academies" for primary education near their homes. These schools often enrolled both girls and boys although they probably separated the sexes during lessons. Such schooling was sometimes of uncertain duration since the schools were easily disrupted and sometimes abruptly discontinued. Isaac T. Avery lamented the postponement of one such school because of illness in the teacher's family: "I was particularly sorry that the school broke up at a time when all the scholars appeared to be studying well except [my son] Lenoir who inclines to study mischief."[25]

Other planters such as John D. Hawkins and William P. Little delayed parting with children by sponsoring a school on the plantation or employing a private tutor or governess. Hawkins' own young ones almost completely composed his school, and he told a prospective teacher, "I live in a most healthy situation but am somewhat secluded owing to not having many wealthy neighbors, and therefore have to depend chiefly upon myself to support a school." Even a par-

---

24. Alexander Gaston to William Gaston, July 9, 1813, in Gaston Papers; Isaac T. Avery to W. B. Lenoir, January 11, 1824, in Lenoir Family Papers; Joseph B. Skinner to Joshua Skinner, June 17, 1823, in Skinner Family Papers; M. S. Henderson Diary, June 30, 1855, in Henderson Papers.

25. Isaac T. Avery to Thomas Lenoir, November 19, 1829, in Lenoir Family Papers. See Charles L. Coon (ed.), *North Carolina Schools and Academies, 1790–1840: A Documentary History* (Raleigh, 1915).

ent so dedicated to education as Hawkins, who built both a school-house and a private dwelling for his teacher, experienced the tran-siency of instructors that was so common to subscription schools. Tutors or governesses could prove unsatisfactory or resign suddenly. Plantation mistress and mother Ann W. Johnson described a com-mon predicament, and probably an equally common solution: "I am now teaching the young children, our Teacher left us about three weeks since. I think she will not return."[26]

When children reached an age, usually between ten and fourteen, parents believed more advanced schooling to be necessary. Most then considered the proper instruction to be at college preparatory schools for boys or female seminaries for girls, both institutions generally lo-cated in large towns or cities of the North and the South. To be sure, some planters thought schooling away from home was different for boys and girls. As John Hope Franklin has pointed out, young men away at school, especially those at northern schools, would not have the opportunities available on the plantation to arrange sexual en-counters with slave women who might be coerced or bribed. Thus straitlaced mothers and fathers could see yet another benefit accru-ing to their sons from the boarding schools. But school did not appear so clearly superior to the plantation as a protector of daughters' vir-tue. Parents believed their daughters to be naturally chaste and in-nocent and feared that the large groups of young women gathered to-gether in seminaries might contain wantons who would then corrupt other students. Thus some planters like John D. Hawkins, who sent sons to preparatory school and extolled the virtues of female educa-tion, flatly refused to enroll daughters in seminaries. For Hawkins, it was "a matter of primary importance as respects the wishes and hap-piness of my Family that my Daughters be instructed at home." Probably the more common reaction to female boarding schools was that of Joseph Pearson, who, after deciding that his daughters should remain in such institutions for at least another year, argued, "I have

26. John D. Hawkins to ABC, August 31, 1828, in Hawkins Family Papers; T. H. Pearce, *Franklin County, 1779–1979* (Freeman, S.D., 1979), 43; William P. Little to William Polk, November 11, 1822, in Polk and Yeatman Family Papers, SHC; Ann W. Johnson to Charles E. Johnson, Jr., May, n.d. [*ca.* 1848], in Johnson Papers.

many objections to boarding schools generally but it is almost impossible to educate our Daughters entirely at home."[27]

Even when parents put aside the question of schools' effect on morals, they—especially mothers—expressed dismay over an impending separation. When William Cain asked that his brother-in-law aid in his eldest son's education by selecting a good school or teacher, Cain also noted that a tutor would be preferable because "Mrs Cain dislikes exceedingly for her children to be sent so far from her and particularly at this time, as her health is not good." James N. McPherson found it difficult to convince his stepmother to send his ten-year-old half sister away to school: "What I shall do with Jane I don't know—Mother is very reluctant to send her anywhere—and unless we can get a school in the neighborhood I am afraid that she will have to remain home a year longer."[28]

Youngsters' absences distressed loving parents. Margaret Collet described her grief to her eldest daughter: "I will now tell you my dear child that it is impossible for me to express my anxiety to see you, the thought is painful to me at this time, when I set and reflect on the distance you are from me and on the uncertainty of earthly things my anxiety is too great for my weak poor heart, were I not to turn my thoughts to that source from which all true comfort flows." Fathers and mothers shared children's sadness at parting and only reluctantly refused some demands for visits home. Duncan Cameron deemed his son Paul's desire to visit home "natural and praiseworthy" and forbade the journey only because winter's approach made it unhealthful. Promising that Paul could visit in a few months, his father added, "Be assured my dear son—that we are all greatly desirous of seeing *you*—and it is with great reluctance that I withhold my consent to your visiting us *this* winter."[29]

27. John Hope Franklin, *A Southern Odyssey: Travelers in the Antebellum North* (Baton Rouge, 1976), 73; John D. Hawkins to Miss Ney, January 20, 1820, in Hawkins Family Papers; Joseph Pearson to William Gaston, July 3, 1823, in Gaston Papers. See Susan Capehart to Robert C. Martin, February 20, 1858, in Martin Papers.

28. William Cain to Willie P. Mangum, May 1, 1836, in Shanks (ed.), *The Papers of Willie Person Mangum*, II, 431; James N. McPherson to Elizabeth McPherson, March 26, 1837, in Ferebee, Gregory, and McPherson Family Papers.

29. Margaret Collet to Eliza Murphy, August 17, 1834, in Walton Papers (similarly Bethell Diary, September 4, 1857); Benjamin F. Hawkins to William Polk, March 24,

Moreover, parents sometimes attempted to cushion the shock of a new school, especially one in an unfamiliar or distant town or city, by ensuring that the child had at least one companion there. Placing two sons or daughters in the same boarding school was a most common device—siblings such as Courtney and Elizabeth McPherson, Thomas and Paul C. Cameron, and Peter E. and William R. Smith attended academies together. Often cousins and occasionally the progeny of very close friends enrolled in the same schools. Such arrangements, which reveal the important role that kinship played, possibly also increased the intensity of same-sex sibling and kin ties. One may speculate that the close friendships among siblings—especially sisters—in such planter families owed some of their intimacy to this earlier shared experience.[30]

Such interested parents often kept close watch over children's schooling. Through letters and visits, planters could monitor welfare and happiness. Parental scrutiny and a willingness to move children to another school tended to restrict somewhat academies' ability to discipline boys and young men. Teachers, whatever their own views, probably realized that parents wished sons well behaved but did not want to see them abused. Joseph Kett has related how the withdrawal of students often injured colleges financially, and the same process probably applied to secondary schools. Certainly two schoolmasters who punished Richard Cuningham were careful in their explanation to emphasize they had used only "a small slender switch" and Mr. Cuningham need not fear ill-treatment of his son. North Carolina's Episcopal School, plagued with financial problems from its inception, blamed its woes upon parents' paying too much attention to "delinquent" boys' complaints.[31]

1826, in Polk and Yeatman Family Papers; Duncan Cameron to Paul C. Cameron, December 24, 1826, in Cameron Family Papers. See also David N. Sills to Gray and Louisa Sills, January 21, 1851, in Sills Papers.

30. William R. Smith to W. J. Bingham, April 10, 1846, in P. E. Smith Papers; Willie McPherson to Courtney and Elizabeth McPherson, May 30, 1835, in Ferebee, Gregory, and McPherson Family Papers; Paul C. Cameron to Mary A. Cameron, July, 1825, in Cameron Family Papers; Thomas Ruffin to Robert Brodnax, March 9, 1845, in J. G. Brodnax Papers, SHC; William Gaston to Susan Gaston, February 14, 1823, in Gaston Papers; Catherine Clinton, "The Plantation Mistress: Another Side of Southern Slavery, 1780–1835" (Ph.D. dissertation, Princeton University, 1980), 40–41.

31. Kett, *Rites of Passage*, 57–59; Solomon Lea and Nicholas Ritter to Alexander Cuningham, October 6, 1845, in Cuningham Papers; "Address of Trustees of the Epis-

Despite calls for hard work, wise spending, and thrift, parents were occasionally indulgent. Margaret Collet gave her two teen-aged daughters permission to attend the University of North Carolina's commencement exercises to compensate for their not being able to visit home during summer vacation. Enclosing money so her son could attend a minstrel show in his town, Susan Capehart remarked that if he already possessed the fee for that entertainment, he could save her gift for the next. Mary S. Henderson believed her son Len lazy and unambitious, but she fretted when temporary postal problems prevented her from sending presents on his sixteenth birthday: "I regret not being able to gratify him, But as he cannot get letters from us, there is not much chance of eatables reaching him." Ten-year-old Josiah Collins told his parents how much he appreciated the watch and box of assorted items they sent for Christmas. In her New York boarding school, Meeta Armistead happily looked forward to the arrival of a package then en route from her home.[32]

Parents highly valued affection in relationships with their offspring. Letters exchanged between parents and children commonly stressed love over respect in terms of address and endearment. Salutations and closing remarks of the younger generation's letters did not, as Greven and Kett have suggested for other Americans, emphasize subordination and honor rather than emotional attachment. In fact, almost all planters' children used the parting remarks "your affectionate son/daughter" and a few even embellished such closings. David N. Sills concluded a letter, "I remain dear parents your loving son until death." Certainly the absence of correspondence signed "your dutiful and obedient son/daughter" does not necessarily indicate any lack of obedience, but it does illustrate the importance placed upon affection within the conjugal circle.[33]

---

copal School of North Carolina to the Public (1836)," in Bailey Papers. See James B. Hawkins to John D. Hawkins, September 28, 1831, in Hawkins Family Papers.

32. Margaret Collet to Eliza Murphy, May 17, 1834, in Walton Papers; Susan B. Capehart to William R. Capehart, January 23, 1849, in W. R. Capehart Papers; M. S. Henderson Diary, November 14, 1857, in Henderson Papers; Josiah Collins, Jr., to Josiah Collins, December 29, 1818, in Collins Papers, NCDAH; Meeta Armistead to Sophia Armistead, October 26, 1854, in M. A. Capehart Papers. Other examples include Thomas Cowan, Jr., to his mother, July 14, 1850, in Thomas Cowan Papers, SHC; Rufus Reid to Jane Camilla Smith and Betsey E. Reid, December 6, 1852, in Reid Papers.

33. Greven, *The Protestant Temperament*, 178–91; Kett, *Rites of Passage*, 45; David N. Sills to Gray and Louisa Sills, January 21, 1851, in Sills Papers. The only exception,

Planters and their children showed much mutual affection. One can only speculate upon love's role in their relationships, but it seems likely that parents' emotional attachment removed some of the harshness their demands might otherwise have held. Mothers and fathers usually couched advice in gentle rather than imperious tones. The fondness they often demonstrated perhaps reinforced their demands, made their requirements more palatable to children, and discouraged rebellion.

Elite North Carolinians continued to shower affection on older children. As in the past, they coupled expectations to emotional attachments; but as their progeny approached adulthood, parents often expressed demands in a more restrained manner with greater consideration for children's sentiments. At times this alteration in parental guidance could cause anguish for both elders and children.

Planters did not mindlessly relinquish power. Rather they came to express authority differently. After years of instruction by parents and school, youngsters were gaining maturity. They had internalized many of the values, such as hard work and self-control, that parents most admired. Planters also wanted successful, self-motivated children and began to further nurture independence and decision making.

Some parents took it upon themselves to change the relationship and refer to themselves as friends and confidants as well as figures of authority. William Cain wrote his sixteen-year-old daughter that he would be willing to counsel her upon any subject, "not . . . to dictate as a parent, but to advise as a friend and an indulgent one too." William Gaston, acknowledged by children and friends as a concerned, kindly father, saw that image of himself assaulted when his twenty-one-year-old son Alexander did not consult him about important plans, and the older man fumed: "Why can he not—why will he not repose confidence in his own father? —where else is he to find a friend on whose attachment and fidelity he can so confidently rely? . . . I am not a tyrant to be feared and hated. . . . He ought at least afford me an opportunity, and *then* it will be time enough to assert his indepen-

and an example of a letter signed "your dutiful son," is an 1803 communication from John Murphy to his father James Murphy, in Walton Papers.

dence by acting as he pleases." Alexander's age convinced his father that he lacked authority, but the latter still wished to have affection and confidence shown toward him.[34]

Older children's new influence first appeared when parents either asked for or allowed youths to voice their desires and took them into account. Susan Polk, whose widowed mother wished her to leave her Philadelphia school, remained after she expressed that preference. Willie P. Mangum gave up a plan to place his son with a French family in Baltimore because of the boy's reluctance to stay there. Margaret Collet doubted her teen-aged daughters should attempt a visit during an upcoming recess but instructed the elder, "let me know the length of the winter vacation and you[r] views and wishes in regard to it."[35]

Parents still desired and expected filial obedience but sometimes hesitated to enforce it among their teen-agers. Intriguingly, some even shrank from using parental authority to forbid plans repugnant to them but important to adolescents. Widowed James S. Battle, a devout Baptist, wrote his sixteen-year-old daughter, then away at school, that her wish to join the Episcopal church left him "with a trembling hand and agitated mind." He continued: "You observe you again ask my consent for you to join the Episcopal Church, it is an embarrassing and delicate subject and what to do in the premises I am at a loss to know, to give my consent willingly I cannot, and to say you shall not I do not feel willing." James believed his daughter to be young, inexperienced, and misled. Despite his lack of confidence in her ability to make that decision, he would not forbid her conversion: "this much I can say, without a change should take place in me, if you unite with them during my day, it will be an unhappy one for me." Willing to defer the decision, James threatened only his unhappiness should his daughter follow her own inclinations. The Devereuxes also found coping with the wishes of a determined adolescent a difficult

34. William Cain to Minerva Cain, February 22, 1837, in Caldwell Papers, SHC; Josiah Collins, Jr., to Josiah Collins, December 29, 1818, in Collins Papers, NCDAH; William Gaston to Susan Donaldson, March 9, 1828, in Gaston Papers.

35. Susan Polk to Sarah Polk, July 21, 1835, in Polk and Yeatman Family Papers; Willie P. Mangum to Charity Mangum, January 10, 1848, in Shanks (ed.), *The Papers of Willie Person Mangum*, V, 90; Margaret Collet to Eliza Murphy, n.d. [ca. 1835–36], in Walton Papers.

matter. When fifteen-year-old Frances Devereux wished to join the Roman Catholic church, the faith in which her father had been reared, her disapproving parents sought their daughter-in-law's aid to counsel Frances. A compromise was reached: Frances agreed to wait until age eighteen before conversion.[36] The Devereuxes had achieved only a limited goal and that through their daughter-in-law's intervention, not the exercise of parental authority. Both Martha Battle and Frances Devereux eventually joined the churches of their choice. Most important, however, was their parents' hesitance to force obedience.

This subtle interaction between parent and youth allowed yet more leeway during young men's decision making about careers. Parental expectations and directions, although still present, were expressed more sporadically. Career choice loosely followed the end of schooling; probably it occurred for most elite young men in their late teens or early twenties. By providing college educations, planters opened occupations other than farming to sons. Since they almost never became artisans and rarely became career military officers, only agricultural, professional, and commercial fields remained. Given the rural nature of much of North Carolina, nonagricultural openings were undoubtedly fewer than in the industrializing Northeast. But a varied pattern of career choice still persisted since in over 40 percent of great planter families, at least one son entered a profession. The Erwin family, for example, included among its eight sons living to maturity, a lawyer, a doctor, a merchant, a clerk, and a farmer.[37]

Both father and son participated to varying extents in the young man's choice of career. Even parents who wished to select a son's occupation did not disregard his wishes. Only two of the ninety-two great planters who drew up wills specified that a son should follow a certain profession. Both of these wills, moreover, illustrate the limitations that fathers placed upon their own power and authority. William Bethell, who granted a tract of land to a son only if he passed the bar examination, also provided that his wife and son-in-law could

36. James S. Battle to Martha Battle, June 19, 1849, in Battle Family Papers; Catherine A. Devereux to Frances Devereux, June 17, 1822, in Gale and Polk Family Papers, SHC.

37. Compare Kett, *Rites of Passage*, 31–35, 93–104. MS Census of 1850, N.C., McDowell County, Sch. I, p. 308, and Burke County, Sch. I, pp. 401, 437; Estate of William W. Erwin, in Burke County Estates.

waive that requirement; and they probably followed that course. Charles E. Johnson ordered his youngest son to study law and to receive his legacy only after practicing law for three years. Charles, however, added a codicil to his will: "I had desired that my son James should study the law which I now much prefer, but as he seems to have such a repugnance to the practice of the law (which I hope however he will overcome) I hereby revoke that part as regards the study and practice of the law and instead thereof he study medicine and practice it." Even those planters who wished to steer a son toward a specific career believed that the inclinations of the young man must be taken into account.[38]

Other elite Carolinians, probably the majority, played a smaller role in career decisions. William Polk had misgivings about his son Leonidas entering the ministry but did not bar the way. Unenthusiastic about his son's becoming a businessman at a young age, William Plummer still allowed the young man to follow his own wishes: "I do not like at all that one of his age (not nineteen) should become Partner in a Mercantile business—and yet I cannot but feel pleasure that at so early an age he should be thought by men like Thomas White and P R Davis Jr worthy from his habits and capacity of such confidence[.] it is by their advice I am induced to consent to it."[39]

Fathers found themselves adjusting to and allowing greater independence as their sons reached maturity, but these changes were not necessarily easy for young men. Because of parents' careful guidance over the years, sons selecting careers and planning for the future looked to fathers for advice. But the elders, as in the exercise of authority over adolescents, had already begun to leave decisions to their offspring. Twenty-two-year-old Franklin Biddle discussed his perplexities in finding a career with his older brother. Believing himself attracted to law, Franklin feared that profession might injure his religious principles. He pronounced his slaveholding too small for farming; still he considered schoolteaching in the Southwest or the

38. Will of William Bethell, in Rockingham County Estates. Mary Bethell's diary, listing events from 1840 onward, does not mention that her husband ever practiced law. Will of Charles E. Johnson, in Chowan County Wills.

39. William Polk to Lucius J. Polk, July 20, 1827, in Polk, Brown, and Ewell Family Papers, SHC; William Plummer to Lucy Battle, April 7, 1854, in Battle Family Papers. Compare M. P. Johnson, "Planters and Patriarchy," 45–72.

mercantile business as interesting possibilities. Franklin also complained about his father's reticence on the subject: "Father has never advised me what to do, and I have broached the subject several times and he, I thought, did not seem disposed to talk about it. I hope he will do it before I graduate for I must come to some conclusion pretty soon." Other young men like Leonidas Polk and B. G. Smith also desired more advice about important decisions than they had received from their fathers. Sons, too, had to cope with the difficulties of the transition to adulthood and independence.[40]

Parents' changing use of authority as their children neared adulthood should be viewed in terms of earlier socialization. Youth was the period when planters' expectations bore most heavily on sons and daughters. Since children had received and internalized parental values, it should be no surprise that planters would be willing to pay more attention to offspring's wishes. A blend of respect for adolescents' and young adults' wishes and affection characterized parent-child interactions in planter families. The pattern continued as sons and daughters began to grapple with the choices involved in courtship and marriage.

40. B. Franklin Biddle to Samuel S. Biddle, March 31, 1852, in Biddle Papers; Leonidas Polk to Lucius J. Polk, September 22, 1858, in Polk and Yeatman Family Papers; B. G. Smith to William R. Smith, April 22, 1858, in P. E. Smith Papers. Also consult William Gaston to Robert Donaldson, May 30, 1828, in Gaston Papers; Thomas Cain to Minerva Caldwell, February 4, 1850, in Caldwell Papers, SHC.

FOUR

Courtship and Marriage Among
the Planters' Offspring

As young men and women attained maturity and began to seek mates, parental affection and expectations remained strong. But in marriage choices, as in career selection, parents continued to exercise authority over young adults increasingly by indirection. Here, as elsewhere, planters who have sometimes been considered all-powerful patriarchs wished to pass some power over to the new grown-ups. In addition, sons and daughters carved out their own areas of independence. This parent-child interaction generally yielded prudent marriages that likely satisfied parental wishes and also provided personal choice for offspring.

Parents, as in the earlier socialization of children, continued to express their values and beliefs, and sons and daughters accustomed to parental guidance could not fail to be affected. Members of the elite held general views about the characteristics of a good match. Although none disputed affection as a basis for marriage, they, like late-eighteenth-century Chesapeake planters, considered suitors' economic and family standing when evaluating a match's desirability. First, the affianced should possess suitable social position. Social status could be interpreted in several different ways, and planters were ambiguous about how to calculate it. Certainly the family's general reputation played a part. Kenneth M. Clark angrily denied rumors of his engagement: "You knew my opinions of the girl and Family better than to think it true." Planters often linked money and family. Richard Hines carefully described to John Buxton Williams the attributes of a young man wooing Williams' orphaned niece: "His family you know are of the first respectability and he will have at the death of his father an estate of some thirty or forty thousand dollars probably more." Such factors pushed Hines to the conclusion: "My opinion is (of course it would have no influence with Mary) that it is a first rate match for her if she is pleased with him &c." An "old" family, however, sometimes commanded little respect if its members lacked wealth. Mary Badger snidely commented about her cousin's fiancé and his family: "It is said that Mary Little made a bad selection, in the choice of her partner for life. Mr Mosby's family are a 'broke down sett' as Grand Papa says[.] he is one of the greatest of the Virginia horse rasers—*Grand Dad* reckon[s] he was so *'fleet upon the heel that he left all his property behind.'*" Derision could await families that had become "broke down."[1]

Elite families discreetly rejoiced at marriages to wealthy heirs or heiresses. Jane Hamilton happily observed that Ann Baskerville's fiancé "is very wealthy; and is the only child of his Mother, and she is a Widow. Her [*i.e.*, Ann's] friends are very much pleased with the match indeed." But planters also liked to disclaim fortune seeking. Although an admirable attribute, money should not form the principal basis for marriage. Tristrim L. Skinner disapprovingly described the interest fortune hunters would show in an heiress of his neighborhood and vowed if he married, love, not money, would be the main motive. Imbued with nineteenth-century romanticism or simply a fear of appearing overly mercenary, planter families could not acknowledge money as the major attraction in a match. Those who chose mates with few desirable traits other than property could also expect derogatory remarks from cynical friends and acquaintances. A young lawyer scornfully remarked that a wealthy Johnston County planter's son "will be married some time this spring to Miss Lucinda Smith—a girl of no accomplishments but worth some ten or fifteen negroes—she is very illiterate." Notions of romantic love and sensitivity to charges of fortune hunting did not dim planter families' appreciation of wealth, but such ideas caused that approval to be expressed in muted form.[2]

1. D. B. Smith, *Inside the Great House*, 126–41; Kenneth M. Clark to Lewis Thompson, June 20, 1851, in Thompson Papers; Richard Hines to John B. Williams, December 16, 1850, in J. B. Williams Papers; Mary B. Polk to Lucius J. Polk, March 16, 1826, in Polk, Badger, and McGehee Family Papers. See also G. G. Johnson, *Antebellum North Carolina*, 191–92.

2. Jane Hamilton to Charles E. Hamilton, October 18, 1844, in Bullock and Ham-

North Carolina planters probably preferred that their children marry people whose family background and circumstances they knew intimately. A great planter's daughter congratulated her niece upon marrying a "young man who was a desirable match for any girl" and added, "It is a great satisfaction to us to know when we marry that we are doing it with the approbation of our friends—as you have done in making choice of one who is known and liked by all your relations."[3]

Suspicions sometimes arose about suitors from other areas. Joseph B. Skinner's actions upon his daughter Penelope's engagement to a young Virginian, Mr. French, reveal that anxiety about strangers. Skinner worriedly wrote his son, then at college in Williamsburg: "Now I scarcely know of whom to inquire and I know nothing of him [*i.e.*, French] but what I have seen." Although French had given permission for an inquiry into his character, the old gentleman advised his son to obtain information simply by remarking to relatives in Williamsburg upon French's visits to Penelope.[4] Skinner obviously believed he needed to know French's background, but learning about a gentleman from another area was a delicate undertaking.

In addition to money and social standing, character was important in determining whether a match was desirable. In that Victorian era, genteel young ladies were presumed chaste. A gentleman could, however, live down past peccadillos. Generally only when a man's drinking and sexual habits continued to be disreputable did previous transgressions outweigh money and position. In Burke County, a great planter's son criticized a female relation's suitor: "I should think it is a serious step for her to marry a man of his habits." Others similarly expected young ladies to be careful to marry only men who had foresworn excesses. William Gaston, though extremely fond of his dissipated son, was relieved when wealthy Eliza Jones rejected the

---

ilton Papers; Tristrim L. Skinner to Eliza Harwood, February 24, 1843, in Skinner Family Papers; Ruffin Wirt Tomlinson to Thomas Ruffin, April 1, 1844, in Daniel S. Hill Papers, Duke. See also Polly Summey to Thomas Lenoir, December 11, 1848, in Lenoir Family Papers; Elijah B. Hilliard to Mary E. V. Biddle, November 24, 1846, in Biddle Papers.

3. Minerva Graham to Sally Watkins, April 28, 1842, in Bullock and Hamilton Papers.

4. Joseph B. Skinner to Tristrim L. Skinner, December 4, 1838, in Skinner Family Papers.

young man's proposal: "I by no means blame Eliza or those with whom she has consulted. Unquestionably as her friend I must have advised the same course. She ought not while his character is yet undecided and uncertain to have made him her Lord— It would have been risquing all upon a most hazardous issue." Other great planters also hoped that debauched young men would show evidence of thorough reformation before marriage, although some believed that marriage could reinforce good intentions.[5]

Although historians such as Bertram Wyatt-Brown and Michael P. Johnson have suggested that wealthy parents directly arranged marriage "alliances" with other families, North Carolina planters took a different part. They, like other close friends and relatives, played only an indirect role in courtship. All sought to encourage suitable and discourage unsuitable matches. They might attempt to kindle romances with promising prospects. The DeRossets excitedly told their daughter about the interest wealthy young Josiah Collins had shown in her. William Baskerville, Jr., in his request that his cousin Charles E. Hamilton serve as groomsman for his wedding, assured Hamilton that "my nicest young female relation," Jane Coleman, would be a bridesmaid. William M. Clark reminded his nephew Thomas Thompson that he should pay a visit and see Clark's "nice" sister-in-law.[6]

Parents and relatives alike became more interested when calls or extended visits indicated that wooing was becoming more serious. Noting that his niece had received a three-day visit from a young man, E. Jones Erwin speculated that something was "on hand." Sarah Ferebee wrote disapprovingly of a younger sister's admirer: "I suppose . . . Billy Noose . . . is a constant visitor[.] from what Lizzy Ferebee told me I think he had better apply for board[.] her account was he

5. E. Jones Erwin to George Phifer Erwin, October 15, 1858, in Erwin Papers; William Gaston to Susan Donaldson, August 20, 1828, in Gaston Papers; Mary B. Badger to Mary Polk, October 13, 1832, in Polk, Badger, and McGehee Family Papers; Kenneth M. Clark to Lewis Thompson, December 8, 1857, in Thompson Papers.

6. Wyatt-Brown, "The Ideal Typology," 9–10; M. P. Johnson, "Planters and Patriarchy," 65–66; Eliza DeRosset to Kate DeRosset, June 9, 1847, in DeRosset Family Papers; William Baskerville, Jr., to Charles E. Hamilton, February 15, 1839, in Bullock and Hamilton Papers; William M. Clark to Lewis Thompson, January 28, 1860, in Thompson Papers. See also Clarence L. Robards to Louisa Hill, September 12, [1851], in D. S. Hill Papers.

came in the morning and remained till dinner[,] after dinner till supper[,] from supper till ten and so on."[7]

Both parents and other relatives were most likely to intervene when they opposed an engagement that might soon be formed. Such interference and advice were usually aimed at the young woman for at least two reasons. First, girls often contemplated marriage at a younger and more immature age than did their brothers. Second, females' social role would not necessarily allow them much independence from husbands, making marriage a more crucial step in their lives. Elizabeth McPherson's older sister and half brother each urged her not to become seriously involved with her beau, Peter Lord. McPherson's sister, Courtney Wilson, bluntly cited Lord's conduct and his debts: "He makes a great many *brags* about you and the *Lord* knows I would not have any *man* who the *Sheriff* is always after them." Lest she be too heavy-handed, Wilson added with a condescending tolerance probably galling to her sister: "But I will say again Elizabeth suit yourself you know best, I have nothing to say if you are satisfied I shall be perfectly so, although I should feel for you." James N. McPherson more tactfully reminded Elizabeth that he liked Lord but believed him incapable of discharging heavy indebtedness. James further remarked that since he believed that she had "better sense" than to become engaged to Lord, his advice should only put her on guard.[8] Wilson's and McPherson's warnings seem to have had the desired effect, for Elizabeth did not marry Peter Lord. A year later she wed a young man belonging to another very wealthy family in that county.

Parental interference in courtship resembled that of other close relatives and probably was similar to that exercised by other nineteenth- and twentieth-century well-to-do parents. Generally these elites have preferred subtle methods of discouragement to flat refusals. William Polk gossiped to his daughter that her cousin Delia's parents had arranged for the latter to leave town to discourage a re-

7. E. Jones Erwin to George Phifer Erwin, March 12, 1858, in Erwin Papers; Sallie Ferebee to Elizabeth M. Proctor, September 6, 1842, in Ferebee, Gregory, and McPherson Family Papers. See Joseph B. Skinner to Tristrim L. Skinner, December 4, 1838, in Skinner Family Papers.
8. Courtney Wilson to Elizabeth McPherson, February 9, [1837], James N. McPherson to Elizabeth McPherson, December 22, 1836, both in Ferebee, Gregory, and McPherson Family Papers. See also Polly M. Summey to Selina L. Lenoir, September 24, 1835, in Lenoir Family Papers.

lationship: "conjecture says she was sent on a visit to Mrs Dudley at Wilmington, to prevent *some body* courting of her—something about courting or marrying." Penelope Skinner's suitor, Mr. French, did not impress her widowed father, who testily grumbled to his son and also intimated to Penelope that dislike.[9] Still Penelope knew that her father would agree to the marriage.

Parents, with their regard for the family connections and wealth of suitors, found an invaluable ally in societal constraints on courtship. The forms that courtship assumes depend upon the way that society allows young men and women to meet. In cultures where marriage is completely arranged, courtship is unnecessary. When young people, however, have some voice, even if only a veto over their parents' selection, meeting places of young men and women reveal, in part, how much choice will be allowed. For example, if male-female encounters are generally limited to areas such as the home, which parents control, the elders may by limiting access eliminate certain suitors and indirectly play an important role in courtship.[10] Wooing among genteel North Carolinians, however, also occurred at places not under parents' direct control. There, society reinforced values planters had tried to inculcate.

Many get-togethers provided opportunities for meeting and courtship. Because of its recreational as well as religious function, church attendance was not restricted to one's own denomination and could introduce or reacquaint young men and women. William P. Biddle, a wealthy Baptist, jokingly recounted his younger daughters' adventures. "The girls and tutoress," he wrote, "went to a methodist meeting Sunday and brought home a great many beaus or sparks or what some people call fleas and in the process of rejecting them have taken slight colds." Moreover, calls upon friends and neighbors also informally brought together possible mates. Visits of well-educated or

9. Marvin B. Sussman, "Parental Participation in Mate Selection and Its Effects upon Family Continuity," *Social Forces*, XXXII (1953), 76–81; Alan Bates, "Parental Roles in Courtship," *Social Forces*, XX (1942), 483–86; Degler, *At Odds*, 12–14; William Polk to Mary B. Polk, January 24, 1824, in Polk, Badger, and McGehee Family Papers; Penelope Skinner to Tristrim L. Skinner, January 22, 1839, in Skinner Family Papers. Other examples are Sarah E. Devereux to Thomas P. Devereux, June 9, 1841, in Devereux Family Papers; Sarah Polk to Leonidas Polk, August 8, 1823, in Leonidas Polk Papers.
10. William J. Goode, "The Theoretical Importance of Love," *American Sociological Review*, XXIV (1959), 38–47; Stone, *The Family, Sex and Marriage*, 270–77.

prominent young men from other areas might provide social excitement for young ladies. Henry Barnard, a recent graduate of Yale College, recorded a pleasant afternoon spent with great planter John Devereux: "My visit was none the less interesting because a lovely granddaughter of some sixteen summers growth was present, and was pleased not to be very coyish."[11]

Numerous parties and balls also formed meeting places for young men and women. There the high spirits of youth could prolong the fun into the early hours of morning. Penelope Skinner thoroughly enjoyed herself at an oyster supper which culminated with dancing. Alice Hilliard in 1856 described a dizzying round of entertainments she had recently attended. Young people mainly went to parties taking place in their neighborhood or given by close friends, but sometimes ventured farther afield. An invitation from the Whitaker family, with whom the Battles were not formally acquainted, surprised Turner Battle and his sisters, but he jokingly told of their acceptance: "we don't know why we are invited. Eliza and Nep think John Henry being anxious to see them, is the moving cause of the favor that has been shown us. I think that Nancy & Elizabeth Whitaker wished to become acquainted with your humble servant[.] Be that as it may we intend going, and John Henry or Nancy and Lizzy will be gratified." Courtship could also be carried on at semipublic events called subscription balls. These dances, sponsored by prominent men in the community, were open to all who "subscribed" the stated fee. Also semipublic were balls sponsored by spas such as Shocco Springs in Warren County.[12]

In all these areas, planters had only limited ability to deny their sons' or daughters' acquaintance to prospective mates, but social

11. William P. Biddle to Sarah F. Norcott, March 17, 1840, in Bryan Scrapbook; Sophia Capehart to Robert Martin, May 9, 1859, in Scotch Hall Papers; Catherine Erwin to Mira Lenoir, September 9, 1826, in Lenoir Family Papers; Henry Barnard, "The South Atlantic States in 1833, as Seen by a New Englander," ed. Bernard C. Steiner, *Maryland Historical Magazine*, XIII (1918), 323.

12. Penelope Skinner to Tristrim L. Skinner, December 8, 1838, in Skinner Family Papers; Alice B. Hilliard to Mary E. V. Biddle, January 27, 1856, in Biddle Papers; Turner W. Battle to Martha Battle, May 7, 1849, in Battle Family Papers; G. G. Johnson, *Antebellum North Carolina*, 152–80; Lucy Battle to William H. Battle, August 15, 1855, in Battle Family Papers; James Hamilton to Charles E. Hamilton, January 22, 1840, in Bullock and Hamilton Papers. See also Moulton Avery to Eliza Murphy, September 30, 1835, in Walton Papers.

conventions and notions of propriety aided the older generation. Social usages barred the poor and those lacking a "respectable standing" from most gatherings attended by genteel young ladies. Likely most artisans and nonslaveholding small farmers (and their wives, sisters, and daughters) rarely interacted socially with the wealthy elite. These social boundaries, fluid enough to include most professional or wealthy groups, still significantly decreased the number of eligible mates encountered by great planters' children.[13]

In the quest for a desirable match, relatives and social conventions aided parents. Offspring's choices were narrowed, both socially and psychologically, to a range of "acceptable" mates that yet included many candidates. Still, parents' self-imposed limits upon their authority were as important as their direct guidance. In part, their self-restraint sprang from successful prior socialization of children. But beliefs about the nature of marriage also increased parental hesitance to interfere directly in courtship.

Building upon ideas that had become common among southern elites during the late eighteenth century, wealthy North Carolinians saw marriage as the most important relationship and firmly approved what Lawrence Stone has called the companionate marriage. Spouses should be loving partners, not two people unwillingly chained together for life. Husbands and wives should be linked by mutual attraction and should provide affectionate support for each other while rearing a family. Reality often approximated that ideal of domestic harmony.[14]

Deep regard frequently appeared in letters that husbands and wives exchanged during separations. William Polk assured his "dearest wife" that he would hurry home from his business trip in Tennessee to be with her and reminded her that "this is my birthday—I wish I had to spend it with you." Robert T. Paine wrote his wife of thirteen years: "Indeed can I give to your love greater bounds than mine for thee? I cannot fathom the depth of my devotion to a wife whom I would not change one jot or tittle in any respect."[15]

13. G. G. Johnson, *Ante-bellum North Carolina*, 152–80; Stone, *The Family, Sex and Marriage*, 316–17.
14. Stone, *The Family, Sex and Marriage*, 328–400; D. B. Smith, *Inside the Great House*, 142–45.
15. William Polk to Sarah Polk, July 9, 1811, in Leonidas Polk Papers; Robert T.

Planter families also believed in frankness between husbands and wives. David Outlaw revealed some of his views on marriage when he cautioned his wife about information he had shared with her: "Of course this is written in that unreserved intercourse which should exist between man and wife, and is not to be repeated to any person whatsoever." Rebecca Cameron reassured her absent husband that she would not conceal the severity of their infant's illness from him. This sharing in marriages could extend to many areas. Catherine Edmondston happily noted that she and her husband had the "same tastes, the same pleasures."[16]

Members of the planter elite believed one's spouse should be the most important person on earth. Although a serious man little given to flights of fancy, Samuel S. Biddle lovingly confided to his absent wife: "Life is robbed of half its pleasures when your smile cannot be seen, nor your voice heard." He worried only that such love might border on blasphemy: "But my dearest wife, we must think of each other [only] as the dearest object on earth, and endeavor to let our hearts and affections ascend to God, who requires of us the supreme affections of us his Creatures." A wife also wrestled with the intensity of her affection: "That you are dearer to me than all else upon Earth, is a confession I make with truth, and without shame; but I am ashamed to say my actions make the decision between you and my Maker." Perhaps Isaac T. Avery most movingly expressed the closeness planters thought should accompany the husband-wife relationship. In a letter written shortly after his wife's death he mused: "I feel that the strongest tie, that bound me to this world has been severed. . . . the heartrending sense of dreary Loneliness that this bereavement has brought me I had never conceived. She had been all in all to me for more than 43 years."[17]

Paine to Lavinia Paine, September 13, 1847, in Paine Papers. Consult William Polk to Sarah Polk, June 22, 1811, in Kenneth Rayner Papers, SHC; Mary N. Biddle to William P. Biddle, May 28, 1815, in Biddle Papers.

16. David Outlaw to Emily Outlaw, March 3, 1848, in Outlaw Papers; Rebecca Cameron to Duncan Cameron, May 22, 1804, in Cameron Family Papers; Beth G. Crabtree and James W. Patton (eds.), *"Journal of a Secesh Lady": The Diary of Catherine Ann Devereux Edmondston, 1860–1866* (Raleigh, 1979), 5.

17. Samuel S. Biddle to Mary E. V. Biddle, November 1, 1851, in Biddle Papers; Anne Cameron to Paul C. Cameron, March 8, 1834, in Cameron Family Papers; Isaac T. Avery to Selina L. Lenoir, August 16, 1858, in Lenoir Family Papers.

This belief in the important emotional content of marriage, though not removing planters' desire that children choose suitable mates, likely convinced parents their role should be restricted. Such a serious choice, bearing so largely upon future happiness, must be left to the individual, who would, however, still have the benefit of parental advice.

Parents' restriction of their role in courtship and marriage is most clearly shown in the absence of financial negotiations and transactions accompanying marriage. In fact, even though such negotiations had begun to play a much smaller role among genteel British families, the amount that a young woman's parents were able and willing to settle upon her helped to determine her marriage prospects. The same interest in financial matters was yet more evident in France. Moreover, the western European marriage contract, drawn up between the young couple but usually arranged by parents, stipulated each family's contribution and what property the young woman would receive, if widowed. Financial negotiations had accompanied marriages in seventeenth- and eighteenth-century New England and Virginia, and both Morgan and Greven have noted the haggling that sometimes took place between two sets of parents over a possible marriage. But nineteenth-century wealthy North Carolinians, like their contemporary northern counterparts, no longer bargained about their children's marriages.[18]

In fact, marriage contracts of great planters' offspring varied a great deal from European documents, in that they were used only to protect property a woman owned in her own right. In planter families, most unmarried women who drew up contracts had inherited property from a deceased father, and only a small number of those women made such agreements. Sometimes when the young woman owned markedly more property than her prospective husband, social pressure would push him to suggest a marriage contract as proof that he

18. Adeline Daumard, *La Bourgeoisie parisienne de 1815 à 1848* (Paris, 1963), 327–35; Stone, *The Family, Sex and Marriage*, 243–44, 289–93; Pierre Bourdieu, "Marriage Strategies as Strategies of Social Reproduction," in Forster and Ranum (eds.), *Family and Society*, 117–44; Robert Forster, *The Nobility of Toulouse in the Eighteenth Century: A Social and Economic Study* (Baltimore, 1960), 120–51, and *The House of Saulx-Tavanes: Versailles and Burgundy, 1700–1830* (Baltimore, 1971), 5–7, 32, 44–49, 118–24, 132–34; G. E. Mingay, *English Landed Society in the Eighteenth Century* (London, 1963), 13, 26–39; Frisch, "Youth Culture," 194–208, 279–97; Morgan, *The Puritan*

was not a fortune hunter. Kemp P. Battle offered to allow the substantial fortune of his orphaned fiancée (and cousin) Martha Battle to be covered by such a contract, but neither Martha nor her siblings showed any interest in such a step. In other cases involving wealthy heiresses, the pressure actually came from the woman and her financial advisors. Margaret Cameron's brother Paul reminded her that her age, which made it unlikely that she would bear children, and the amount of her fortune should lead her to protect her property: "If my advice would avail anything: it would be offered in the five words 'take care of your self' but it may be that a manly and generous spirit will secure to you your own—this is but justice to *you* considering the age and circumstances of the contracting parties." Margaret took this advice and subtly maneuvered her fiancé into entering a marriage contract.[19]

Such marriage contracts might cover only part of a young woman's estate. The document drawn up between Frances H. Pugh and Stephen A. Norfleet covered only seven thousand dollars due her from sales of her father's Louisiana lands, and her sister Laura's agreement with Henry F. Williams included only five thousand dollars due from western property and a tract of land purchased from a younger brother. Since both Pugh women had inherited slaves and other land, probably they and the relatives who advised them were willing for that property to vest in the young women's husbands.[20]

Marriage contracts served yet another purpose for planters' widowed daughters, who sometimes drew up such agreements upon remarriage. Since they or their prospective husbands often had children by former marriages, contracts protected offspring's property rights and kept the bargainers' estates separate. In exchange for retaining all her property in trust, Delha Foreman agreed not to press

Family, 54–58, 81, and *Virginians at Home*, 30–34; Greven, *Four Generations*, 74–76, 78–82.

19. Kemp P. Battle, *Memories of an Old Time Tar Heel* (Chapel Hill, 1945), 124; Paul C. Cameron to Margaret Cameron, April 23, 1853, Margaret Cameron to Paul C. Cameron, May 6, 1853, both in Cameron Family Papers; George W. Mordecai and Margaret Cameron to Paul C. Cameron *et al.*, 1853, in Wake County Deeds, Vol. 19, pp. 590–95.

20. Frances H. Pugh and Stephen A. Norfleet to William A. Pugh, 1844, Laura S. Pugh and Henry F. Williams to William A. Pugh, 1846, both in Bertie County Deeds, Vol. GG, pp. 174–76, 422–24. Other typical marriage contracts are Mary Ellis and George B. Douglas to John W. Ellis, 1843, in Davidson County Deeds, Vol. 9, pp. 72–74, and

any claim as her second husband's widow to dower, the lifetime use of one-third of his real estate, or to a distributive share of his personal property. These contracts involved the couple planning marriage; parents did not arrange or negotiate the agreements.[21]

Probably most planters believed that as long as a young woman had a living father, he would take precautions necessary to protect property given to her. Young women who had only a possible future legacy never entered into contracts before marriage. Thus the marriage contract, rarely used in antebellum North Carolina, even then did not serve the same purpose the European agreement did.

As planters had relinquished financial bargaining in their progeny's matches, they also took little part in the actual activity of courtship. Young people expected to seek out and select their own spouses, even if from candidates prescribed by convention. Men proposed marriage; women accepted or rejected. Courtship, however, was also an elaborate game in which both men and women competed. For young adults who had been somewhat cloistered from the opposite sex by single-sex schools, it was a new, exhilarating—though not always pleasant—experience that reintroduced male to female. Young women vied to become the reigning belle and have the delicious choice of suitors that the role provided. Becoming the most-sought-after offered a certain distinction and celebrity to the coquette among not only peers but also those younger and older. Alice Hilliard reported about her older cousin: "Cousin Lucy I learn is quite a belle and has thrown Pattie Wiggins completely in the shade." Elderly William Polk described the Raleigh social season: "Miss Graham, Miss Turner of Warren—two Misses Hawkins, with several others have been the admiration of all."[22]

Frances A. Waddell and John Swann, Jr., to Francis N. Waddell, 1841, in Chatham County Deeds, Vol. AF, pp. 111–12.

21. Delha M. Foreman and Robert H. Austin to John S. Dancy, 1860, in Edgecombe County Deeds, Vol. 28, pp. 378–79. See also Mary Southerland and Willie N. White to William M. Green, in Mangum Family Papers, Series II, SHC.

22. Alice B. Hilliard to Mary E. V. Biddle, May 18, 1853, in Biddle Papers; William Polk to Lucius J. Polk, December 11, 1828, in Polk, Brown, and Ewell Family Papers. Consult Mary Lucas to Melissa Williams, July 16, 1836, in Badger Family Papers. My understanding of the relationship between single-sex schooling and courtship has been greatly enriched by discussions with Steven Mac Stowe and by his article, " 'The Thing, Not Its Vision': A Woman's Courtship and Her Sphere in the Southern Planter Class," Feminist Studies, IX (1983), 113–30.

In the game of courtship, young men clamored for the attention of the most scintillating young ladies, and the "score"—kept by participants and spectators alike—depended upon the number of admirers attracted and rejected. A young woman was not "successful" unless the enthralled suitor pledged his devotion and offered marriage. A Virginia lady chronicled the social failure of a visiting North Carolina planter's daughter who charmed men but did not make any "conquests." Flushed with victory, Penelope Skinner boasted of her belledom to her brother: "I can not see any one to suit my fancy and beaux are not *very* scarce with me. Do not tell if I tell you something[:] I refused three or four week before last. So you see your little sister is not forgotten in the crowd[.] a Lady told me the other day she expected I had had more offers than any other Lady in the state I said nothing but thought it very probable."[23]

In fact, elite families recognized courtship as a battle—or at least a skirmish—between the sexes. To the elders, it seemed an activity controlled by young women, whose charms made men their captives. Sarah Polk, herself a strong, capable woman, probably expressed a commonly held view when she commented upon her engaged daughter Susan's proposed visit to relatives in Warren County: "I suppose she thought she would pay the visit while she could, But she tells me, the Gentleman says he will never ask her to do anything against her will, all this is very clever before Marriage, when Right its that the Woman should Reighn [*sic*], but after, It's certainly Right the Husband should, as the Good Book says be the 'Head of the Wife.'" This very limited nature of young women's dominance and the toleration afforded their perversity probably encouraged many to be capricious. "My *expectations* that you so delicately hinted at," stormed Kenneth M. Clark to his brother-in-law, "by some unaccountable frieck [freak] of woman's nature, are all blasted." Another great planter's son perceptively, though in part teasingly, commented upon the lovelorn plight of a friend: "I feel sorry for him, as I do for every man in like condition and yet I cant blame women for exercising the only valued prerogative left them. He must practice now the simple but effective philosophy which you and I, and a great many other

23. Jean S. Syme to Mary A. Cameron, April 2, 1822, in Cameron Family Papers; Penelope Skinner to Tristrim L. Skinner, September 4, 1837, in Skinner Family Papers.

clever fellows have had to put on when cast off by the 'provoking little Darlings' and that is throw up his coat Tail, say Heigh ho loona
three times and laugh as loud as lungs will let you—and away will go
the spell."[24]

Emphasis upon young women's power during courtship also yielded
a dual vision of females—the normal sentimental view of innocent,
unworldly charmers was supplemented by that of coldly conniving,
heartless belles. John W. Ellis knew where to place the emphasis when
he remarked that "*all* men & some women have hearts." Still Ellis,
like other bedazzled young blades, was willing to visit a spa full of
"fascinating" young ladies despite his professed fears of being "caught
in a web."[25]

While elite young Carolinians chose from groups limited by social
conventions and during activities that caught the notice of all ages,
the young set some rules of their own for the conduct of engagements
and love affairs. Engagements quite often began—and sometimes even
ended—with little parental knowledge. D. T. Tayloe's engagement
to Meeta Armistead illustrated how informal and tenuous commitments could be. He assured her, "Have I ever murmured at your many
little 'affaires du couer' [sic]? Not at all—And why not? When we made
the engagement, I expressly told you to follow the dictates of your
heart, that many difficulties were in the way—that I hoped but little,
and loved much." This young couple probably dissolved their engagement without ever consulting parents. Other young lovers not
only made but broke their own engagements. Penelope Skinner felt
humiliated when, after her numerous refusals of young men, an admirer did not follow up on her acceptance and her father's consent.
She did not, however, expect her father to intervene. "Nothing has
been heard of or from Mr. S. I do not believe he is coming," fumed
Penelope. "I think it is time for me to take it in hand. I wish to hear
from him in some way or other—to think *I* should have been disap-

24. Sarah Polk to Mary Polk, March 17, 1842, in Polk and Yeatman Family Papers;
Herman R. Lantz *et al.*, "Pre-Industrial Patterns in the Colonial Family in America: A
Content Analysis of Colonial Magazines," *American Sociological Review*, XXXIII
(1968), 413–26; Kenneth M. Clark to Lewis Thompson, December 29, 1849, in
Thompson Papers; James S. Green to Gaston Meares, September 11, 1849, in DeRosset
Family Papers.

25. John W. Ellis to Lucy E. Williams, April 2, June 25, 1854, both in Noble J. Tolbert (ed.), *The Papers of John Willis Ellis* (2 vols.; Raleigh, 1964), I, 135, 138.

pointed." She later heard that her suitor had told people that she had rejected him, a lie which she resolved to make true. Her father played no part in ending that engagement.[26]

Most often parents were formally consulted when the engaged couple began to contemplate marriage and plan a wedding. The prospective bridegroom then informed his fiancée's father of the commitment and asked approval. Archibald Glenn plainly stated his purpose to Alexander Cuningham: "The object . . . is to inform you that Mary and myself have our own consent to be married, and are engaged but knowing that I have to appeal to you—it would be very gratifying if you would approve of it—at least give your consent." Paul C. Cameron, in a more formal letter, presented himself as a petitioner rather than as a partner as had Glenn, but clearly indicated that he and his prospective fiancée had entered into the engagement: "To be plain, I have loved, courted and been *accepted* by *Her*: and I now offer myself to you and your lady, as one worthy of your Daughters affection."[27]

Parental consent served more as a formality than an actual hurdle for young people. Parents generally assented to offspring's commitments. James Turner told his cousin that he expected approval of his engagement to Ann Hawkins. Both the Waddells and DeRossets were pleased by Moses DeRosset's choice of Sarah Waddell. Even those planters who did not particularly like their child's decision agreed to the wedding. According to family tradition, Charity Cain's wealthy parents preferred a well-to-do suitor over Willie P. Mangum, a struggling local lawyer who was Charity's choice. After being rebuffed by William Cain two times, Mangum sought a third audience and gained parental permission for the marriage. When Jane Dudley chose a young Roman Catholic army officer, her parents consented, although as a friend cattily reported, "the family (one and all) dislike the match exceedingly." Believing in the companionate marriage, parents thought themselves obliged to ratify their offspring's selec-

26. D. T. Tayloe to Meeta Armistead, March 11, 1855, in M. A. Capehart Papers; Penelope Skinner to Tristrim L. Skinner, January 15, 31, 1840, both in Skinner Family Papers. See Sally Tarry to William Tarry, March 14, 1842, in John Bullock Papers, Duke;[?] to Walter W. Lane, April 5, n.d., in Lane Papers.

27. Archibald Glenn to Alexander Cuningham, July 5, 1830, in Cuningham Papers; Paul C. Cameron to Thomas Ruffin, June 7, 1831, in Cameron Family Papers.

tion, unless such serious objections existed that the son's or daughter's future happiness might be jeopardized. Joseph B. Skinner gravely wrote about his daughter Penelope's fiancé: "I cannot say from the slight acquaintance I have with him that he is such a one as by any means would receive my cordial approbation—but if he is her choice She must take her destiny in her own hands, unless I hear something so objectionable, that I should ever reproach myself, if I did not use my Parental authority as far as that would operate to prevent her future wretchedness."[28]

The younger generation's beliefs about consent probably encouraged parents not to withhold it. Although offspring, especially daughters, believed they should seek parental approval, some did not deem it essential to marriage. Sophia Devereux clarified this view in a letter to her future husband. Her criticism of those who married without asking approval rested on the pain it would cause parents—a wound that Sophia had probably witnessed firsthand when one older sister eloped and yet another married before receiving, though after asking for, parental consent. "Where must a woman's heart go to who can cooly marry without letting her father know," motherless Sophia rhetorically queried. But like other romantic young people of her day, she believed parents should not be able to veto a choice. She discussed her solution: "I would wait a reasonable time and then if my father would not consent I would marry but it should be in his house." Parental consent to Sophia was a thoughtful formality, not an indispensable preliminary to marriage. Other young women such as Ann Hawkins, Penelope Skinner, and Elizabeth Johnson also indicated that they would follow their own hearts, regardless of obstacles.[29]

28. James B. Turner to Charles E. Hamilton, December 24, 1839, in Bullock and Hamilton Papers; Sarah Waddell to Catherine DeRosset, September 1, 1826, in DeRosset Family Papers; Shanks (ed.), *The Papers of Willie Person Mangum*, V, 759; Eliza DeRosset to Catherine DeRosset, March 1, 1845, in DeRosset Family Papers; Joseph B. Skinner to Tristrim L. Skinner, January 30, 1839, Penelope Skinner to Tristrim L. Skinner, March 13, 1839, both in Skinner Family Papers. See Mary H. Walker to Susan Cabanne, August 27, 1841, in Battle Family Papers; Leonidas Polk to Lucius J. Polk, July 3, 1828, in Gale and Polk Family Papers; B. Franklin Biddle to Samuel S. Biddle, March, 1848, in Biddle Papers.

29. Sophia Devereux to Josiah Turner, Jr., December 6, 1855, in Turner Papers; James B. Turner to Charles E. Hamilton, December 24, 1839, in Bullock and Hamilton Papers; Elizabeth E. Johnson to Sarah A. B. Granberry, November 10, 1832, in Bailey Papers; Penelope Skinner to Tristrim L. Skinner, January 15, 1840, in Skinner Family Papers.

The few cases in which parental consent was not immediately forthcoming indicate how much a formality it was. Young people married, even without parental approbation. Honoria Devereux did not wait for her father's assent before marrying and leaving the area. Although temporarily angered, he later visited her distant home. William Gaston commented that another rich father would soon forgive his daughter's headstrong marriage. Even in the most unusual case, lack of parental consent caused only a temporary delay. Elderly Duncan Cameron did not wish his mid-thirtyish daughter Margaret, who managed his household and cared for her invalid sister, to marry George W. Mordecai, a banker of Jewish descent. Still, Cameron, who cited "domestic" reasons in his refusal, took no steps to guard against Margaret's marriage in his will drawn up shortly after. The not-so-young lovers complied with Cameron's waiting game and married shortly after his death less than a year later.[30] That some parents could be successfully defied likely influenced others to consent to matches they did not particularly like. Possibly some planters believed it better to retain influence with their sons and daughters by careful counseling rather than to squander it through futile prohibitions.

Young couples also set the tone of their engagement. Some sought to move their relationship from the flirtatious game of courtship toward the more sober and intimate sharing associated with marriage. In the same letter that pleaded for the honor of addressing his fiancée as "Dear Anna," Paul C. Cameron also informed her in a stylized yet sincere manner: "This you must know[:] that such is the light in which I view the happy relation existing between us, that I will never conceal a single thought from you. I consider it a mutual *duty*, that we owe to *each* other during our engagement, to *communicate* with each other, in a spirit of the *utmost* frankness and candor; Yes 'loved and lovely one' let it be done with unlocked bosoms." Other engaged couples attempted to be frank in their discussions and sometimes

30. Sophia Devereux to Josiah Turner, Jr., December 18, 1855, in Turner Papers; Sarah E. Devereux to Thomas P. Devereux, March 18, 1858, Ann W. Mordecai to Margaret M. Devereux, February 8, 1852, both in Devereux Family Papers; William Gaston to Susan Donaldson, January 14, 1840, in Gaston Papers; Will of Duncan Cameron, in Wake County Wills. See also Samuel S. Downey to John Downey, August 16, 1845, in Downey Papers; Nancy Turner to Charles E. Hamilton, March 18, 1838, in Bullock and Hamilton Papers; G. G. Johnson, *Ante-bellum North Carolina*, 193–94.

criticized their own and their prospective mate's shortcomings. Tristrim L. Skinner mildly rebuked his fiancée, Eliza Harwood, for not wearing the ring he had given her: "I only dislike it for the reason that it shows that you care, (as I tell you perhaps too often) too much for the world's remarks."[31]

Young people's important role in courtship and marriage also meant that they often chose the kind of wedding they wished. Couples might, like Anne Ruffin and Paul C. Cameron, decide that the sacredness of the occasion meant only close relatives should attend. Others had large, joyful assemblages of neighbors, friends, and relatives. Young friends and relatives also exuberantly participated in the wedding festivities. Often they served as attendants during the ceremony. One great planter's daughter described her sister's "small but pleasant" wedding including four attendants, three of whom were siblings of either bride or groom. Minerva Cain had four bridesmaids: her cousins Alice Ruffin and Mary White, her younger sister Martha, and her future sister-in-law Martha Caldwell.[32]

Peers provided much of the humor that accompanied weddings. Joking that rumors of his brother Moulton's impending marriage were "*lamentably* but too true," Waightstill Avery invited a cousin to the wedding since Moulton "thinks he will require the presence of some of his Friends on that trying occasion." Brides too might announce their nuptials humorously. Mary B. Polk told her cousin, "What do you think? I am actually *going to be married (excuse my blushes)* and that too, the week after next or *thereabouts*, provided Papa returns by that time from Charlotte." Martha Cain reported that during her older sister's wedding, the bridegroom said "I do" too early, sending all the girls into peals of laughter. Some joking and teasing by friends and young relatives accompanied the couple's change in status and enlivened the wedding and its preparations. But organized harass-

31. Paul C. Cameron to Anne Ruffin, July 8, 1831, in Cameron Family Papers; Tristrim L. Skinner to Eliza Harwood, December 10, 1848, in Skinner Family Papers. Consult George E. Badger to Mary B. Polk, September 6, 1826, in Polk, Badger, and McGehee Family Papers.

32. Paul C. Cameron to Anne Ruffin, November 21, 1832, in Cameron Family Papers; Josiah Turner, Jr., to Sophia Devereux, November 18, [1855], in Turner Papers; Lavinia B. Battle to Mary L. Gordon, December 18, 1855, in Battle Family Papers; Delia Erwin to Selina Lenoir, April 25, 1828, in Lenoir Family Papers; Martha Cain to Catherine de Roulhac, February 7, 1841, in Caldwell Papers, SHC.

ment by peers, such as charivaris, does not seem to have existed among this elite.[33]

Marriages arising from sons' and daughters' choices influenced by parental views had a predictable pattern: choices generally were prudent but showed a certain level of personal preference. Most North Carolina planters' children wed members of slaveholding families. All spouses from slaveholding states whose socioeconomic background can be determined—at least 114 husbands of planters' daughters and 77 wives of sons—belong to this category. For example, Mary Eaton in 1827 wed James H. Taylor, whose father owned sixty-three slaves. William Bethell married Mary Jeffreys, whose father in 1830 owned thirty-four slaves. Lucius J. Johnson chose Mary Isabella Granberry, whose father's holdings totaled forty-six bondsmen.[34]

Some marriages were completely intragroup as rich young scions married wealthy heiresses of the planter elite. But since only about 15 percent of children's marriages were to members of the 1830 slaveholding elite or their descendants, most sons and daughters married outside the state's richest families.[35] Still most marriages outside this inner circle could be called sagacious.

The younger generation of the elite sometimes wed those of similar standing from other states. Sally Turner married a Virginia congressman, and Penelope Benbury's father-in-law, John A. Selden, owned the famous plantation Westover in Virginia. George P. and Thomas P. Devereux, great-grandsons of New England divine Jonathan Edwards, married well-connected young women from Connecticut, and Thomas' second wife was the daughter of a wealthy New York merchant.[36]

33. Waightstill W. Avery to I. T. Lenoir, May 11, 1841, in Lenoir Family Papers; Mary B. Polk to Sarah L. Blount, October 26, 1826, in Polk, Badger, and McGehee Family Papers; Martha Cain to Catherine de Roulhac, February 7, 1841, in Caldwell Papers, SHC.

34. MS Census of 1830, North Carolina, Granville County, p. 23, Perquimans County, p. 101, and Person County, p. 23; Raleigh *Register*, August 16, 1827; Descendants of Colin Clark, in Compiled Genealogies, NCDAH; Stuart Hall Hill Papers, III, 13, in North Carolina Division of State Library, Raleigh.

35. Thirty-eight of 303 marriages (12.5 percent) contracted by great planters' daughters and 42 of 182 marriages (23.1 percent) by sons were to another great planter of 1830 or a descendant.

36. Raleigh *Register*, June 16, 1831, June 29, 1827; John A. Selden, Jr., to Penelope

Others chose spouses from politically prestigious and influential families. For example, Ann Bullock's husband, Archibald Henderson, was the son of a state supreme court justice. Frances Iredell, second wife of Charles E. Johnson, Jr., belonged to a politically prominent family; and Peter G. Evans and Waightstill W. Avery married daughters of North Carolina governor John M. Morehead.[37]

Some North Carolina great planters' daughters married young professional men. Approximately 11 percent of their unions were to lawyers, and 15 percent were to physicians. Some professional men also belonged to wealthy elite families. For example, Mary E. Williams' husband, Peter B. Hawkins, was a member of that rich Warren County clan. Dr. William S. M. Davidson, who wed Jane Torrence, came from a respected western North Carolina family. Other men with more modest origins were likely to become prominent in their professions. Ann Slade's choice, Joseph Lloyd, was an aspiring young lawyer and politician. Lucy Boddie's husband, Bartholomew F. Moore, not only had a successful law practice but also later served as state attorney general.[38] Marriage could then closely link rising young professional men to the planter elite.

Not only did planters' sons and daughters generally marry those in comfortable circumstances, they also cautiously chose those who by kinship or geography were well known to them and their families. One form of this parochial orientation emerged in cousin marriage; matches with first or second cousins comprised almost one-tenth of the total known.[39]

Some North Carolinians—black and white—did not approve of cousin marriage. Herbert G. Gutman has documented the taboo

Benbury, November 15, 1853, in Chowan County Marriage Bonds; John S. Bassett (ed.), "The Westover Journal of John A. Selden, Esqr., 1858–1862," *Smith College Studies in History*, VI (1921), 253–330; Crabtree and Patton (eds.), "*Journal of a Secesh Lady*," xxi–xxv.

37. Samuel T. Peace, "*Zeb's Black Baby*": *Vance County, North Carolina: A Short History* (Henderson, N.C., 1955), 370; *North Carolina Standard*, April 18, 1849; W. W. Avery to Mary C. Morehead, May 27, 1846, Peter G. Evans to Anne E. Morehead, January 13, 1850, both in Guilford County Marriage Bonds.

38. Thirty-three of 303 marriages (10.9 percent) were to lawyers and 47 (15.5 percent) were to physicians. Raleigh *Register*, October 26, 1821, June 2, 1835, January 3, 1845; Peter B. Hawkins to Mary Elizabeth Williams, June 14, 1844, in Warren County Marriage Bonds.

39. Twenty-four (7.9 percent) of planters' daughters' marriages and twenty-six (14.3 percent) of sons' marriages were to first or second cousins.

against cousin marriage in the slave community. Local newspapers also sometimes carried items suggesting such matches were not quite acceptable. For example, a long, sad poem in the Cape Fear *Recorder* detailed a romance that, because it was between cousins, had been to the narrator "the ruin of me." Doubts about the propriety of courting close kin also arose in at least one planter family. Eighteen-year-old Willie Hardy described the highlight of his recent visit to South Carolina: "I fell in love with a cousin of mine Miss Sallie Douglass she is my 4th or 5th cousin so you see there is no harm in my having an affection for her."[40]

Much of upper-class North Carolina society, however, seems to have accepted cousin marriage. One lady tacitly endorsed such matches in her joking remark to her brother, the father of a newborn daughter: "[My son] Walker is already promised a wife in his new cousin, & you must write her name as he may be made acquainted with it." Cousins, other than those marrying, are also known to have courted one another. A young lady recounted a visit to great planter Edward B. Dudley's two oldest daughters: "Eliza Anne is not married yet, her cousin is gone, whether or not he is discarded I cant say." Ann Downey received love letters from at least two cousins—one a first cousin.[41]

Although historians studying such diverse groups as eighteenth-century Boston merchants and English aristocrats have suggested cousin marriages were arranged to consolidate or retain property within the family, no evidence to substantiate that hypothesis has been found for wealthy North Carolinians. In his study of the English peerage, Randolph Trumbach discovered that the typical cousin marriage was between a woman and her paternal cousin—the son either of her father's brother or of her father's sister. Such unions thus protected patrilineal wealth. But that pattern had no parallel among wealthy North Carolinians: ten of the thirteen marriages of first

40. Gutman, *The Black Family*, 88–90; Cape Fear *Recorder*, July 1, 1829, p. 4; Willie H. Hardy to George Phifer Erwin, March 16, 1860, in Erwin Papers. See also Raleigh *Register*, July 9, 1833.

41. M. Anderson to Duncan Cameron, January 23, 1804, in Cameron Family Papers; S.C.A. to "Dear Laura," October 26, 1840, in Battle Family Papers; James A. Amis to Ann Downey, October 1, 1852, James R. Hunt to Ann Downey, December 2, 1852, both in Downey Papers. Consult D. T. Tayloe to Meeta Armistead, March 11, 1855, in M. A. Capehart Papers.

cousins (with no generational "removes") involved what anthropologists call parallel cousins, that is, offspring of siblings of the same sex. In eight of these cases, however, the young woman wed her mother's sister's son; only two matches were with a father's brother's son. Such marriages of sisters' children were almost unknown among the English aristocracy—Trumbach found only a single case. Moreover, Peter Dobkin Hall in his examination of cousin marriage among Boston merchants has characterized such marriages of sisters' children as the least patriarchal form of cousin marriage because the parties shared no patrilineal ancestor whose authority would be increased by the match. Overall, Carolinian first-cousin marriages were to maternal rather than paternal relatives. This phenomenon does not appear to indicate any increased maternal power over mate selection; rather, it most likely highlights the importance of bilateral kinship, ties to both maternal and paternal kin.[42]

Instead of being prompted by parents or property arrangements, cousin marriages took place mainly in response to two different social situations. In older, long-settled communities—where much of the cousin marriage occurred—descendants of large families often found much of the local gentry to be relatives. Kin formed a large part of the pool of possible mates. Mary B. Polk exaggerated when she claimed that most of Warren County was kin to her mother's family, the Hawkinses, but that big clan had many blood and affinal relations in society's higher echelons. In this context, the marriage of George Little, son of Ann Hawkins Little, to one of his numerous first cousins, Margaret Haywood, daughter of Eleanor Hawkins Haywood, is not so surprising.[43]

A second set of circumstances producing cousin marriage was social and economic isolation. Like twentieth-century Kentucky

42. Peter Dobkin Hall, "Family Structure and Economic Organization: Massachusetts Merchants, 1700–1850," in Tamara K. Hareven (ed.), *Family and Kin in Urban Communities, 1700–1930* (New York, 1977), 38–61; Trumbach, *The Rise of the Egalitarian Family*, 17–22. Contrast my interpretation to Clinton, "The Plantation Mistress," 44, 135–45; Guion G. Johnson, "Courtship and Marriage Customs in Antebellum North Carolina," *North Carolina Historical Review*, VIII (1931), 386.

43. Mary B. Polk to George E. Badger, October 22, 1826, in Polk, Badger, and McGehee Family Papers; Allan Kulikoff, "Tobacco and Slaves: Population, Economy, and Society in Eighteenth Century Prince George's County, Maryland" (Ph.D. dissertation, Brandeis University, 1976), 363–406.

mountaineers of very high or very low status who tended to marry within their extended families, some North Carolinians, faced with great disparities of wealth between themselves and their neighbors, for lack of other eligible partners turned to kin. Illustrative is the marital history of the Hairston family. Great planter Peter Hairston's only daughter Ruth first married Peter Wilson, a wealthy Virginian. After Wilson's death, Ruth married her first cousin, Robert Hairston. To complicate further the family's relationships, Agnes J. P. Wilson, Ruth Hairston's only child by that first marriage, wed Robert Hairston's brother Samuel, thus making mother and daughter also sisters-in-law. Marriages within the next generation further tangled the intricate web of kinship. Since the Hairstons' section of North Carolina contained many nonslaveholders and few large planters, family members may have constituted many of the eligible matches. A similar isolation may have influenced Mary Brodnax of Rockingham County to marry her second cousin, John G. Brodnax.[44]

Another less frequent marriage pattern, similar to cousin marriage in its narrow orientation, arose when more than one union linked two families. One form of these marriages, known to anthropologists as sibling exchange, involved two children of Family A each marrying different members of Family B. For example, three of Thomas Norfleet's four daughters wed members of the Urquhart family of Southampton County, Virginia. The eldest daughter Mary married Dr. Richard A. Urquhart; her sister Louisa wed his brother James B. Urquhart, whose first wife had been Antoinette Hill, the Norfleets' first cousin. Urquhart's son from that earlier marriage, Whitmell H. Urquhart, married Frances, a third Norfleet sister. The Norfleet sisters' marriages to Urquhart brothers illustrate sibling exchange, and all three show the Norfleet family allying itself to one family by multiple marriages.[45]

Others in great planter families also forged strong links to a family by more than one marriage. Among the examples, brothers William, John D., and Joseph W. Hawkins married sisters Ann, Jane, and Mary

44. James Stephen Brown, "Social Class, Intermarriage and Church Membership in a Kentucky Community," *American Journal of Sociology*, LVII (1951), 232–42; John Wilkins Brodnax Papers, SHC. Peter W. Hairston was kind enough to explain the complicated Hairston genealogy to me.
45. S. H. Hill Papers, II, 26–28, 39–40; P. D. Hall, "Family Structure," 42–43.

Boyd. Siblings Mary Martha and Justina Avery wed cousins, Joseph F. and Pinckney Chambers. John J. Alston and his brother Nathaniel M. Alston chose sisters, Adeline and Patsy K. Williams, who were also the Alstons' cousins. Multiple ties to a single family might also be created when a widow or widower, usually the latter, married the deceased spouse's sibling. After his young wife Louisa's death, Bartholomew F. Moore married her sister Lucy Boddie. William J. Hawkins first wed Mary Alethea Clark, and then her younger sister. Among the practical reasons influencing such marriages was child care. Common belief held that a second wife who was also an aunt would be a kinder and more concerned stepmother.[46]

Parochial as sibling-exchange unions and marriages with cousins and affinal kin were, they did not necessarily indicate the successful intervention of parents and relatives in mate selection. In fact, some such marriages caused great unhappiness among families. When Margaret McDowell wed her first cousin Marcus Erwin, their relatives were depressed, not elated, because of Erwin's dissipated habits. Nor were the Collins family at all pleased when Henrietta Collins married her widowed brother-in-law Matthew Page. A neighbor reported that "the family are *all* very much distressed at it, and the young men talk very fiercely."[47]

Geographical origins of their mates further reveal a narrowness of vision among the planter elite. Like sons and daughters of Alabama planters, most wealthy young North Carolinians chose spouses within their county or the area immediately surrounding it.[48] As Table 2 shows, over three-fourths of planters' sons' marriages and almost four-fifths of daughters' were to people living within a two-county, roughly twenty-five- or thirty-mile radius. For example, three of Francis L. Dancy's four children married other Edgecombe County

---

46. Groves, *The Alstons and Allstons*, 126–27; Chambers Family Papers, SHC; S. H. Hill Papers, III, 258–59; Hawkins Family Papers; Raleigh *Register*, December 12, 1828, June 2, 1835; Descendants of Colin Clark, in Compiled Genealogies, NCDAH. See Verena Martinez-Alier, *Marriage, Class and Colour in Nineteenth Century Cuba: A Study of Racial Attitudes and Sexual Values in a Slave Society* (Cambridge, 1974), 88–90.

47. Polly M. Summey to Selina L. Lenoir, July 29, 1854, in Lenoir Family Papers; E. L. Skinner to Tristrim L. Skinner, January 5, 1849, in Skinner Family Papers.

48. Boucher, "Wealthy Planter Families," 93–97.

residents, and at least five of James Hilliard's six children wed people living in their own or adjacent county.

Unions with those from outside this geographically restricted area tended to fall into two groups. First, many marriages between people from two different locales involved relatives, former residents, or those with ties to the area. At least five of Joseph J. Alston's sons married women from Franklin or Warren County. Both Alston and his wife had grown up in that northern tobacco belt and still had numerous friends and relatives there. William H. Pugh of Louisiana, who married W. Ann Thompson, was a relative of her stepfather and had probably lived in the same county.[49]

Second, lawyers, politicians, merchants, ministers, and doctors, who tended to know many people outside their locality, also married women from more distant areas. In fact, over 40 percent of the marriages involving a spouse from an area more remote than the two tiers of neighboring counties were contracted by men in one of those professions. Lawyers and judges who rode circuit perhaps had the most far-ranging circle of friends and acquaintances throughout the state. Lawyer Clement G. Wright of Fayetteville married a young lady from Greensboro, and western Carolina lawyer and jurist John W. Ellis married Mary Daves of New Bern, a coastal town.[50]

Marriage patterns among wealthy planters' offspring reveal both prudence and provincialism. Generally they chose members of North Carolina's slaveholding group, the upper 25 percent of the state's population, although a few wed well-to-do people from other states. Marriages to a relative or more than one marriage uniting two families also illustrate the limited scope of their social world. Had planters been less provincial, more unions to solidify the state's planting elite, rather widely dispersed geographically, might have occurred.

Yet these choices, which partly reflected socialization by the older generation, also show the freedom exercised by young men and women. One indicator of parental interference in mate selection, the

49. Groves, *The Alstons and Allstons*, 126–27; Alston-Kearney-Kinchen Papers, in Isaac London Collection, Compiled Genealogies, NCDAH; Raleigh *Register*, September 8, 1831.
50. *North Carolina Standard*, October 17, 1855, August 14, 1858.

Table 2. Residence of Those
Marrying Great Planters' Offspring

| Those Marrying Sons | | |
Location	Number	Percentage
Same county	69	42.1
Adjoining county	47	28.7
Two counties away	10	6.1
More distant	38	23.2
TOTAL	164	100.1

| Those Marrying Daughters | | |
Location	Number	Percentage
Same county	85	42.1
Adjoining county	52	25.7
Two counties away	23	11.4
More distant	42	20.8
TOTAL	202	100.0

relation of birth order of daughters to the order in which they marry, reveals that young women in planter families enjoyed a certain latitude. Daniel Scott Smith, in his long-term analysis of parental power in Hingham, Massachusetts, has examined this relation between birth order and marriage order to measure parental control. According to Smith's hypothesis, parental interference would strengthen the natural tendency of daughters to marry in order of birth because to skip over a daughter would suggest that she was not as marriageable as her sisters. He found a great increase in the nineteenth century in women marrying out of birth sequence: if spinsters are excluded, approximately 15 to 20 percent wed before an older sister. If one includes those women who never married, approximately 25 percent wed out of turn. Such findings contrast dramatically with Bonnie Smith's for marriages among nineteenth-century bourgeois women of northern France. In such French families where parents played an important role in matchmaking, a mere 3 percent of the young ladies married out of birth order. North Carolina elite women more resembled their counterparts among Hingham residents and wealthy Alabamians. Of eighty-five daughters of Tar Heel planters, about 30 percent including spinsters, or 20 percent if the never-married are excluded, eschewed birth order. Such proportions further indicate that in North Carolina the younger generation's preferences and desires played a role in marriage choice.[51]

Age at marriage can also provide clues about direct parental involvement. Historians and demographers have tended to interpret age at marriage in two general ways. They have attributed youthful unions to parental control and those made at an older age to economic constraints. Thus Anne Firor Scott's and Bertram Wyatt-Brown's emphasis upon the young age at marriage of southern upper-class women suggests parental prominence in marriage. Wealthy North Carolinians' daughters, however, married neither extremely early nor extremely late (see Table 3). Although they probably married a couple of years younger than wealthy New Englanders and native-born Buf-

Table 3. Age at First Marriage
of Great Planters' Daughters

Age	Number Marrying	Percentage Marrying
15 or under	6	3.9
16	9	5.8
17	11	7.1
18	17	11.0
19	32	20.7
20	17	11.0
21	14	9.0
22–24	31	20.0
25–29	16	10.3
30–34	0	0
35 or over	2	1.3
TOTAL	155	100.1

51. Daniel Scott Smith, "Parental Power and Marriage Patterns: An Analysis of Historical Trends in Hingham, Massachusetts," *Journal of Marriage and the Family*, XXXV (1973), 424–25; Bonnie G. Smith, *Ladies of the Leisure Class: The Bourgeoises of Northern France in the Nineteenth Century* (Princeton, 1981), 60; Boucher, "Wealthy Planter Families," 91.

falo women of that time, their average age of 20.5 years is almost the same as that of women in the Alabama elite. And, in fact, the median age of 20 for the North Carolinians approximates the U.S. national median for women first marrying between 1950 and 1970.[52]

The range of ages at marriage in the same family testifies to differing preferences and opportunities of young women. Some of William K. Kearney's older daughters married early. Matilda was only fifteen when she wed John Somervell, and her sisters Martha and Cornelia married at ages sixteen and seventeen respectively. But even though William remained rich and as able to provide property to his younger as to his older daughters, two of the younger girls waited until age twenty-five and another until age twenty-two for marriage.

Not wishing the dependent role thrust upon spinsters, some young ladies believed they should not wait too long before accepting a proposal. Twenty-year-old Penelope Skinner only half-jokingly described the visits of local schoolgirls between ages twelve and fifteen: "So you see we have the Town full of young girls who will soon be Ladies—I pray some of the old stock may be off of the carpet before that time arrives, myself for one." Although most women not physically or mentally incapacitated married, planters' daughters also wished to wed men who satisfied their notions of romance and propriety. Sometimes a scarcity of eligible men existed. Catherine Erwin of western North Carolina frequently complained about the shortage of beaux and at one point remarked, "I fear we shall have a dull winter[,] not a word about weddings in this County[.] I do believe it will never become fashionable here again to get married." Perhaps this lack of suitable suitors was the reason that Erwin herself did not marry until age twenty-eight.[53]

Since nineteenth-century North Carolina upper-class men not only

52. E. A. Wrigley, *Population and History* (New York, 1969), 47–48, 100–105; Stone, *The Family, Sex and Marriage*, 190–94, 318–20; A. F. Scott, *The Southern Lady*, 23–26; Wyatt-Brown, "The Ideal Typology," 10; Rudy Ray Seward, *The American Family: A Demographic History* (Beverly Hills, Calif., 1978), 54–61; Laurence A. Glasco, "The Life Cycles and Household Structure of American Ethnic Groups: Irish, Germans and Native-born Whites in Buffalo, New York, 1855," in Hareven (ed.), *Family and Kin*, 133–34; Greven, *Four Generations*, 33–35, 120–22, 208–209; Boucher, "Wealthy Planter Families," 84–89.

53. Penelope Skinner to Tristrim L. Skinner, April 22, 1839, in Skinner Family Papers; Catherine Erwin to Mira Lenoir, November 3, 1826, in Lenoir Family Papers.

had a more extended period of schooling than females but also usually married women their own age or younger, their pattern of ages at first marriage differed. Young men married later than their sisters, but still as young adults. Almost three-fourths of planters' sons married between ages twenty and twenty-nine (see Table 4). Their median age was but 24, only slightly higher than that of U.S. men marrying for the first time between 1950 and 1970. And the North Carolinians' average age of 25.2 was almost the same as that of their wealthy Alabama counterparts, whose mean age was 25.7 years.[54]

Marriage among the sons of elite Carolinians also had more to do with personal preference than with parental control or economic fac-

Table 4. Age at First Marriage
of Great Planters' Sons

Age	Number Marrying	Percentage Marrying
19 or under	8	6.7
20	3	2.5
21	15	12.5
22	14	11.7
23	10	8.3
24	17	14.2
25	9	7.5
26	4	3.3
27	10	8.3
28	8	6.7
29	3	2.5
30	3	2.5
31–34	9	7.5
35–39	5	4.2
40 or over	2	1.7
TOTAL	120	100.1

54. All but seven of two hundred marriages of planters' sons and daughters extant in 1850 involved a husband who was the same age or older than his wife. Seward, *The American Family,* 54–61; Greven, *Four Generations,* 117–19, 206–208; Boucher, "Wealthy Planter Families," 84. Compare American ages at first marriage to the older ages of the "European" pattern described in J. Hajnal, "European Marriage Patterns in Perspective," in D. V. Glass and D. E. C. Eversley (eds.), *Population in History: Essays in Historical Demography* (London, 1965), 101–143.

tors. In theory, a wealthy man's death while his son was young could enable the young man to marry earlier through the property it brought him and the paternal control it removed. Yet in actuality the father's decease does not appear to have encouraged early marriage. In fact, a larger percentage of those who had a living father married before age twenty-five than those whose fathers were deceased. Of the 120 elite sons whose age at first marriage can be determined, 62 percent of those marrying before a father's death wed under age twenty-five; only 48 percent of those marrying after paternal demise did so by that age. For example, James Turner during his father's lifetime married at age nineteen, and Richard Boyd saw three of his sons marry at ages nineteen, twenty-one, and twenty-two. Sometimes a long bachelorhood seems to have been self-imposed. Tristrim L. Skinner, only son of a wealthy father, delayed marriage until age twenty-eight because of his affection for a young lady he met during his college days in Williamsburg, Virginia. Then she was in her early teens, but the two corresponded, first in friendship, later in courtship. Skinner eventually sought her hand and was rejected, but two years later they married. Other similar situations existed. In 1848, Frank Hawkins expressed pleasure that two of his younger brothers, then in their early twenties, were likely to marry soon. In fact, over ten years passed before either married. The vagaries of romance rather than parental constraint were more in evidence for those who married relatively late in life.[55]

Aided by social conventions, elite North Carolinians could subtly limit the range of their offspring's courtship prospects. But as strong supporters of the companionate marriage, parents restricted their direct role in courtship and consented to marriages they did not like. Generally children chose marriage partners who satisfied their parents' wishes but these selections resulted from the younger people's desires, nurtured by years of socialization, meshing with those of their parents.

55. Sally A. Tarry to William Tarry, March 14, 1842, in Bullock Papers; Boyd Family Records, in Compiled Genealogies, NCDAH; Penelope Skinner to Tristrim L. Skinner, January 31, 1840, Tristrim L. Skinner to Eliza Harwood, October 30, 1842, March 28, 1846, October 14, 1848, all in Skinner Family Papers; Frank Hawkins to John D. Hawkins, November 29, 1848, in Hawkins Family Papers.

This parent-child interaction in courtship and marriage among planter families should be viewed as part of a trend among well-to-do nineteenth-century parents. Young people's growing influence in these areas has been documented for eighteenth- and nineteenth-century England and America. Parents increasingly assumed an indirect role, relinquishing or downplaying direct financial bargaining. Like middle-class northerners, elite Carolinians had turned over much decision making to their offspring.

FIVE

Parent–Adult Offspring Relations

Parental affection continued unabated as sons and daughters attained adulthood. But the close guidance of earlier years, already more sporadic and less apparent, further withered away. Planters' relinquishing of controls came about for several reasons. During the formative years, they had attempted, usually with success, to lead children into paths of virtue and achievement. Parents could view with equanimity this internalization of values in adult offspring, especially as the latter made judicious, acceptable marriages and formed ambitious, self-reliant, and self-controlled families of their own.

Continuities and changes wrought in parent-child relations can best be viewed by examining divisions of property as well as the more routine parent-child interaction. Transfers of land and slaves, both during the planters' lives and at their deaths, illustrate parental renunciation and forfeiture of power over offspring. And the relationships themselves also show the continuity of affection as well as a mutuality that signaled the decline of one-way control.

Parents and adult offspring developed a system of mutual aid. In times of illness, each looked to the other for assistance and comfort. Mothers sometimes nursed and advised sick adult sons and daughters. Margaret Lane of New Hanover County accompanied her tubercular daughter Virginia on a trip through western North Carolina. Missouri Alston sought her mother's presence and advice: "I am anxious to see you Mother for my health has been very feeble all this spring. Mr Alston would have sent for you several times but thought you were expecting our relations and would be up very soon. . . . he feels very uneasy about me[,] thinks he will take me to Philadelphia soon and would like to see you before doing so." Most likely her mother quickly answered that call. Several years earlier the older woman had responded to mere rumors of Missouri's "delicate" health: "if anything is the matter I will come down at any moment."[1]

Mothers frequently assisted daughters through the ordeal of childbirth. Sometimes the older women then remained for a time at their daughters' homes. Patsy Cuningham, for one of many examples, not only was present at the birth but also stayed to help her daughter recover and to care for the infant. Other young women wishing maternal aid returned to the parental home. Because difficulties of travel were considerable for pregnant women and women with infants, some daughters spent a long period there before and after the delivery. Adelaide Avery described her sister's two-week-old baby and added, "Mr Chambers wants to take her home in a few weeks, but I don't think it will be possible if this weather continues, We cant say much to him for she has been away from home seven months." Levin Lane's daughter arrived at his home in early December, either miscarried or delivered a dead infant in January, and remained until mid-May because of bad weather and ill health.[2]

In turn, adult offspring aided parents during illness. Both married and unmarried daughters helped to nurse their ailing fathers or mothers. Mary Turner cared for her father during a long siege of poor health. Penelope Skinner Warren, often irritated by her father's behavior, was dismayed to hear of his illness while she was away, since "he is the poorest person in the world to bear pain of any sort—it makes him impatient & must go hard with him, I wish sincerely that I was at home to nurse him and amuse him." Martha Urquhart became so upset at reports of her mother's ill health that only her own feeble condition prevented her from visiting the elderly lady, then at another daughter's home.[3]

1. Eliza DeRosset to Kate Meares, August 15, 1858, in DeRosset Family Papers; Missouri F. Alston to Sarah M. Alston, June 13, 1859, in Alston Papers (similarly W. P. Biddle to Samuel S. Biddle, October 8, 1848, in Simpson and Bryan Family Papers); Sarah M. Alston to Willis Alston, February 10, 1854, in Alston Papers.

2. M. M. Harrison to Alexander Cuningham, September 9, 1845, in Cuningham Papers; Adelaide Avery to Sarah Lenoir, January 5, 1857, in Lenoir Family Papers; Levin Lane to Walter W. Lane, May 14, 1856, in Lane Papers. Also see Jane A. Hawkins to John D. Hawkins, February 9, 1840, in Hawkins Family Papers.

3. Will of James Turner, in Warren County Wills; Penelope Warren to Thomas D.

Above all, both sons and daughters attempted to be present during serious and possibly fatal maladies, even though the watch might be lengthy. During prolonged illnesses, adult offspring often took turns spending the night with the patient. On William Cain's last night, his son Thomas attended him. A son-in-law, Pride Jones, dropped in and, finding other members of the family present, decided to spend the following night. As Cain's condition worsened, other children were summoned so that only one, who a few days earlier had left for her distant home, was not present at his death. Seven of Harriet Avery's nine children were at the dying woman's bedside. Both Samuel S. Biddle and Paul C. Cameron tried to comfort their fathers as the old men slowly and painfully expired. Nineteenth-century Americans believed the terrifying prospect of death was best faced with the aid of others; to die alone meant, in one wealthy North Carolinian's words, an "awful death." In planter families, concerned children sought to prevent such solitary suffering.[4]

Long before deathwatches became necessary, adult sons and daughters gave and received aid from parents in business and in domestic concerns. Many young men traveled to the Southwest to transact business and oversee plantations for their fathers. Those trips, although deemed valuable business experience for the sons, also saved the older folks much time and money. Sarah Polk told her oldest son, "I hope my son you will be able to take care of the trouble and vexation of your Fathers Tennessee business. . . . he tells me that he thinks with a little experience you will make and [sic] excellent agent[.] its a fine school for a young man to learn to deal with those Tennesseans." Mary E. Hamilton felt both satisfaction and loneliness at her son's activities in the Southwest: "When I think how far

---

Warren, September 17, 1840, in Skinner Family Papers; A. B. Urquhart to Lewis Thompson, June 20, 1843, in Thompson Papers. See Frances A. Polk to Sarah Polk, March 25, 1839, in Gale and Polk Family Papers.

4. Mary Cain to Minerva Caldwell, October 6, 1857, in Caldwell Papers, SHC; Lizzie Avery to her cousin, August 9, 1858, in Lenoir Family Papers; Paul C. Cameron to Anne Cameron, n.d., in Cameron Family Papers; Samuel S. Biddle to Mary E. V. Biddle, August 8, 1853, in Biddle Papers; Sarah Polk to Mary Polk, October 25, 1842, in Polk and Yeatman Family Papers; Hallie [?] to her cousin, November 29, 1853, in Presly C. Person Papers, Duke; Saum, "Death in the Popular Mind," 489–95; Blake, "Ties of Intimacy," 157–96; Philippe Ariès, *Western Attitudes Toward Death from the Middle Ages to the Present*, trans. Patricia M. Ranum (Baltimore, 1974), 59–60. Consult Eliza M. Walton to John Murphy, September 9, 1842, in Walton Papers.

my Charles is from me, it almost kills me, and then when I think he is trying to do something to help his Pa and trying to do for the best, I feel proud of such a son."[5]

Other sons took charge of business closer to home. Tristrim L. Skinner gradually assumed management of his father's large holdings in Chowan and Perquimans counties. George Collins, twenty-three-year-old son of Josiah Collins, Jr., supervised preparation of wheat for market. Charles E. Johnson yielded managerial powers to his twenty-nine-year-old son: "Lucius is still with me and has taken charge of the farm as he did the fishery, and attends very closely to it."[6]

Generally when a son acted as his father's agent, he received and exercised much responsibility in parental business affairs. James W. Downey, supervising his father's Mississippi enterprises, sacked the overseer for incompetence, employed a highly recommended young man at an annual salary of four hundred dollars, bought four hundred bushels of corn, and planned to purchase two hundred more. Simmons J. Baker left the sale of his Florida cotton and molasses to the direction of a son residing there. Robert B. Cuningham, who managed various aspects of his father's southwestern business concerns, advised the older man to sell or consolidate his interests there. In 1840, John T. Branch and his father formed a partnership to farm together in Southampton County, Virginia, and Northampton County, North Carolina, and continued collaboration until the younger Branch sent slaves to the Southwest in 1844.[7]

Fathers also followed sons' advice or opinions on important business issues. In a letter to his brother-in-law, John D. Hawkins noted

5. Sarah Polk to Lucius J. Polk, August 31, 1823, in Polk, Brown, and Ewell Family Papers; Mary E. Hamilton to Charles E. Hamilton, January 3, 1836, in Bullock and Hamilton Papers; R. H. Taylor, *Slaveholding*, 58–59.

6. Depositions in the lawsuit, *Skinner* v. *Warren*, Estate of Joseph B. Skinner, in Chowan County Estates; Tristrim L. Skinner to Joseph B. Skinner, January 8, 1849, in Skinner Family Papers; Josiah Collins, Jr., to Brown, DeRosset and Company, September 6, 1849, in Collins Papers, NCDAH; Charles E. Johnson to Charles E. Johnson, Jr., June 6, 1849, in Johnson Papers. See also Thomas L. Avery to Isaac T. Avery, March 3, 1843, in Alphonso C. Avery Papers, SHC.

7. James W. Downey to Samuel S. Downey, May 7, 1850, in Downey Papers; Simmons J. Baker to Joseph H. Saunders, March 9, 1849, in J. H. Saunders Papers; Robert B. Cuningham to Alexander Cuningham, January 22, 1842, in Cuningham Papers; Estate of Thomas Branch, in Northampton County Estates. See Samuel Simpson to William P. Biddle, July 29, 1812, in Simpson and Bryan Family Papers.

his father's reaction to a property settlement: "The old gentleman has been to see me, and is well satisfied with the negro arrangement. I believe because you and the Mr. Haywoods [John's brothers-in-law] and myself settled it." Peter Evans told his two sons-in-law that he would either give them a plantation or sell it "so it may be optionary with you . . . which way I shall act." Some planters called upon sons' professional expertise and recognized that the younger men should be paid for special services. Philemon Hawkins, in a will made in 1810 but never probated, noted that "my son John D Hawkins has been at considerable trouble & expense respecting lawsuits that I have been engaged in & for which he is justly Entitled to compensation Extra and for it I give him 150 acres of land I own Joining to him and Green Garrett." Although it is not clear that John received possession of that specific lot, Philemon in 1820 gave him another tract of land and four slaves as recompense for aid in lawsuits.[8]

Assistance in business matters did not flow in only one direction. Fathers also aided young men in such affairs. Frank Hawkins, living in Mississippi, often asked for and received his father's attention to matters such as the sale of land or care of slaves in North Carolina. Philo White helped his son-in-law by negotiating and receiving payment in Wisconsin for a fugitive slave belonging to the younger man.[9]

Even financial services such as lending money or cosigning notes could sometimes be reciprocal among planters and their adult progeny. Since parents generally had greater resources, they more often aided sons and daughters. For example, Thomas Benbury over a five-year period lent his son-in-law Robert T. Paine over one thousand dollars. William Hunt served as surety for two thousand dollars his son Memnucan borrowed from wealthy neighbors. On occasion, sons, but mainly sons-in-law, aided indebted planters. Here the financially

8. John D. Hawkins to William Polk, January 16, 1822, in Polk and Yeatman Family Papers; Peter Evans to William R. Smith, October 29, 1847, in P. E. Smith Papers (similarly William Cain to Minerva Caldwell, June 5, 1842, in Caldwell Papers, SHC); Will of Philemon Hawkins, March 5, 1810 (never probated), Philemon Hawkins to John D. Hawkins, December 20, 1820, both in Hawkins Family Papers; Philemon Hawkins to John D. Hawkins, 1820, in Warren County Deeds, Vol. 26, pp. 266–67. See James Somervell to James G. Brehon, 1832, in Warren County Deeds, Vol. 26, p. 316.

9. Frank Hawkins to John D. Hawkins, November 29, 1848, April 16, 1852, both in Hawkins Family Papers; Philo White to John W. Ellis, December 24, 1852, in Tolbert (ed.), *The Papers of John Willis Ellis*, I, 117–18. Consult Peter Evans to William R. Smith, December 22, 1839, in William R. Smith Papers, SHC.

prudent marriages children had contracted provided benefits to parents. William M. Clark, Jr., not only served as surety on a four-thousand-dollar mortgage his father-in-law Mark H. Pettway gave the Bank of North Carolina but also borrowed over three thousand dollars for the latter's use. Daniel McDiarmid lent money to his father-in-law Isaac Wright, assuring him that he could pay it back at his convenience.[10]

Parents and adult offspring also exchanged domestic services such as baby-sitting and boarding children during school attendance. Planters who had been loving parents were doting grandparents. Sarah Polk assured her daughter, then visiting the seashore for her health, that her children were well and happy. Charles E. Johnson greatly enjoyed his grandchildren's visits. Although such sojourns were arranged to suit the younger generation's convenience, they also delighted the old folks. David Sills boarded and sent his widowed daughter's children to school with his own young daughters. Adult sons and daughters could also aid parents in the care of younger siblings. Robert T. Paine escorted his teen-aged sister-in-law to her Raleigh boarding school and frequently visited her while the legislature was in session. One of Isaac T. Avery's younger sons lived with an older, married brother during the school year.[11]

Parents and children, whether living close together or far apart, cemented reciprocity by exchanging gifts. Frances Devereux shipped a barrel of fish to her daughter and son-in-law in Louisiana, and Charles E. Johnson sometimes sent hams to his son in Raleigh. Children also gave parents small tokens of esteem. Ariella Hawkins sent some handworked caps to her mother and admonished her, "Mother don't go to saying they are too fine and nice to ware [sic], or you will get them dirty, but put them on and ware them everyday, and when they

10. Estate of Thomas Benbury, in Chowan County Estates; Will of William Hunt, in Granville County Wills, Vol. 12, pp. 467–69; Mark H. Pettway to John B. Williams, 1848, in Halifax County Deeds, Vol. 32, pp. 423–24; D. McDiarmid to Isaac Wright, July 4, 1849, in Gillespie and Wright Family Papers. See also Richard Boyd to Richard Davison, 1833, in Warren County Deeds, Vol. 26, pp. 380–81.

11. Sarah Polk to Mary B. Badger, March 5, 1834, in Polk, Badger, and McGehee Family Papers; Charles E. Johnson to Charles E. Johnson, Jr., December 18, 1849, in Johnson Papers; Will of David Sills, in Nash County Wills; Robert T. Paine to Lavinia Paine, November 15, 19, 1844, both in Paine Papers; Adelaide Avery to Selina L. Lenoir, January 23, 1847, in Lenoir Family Papers.

get dirty or ware out I will make you plenty more." From the family fishery's catch, George W. Capehart presented his father-in-law with two barrels of fish.[12]

Other aspects of parent-child relationships likewise reveal more reciprocity than deference. Adult offspring asked for favors in an off-hand manner and expected parents to comply. Archibald Glenn instructed his father-in-law to have a good two-horse wagon built for him and barter it to him for bacon. Penelope Skinner Warren, pregnant and spending the summer in Hillsborough, advised her husband to borrow her father's carriage for her return to Chowan County: "ask him for the Carriage by all means[,] I should be affraid to go home with any other." Robert B. Cuningham decided to erect a double kitchen on land promised to him by his father-in-law and asked his father to send three skilled slaves, Robinson, Anderson, and Burwell, for the four to five weeks necessary to complete the building. Robert, in closing, also directed that the workmen bring all necessary tools and a crosscut saw.[13]

Sons and daughters, accustomed to affectionate support, did not believe self-abnegation to be essential in the face of parental wishes. Young people did not wish to offend needlessly or to carelessly disregard parental concerns. Still, they arranged their lives to suit themselves. William Cain's attempt to persuade his eldest son to write to a recently married sister was completely unsuccessful: "I have asked & beged [sic] Wm to write to you and his reply was, that he wrote to *nobody.*" Frank Hawkins told his father that he and his wife did not find it convenient to perform an errand as they had earlier agreed. M. M. Harrison assured his father-in-law Alexander Cuningham that he and his wife were anxious to visit, but the state of the wheat crop prevented their departure. In the meantime, he suggested that the

12. Frances Devereux to Catherine Polk, December 25, 1844, in Gale and Polk Family Papers; Charles E. Johnson to Charles E. Johnson, Jr., October 10, 1849, in Johnson Papers; Ariella Hawkins to Sarah M. Alston, June 26, 1846, in Alston Papers; George W. Capehart to Peter Martin, June 9, 1837, in Scotch Hall Papers.

13. Archibald Glenn to Alexander Cuningham, July 25, 1840, Robert B. Cuningham to Alexander Cuningham, August 12, 1845, both in Cuningham Papers; Penelope Warren to Thomas D. Warren, September 17, 1840, in Skinner Family Papers. See also Frank Hawkins to John D. Hawkins, April 16, 1852, in Hawkins Family Papers.

Cuninghams come to his house. Rather than being at their parents' beck and call, the young adults acted on their own.[14]

Sons' and daughters' independent actions did not arise only from parents' immediate encouragement and treating them as equals. Members of the younger generation, like their peers in other times and places, desired control over their own lives. Past socialization had also inclined them to prize self-determination and independence. Their own push for autonomy can be found in their establishment of their own households and resistance to parental actions that might compromise their adult status.

Newlyweds sometimes could not immediately afford to procure their own home. Some lived for a short time with parents. William and Mary Bethell spent over four months with his widowed mother before moving to their own place. Penelope Skinner Warren and her husband lived with her father for several months. Other young couples rented rooms in a private home or a respectable boardinghouse. Patty and Kemp Battle, after a short visit with his parents, became lodgers in Raleigh; and William B. Hamilton planned to find hotel accommodations for himself and his bride in Richmond.[15]

Newly married couples, despite parental aid in providing lodging, wanted to "set up housekeeping," as they termed it, as soon as possible. Anne Cameron felt that such a desire was perfectly normal: "My dear I am afraid you will think me very ungrateful in being so anxious to have a house of my own. Altho' I have been treated as kindly and affectionately as it was possible in your father's home, still it has not altered my *natural* wish of being settled, and I had much rather live in a hut of *my own*, than a palace of any one else's." In fact, no young couples expressed a preference for living with their parents. Young people silently testified to their predilections by securing their own

14. William Cain to Minerva Caldwell, December 18, 1841, in Caldwell Papers, SHC; Frank Hawkins to John D. Hawkins, December 17, 1836, in Hawkins Family Papers; M. M. Harrison to Alexander Cuningham, June 9, 1848, in Cuningham Papers (similarly Ariella Hawkins to Sarah M. Alston, June 26, 1846, in Alston Papers).

15. Bethell Diary, p. 6; Penelope Warren to Tristrim L. Skinner, May 22, 1840, Tristrim L. Skinner to Eliza Harwood, January 5, 1841, both in Skinner Family Papers; Lucy Battle to Susan Cabanne, September 12, 1856, in Battle Family Papers; William B. Hamilton to Charles E. Hamilton, March 15, 1839, in Bullock and Hamilton Papers. See also William Gaston to Susan Donaldson, April 3, 1831, in Gaston Papers.

abodes; and their appreciative comments about their residences indicate how important that was. Significantly, only financially embarrassed older couples lived with parents or parent.[16]

Recognizing children's wish for a separate establishment, some parents directly aided them. Mary K. Williams bought a house in Warrenton after her daughter's marriage and allowed her son-in-law and daughter to live at the plantation. William R. Smith, Sr., and his wife purchased a house on the Halifax road, leaving their home, Magnolia, to be occupied by their son and daughter-in-law.[17]

Sons' and daughters' beliefs about autonomy can also be found in the way they acted to protect that independence. Parental encroachments upon what offspring perceived to be their self-determination might be gently but firmly resisted. When Duncan Cameron's grandson and namesake died after a prolonged illness, the old man quietly paid all medical bills. Paul C. Cameron, despite his loving letter to his father, insisted upon repaying the sum. That action too closely resembled a usurpation of what Paul believed to be his duties as a father and household head. Jane Hamilton liked her father-in-law and stayed on his nearby plantation when her husband traveled to the Southwest. But Jane cut that visit short when she felt that her authority and responsibility as mother and plantation mistress were lessening.[18] Here, as elsewhere, loving but undaunted sons and daughters might quietly, and determinedly, express their viewpoint and independence.

A diminution of parental control can also be found in the distribution of property to children. This division or portioning took two forms: first, large gifts of property made during the planter's lifetime; second, legacies provided after death. Together, they reveal transfer-

16. Anne Cameron to Paul C. Cameron, March 8, 1834, in Cameron Family Papers; Susan Capehart to Peter Martin, January 16, 1835, in Scotch Hall Papers; Josiah Turner, Jr., to Sophia Devereux, December 16, 1855, in Turner Papers; Adelaide Avery to Sally Lenoir, March 1, 1847, in Lenoir Family Papers; William M. Clark to Lewis Thompson, December, 1854, in Thompson Papers.

17. Lucy Battle to William H. Battle, January 25, 1856, in Battle Family Papers; Lena H. Smith, "Magnolia" (newspaper clipping), in W. R. Smith Papers.

18. Paul C. Cameron to Duncan Cameron, November 29, 1848, in Cameron Family Papers; Jane Hamilton to Charles E. Hamilton, January 10, 1845, in Bullock and Hamilton Papers.

ral of property to the next generation in a relatively nondirective, egalitarian manner.

Gift giving was common among great planters who settled property upon both sons and daughters. The informal nature of these distributions sometimes left presents unrecognized either in deed or by will. Tracing all formal transfers also poses formidable problems. Still, much gift giving can be discovered among great planters. Forty-two of the ninety-one planters with adult sons—over 45 percent—definitely gave one or more sons property, usually land, by deed of gift. For example, in 1846, William Baird granted his son Benjamin a 1,150-acre tract of land. Another twelve men— or 13 percent—placed sons in possession of property through what they called "advancements" or advances on the son's share of the estate. For instance, Robert Brodnax, in his will of 1853, bequeathed his son John a 1,500-acre tract of land "of which I put him in possession of in 1845 and on which he now resides."[19]

More can be discovered about presents given to sons than to daughters, but women were not neglected. Daughters' gifts, more likely to be slaves than land, often went unrecorded. Although twenty-four North Carolina planters' deeds of gift to their daughters were discovered, gift giving was much more widespread than that number would indicate. At least thirty-two planters recorded in their wills presents of slaves or other property given informally to their daughters. The Kearney family's actions are revealing. William K. Kearney transferred two tracts of land to his son Whitmell, but no deeds of gift to any of Kearney's eleven daughters can be found. Still it is likely that they too received advances. A legal document Kearney drew up after a son-in-law's death indicates the older man had "advanced" slaves to at least one daughter: "part of the above negroes I put in possession of Conrad Boyd who married my daughter Mary Ann[.] I never made him a right to them, I therefore relinquish to my daughter Mary Ann and her two children Virginia T and Conrad S Boyd all my right[,] title and interest to said negroes together with the increase."[20]

19. William Baird to Benjamin R. Baird, 1846, in Person County Deeds, Vol. Q, pp. 189–90; Will of Robert Brodnax, in Rockingham County Wills, Vol. C, pp. 183–86.
20. William K. Kearney to W. H. A. Kearney, 1859, in Warren County Deeds, Vol. 31, pp. 924, 960; Estate of William K. Kearney, in Warren County Estates.

Although property in many societies has formed a major lever for controlling adult offspring, North Carolina planters' gifts tended to relinquish rather than reinforce control. Their formal gifts, the deeds to land and slaves, did not abrogate children's freedom. In contrast to the seventeenth-century Andover, Massachusetts, men who filled gift deeds with restrictions, obligations, and duties, wealthy nineteenth-century Carolinians made deeds amazingly simple and absolute. Planters did not require payments or support of their widows; neither did they allow title to vest only after their deaths. To be sure, a few planters like James Somervell provided in gift deeds that their children renounce rights to other lands on which they would have a claim. Although such clauses appear somewhat coercive, they were absolutely necessary to avoid division of tracts of land and to secure the property settlements these men wished to make. Attaching almost no strings to their gifts, elite North Carolinians transferred property quickly and absolutely.[21]

Moreover, the timing of deeds of gift and informal transfers of property makes apparent planters' purposes. Not only were wealthy North Carolinians eschewing control by property, they were actually attempting to secure their offspring's independence. Most young elite men receiving property by deed of gift in North Carolina, as in Alabama, were few years beyond the age of majority. The Tar Heelers' average age was but twenty-four, and only 15 percent of those receiving gifts had attained age thirty before their first grant. For example, Thomas Speller in 1823 transferred a tract of land bordering the Roanoke River to his twenty-two-year-old son. Although the timing of informal gifts can seldom be accurately pinpointed, likely they too went to the young. For example, James Bullock in his will authorized his wife Nancy to make "advancements" to children as they reached age twenty-one or married, whichever came first.[22]

This granting of financial autonomy was related to age but was even

21. W. M. Williams, *The Sociology of an English Village*, 42–52; Greven, *Four Generations*, 69–148; James Somervell to Joseph B. Somervell, 1836, Warren County Deeds, Vol. 27, pp. 48–49.

22. Boucher, "Wealthy Planter Families," 81–87; Thomas Speller, Sr., to Thomas Speller, Jr., 1823, in Bertie County Deeds, Vol. BB, p. 49; Will of James Bullock, in Warren County Wills. Only nine of the fifty-seven sons of the North Carolina elite receiving deeds of gift whose ages can be determined were aged thirty or older. Ages cannot be determined for eleven others.

more closely tied to marriage. That event signaled the need for independence, and planter families sought to provide it. Ninety percent of formal gifts to young men came just before or during their first five years of marriage. For instance, approximately eight months after Baldy Sanders married, his father John presented him with a 1,250-acre tract and nine slaves. Furthermore, some men who first received land after age thirty probably were landless because unmarried rather than unmarried because landless. Bachelor Philemon B. Hawkins attained age thirty-one before he obtained land from his father. The elder Hawkins, however, granted land to other sons marrying in their early twenties, at the time of each marriage. Over 75 percent of gift deeds to daughters or their husbands also coincided with the early years of marriage. Other sources on informal gifts further support this view. For example, William Plummer called in some debts he thought could easily be repaid because he wished to "advance" money to a recently married daughter. Some planters' wills, like those of James Turner and Isaac T. Avery, noted that property had been given to a daughter shortly after marriage.[23]

The distinction in property given—sons more often receiving land; daughters, slaves or money—arose not from the desire that sons receive more valuable property but from assumptions about sexual roles and independence. Planters believed sons needed tracts of land to support themselves and rear a family. In contrast, they assumed that their daughters' husbands, usually professionals or planters, should be able to maintain the young women and any children. Presents to daughters, then, constituted helpful additions to family income and autonomy rather than necessities for independence.

Although planters' deeds of gift and large informal transfers of property indicate what parents thought necessary to give children, especially sons, a proper start in marriage, these transactions reveal

23. Twenty-six of the twenty-nine sons whose age and marriage date can be correlated with a first deed of gift received that gift either before marriage or within five years of their weddings. John Sanders to Baldy Sanders, 1822, in Johnston County Deeds, Vol. L, pp. 420–21; John D. Hawkins to Philemon B. Hawkins, 1855, in Franklin County Deeds, Vol. 32, p. 389; John D. Hawkins to Frank Hawkins, 1837, in Granville County Deeds, Vol. 11, pp. 307–308; John D. Hawkins to William J. Hawkins, 1844, John D. Hawkins to John D. Hawkins, Jr., 1845, both in Franklin County Deeds, Vol. 29, pp. 62–63, 246–47; Will of James Turner, in Warren County Wills; William Plummer to Daniel S. Hill, December 6, 1853, in D. S. Hill Papers.

only part of the portioning system. Inheritance, particularly as guided by wills, shows planters' final disposition of property. Such bequests display a similar failure to use property as a means of control. Inheritance, instead, was aid for all sons and daughters.

Many forms of property division among children are possible. The abolition of primogeniture in North Carolina during the Revolutionary era meant that in cases of intestacy (failure to draw up a valid will), all landed property would be divided equally among children rather than going to the eldest son. Planters still remained free to favor the eldest son or any other child in their wills. And, in fact, this was a course that planters' widows frequently followed. Elite women such as Susan Eaton, Ann Little, and Elizabeth Proctor tended to divide their property unequally, and some gave most of their possessions to one child. However, women most likely felt free to make such arrangements because their husbands' wills or the settlement of the men's estates had already disposed of the bulk of these families' property and had given each child his or her rightful share. Planter fathers, able to award each child as little or as much as they wished, not only chose partible inheritance but also granted much—sometimes complete—equality among children. Younger offspring received the same amount of property as older siblings, and any distinctions were generally based upon sex. Indeed, almost all of the eighty-two wills drawn up by male North Carolina planters to allocate property among their children fall into two main categories: one divided property fairly equally among all children, the other gave sons larger shares than daughters.[24] Both groups used partible inheritance, but the second held a narrower vision of equality among children.

Seventy percent of these elite Carolinian men leaving wills were relatively egalitarian in the matter of inheritance. Part of this group, slightly over 30 percent of the men with wills, explicitly espoused

24. On inheritance in antebellum North Carolina, see "Widows," "Wills and Testaments," and "Legacies, Filial Portions and Distributive Shares," *Revised Statutes of the State of North Carolina* (Raleigh, 1837), 612–18, 619–25, 369–71; Will of Susan Eaton, in Granville County Estates; Will of Ann Little, in Warren County Wills; Will of Elizabeth Proctor, in Camden County Wills, Box 44, Bk. C, pp. 126–27. Although I discovered ninety-two wills drawn up by male planters, ten of them gave property to an only child or left division to a wife or third party and thus are not included in my analysis of property division among children. Another two men decreed an unequal disposition of property, not necessarily sex-linked, and will be discussed separately.

such equality. John Waddell affirmed his belief in the justice of complete equality when he bequeathed rice lands to his second son,
Maurice, but required a settlement with the other children: "It is my
Will that he come into account with his Brothers and Sisters for the
same, acre for acre, or an equivalent in Money at their option, before
he shares in the rest of my Estate—as it is my Will and wish to do
equal and impartial Justice between them, and well I may, for they
are alike, upright, virtuous and dutiful."[25]

The remainder of the egalitarian group, almost 40 percent of these
testate planters, granted both lands and slaves to sons and daughters.
It is impossible in some cases and difficult in others to determine if
legacies were exactly equal. Obvious inequalities are not present, although Bertram Wyatt-Brown has suggested that planters tended even
in partible inheritance to give daughters less fertile land and less
valuable slaves, often house servants, than their brothers received.[26]
Comparing the value of land bequeathed is not feasible, but some
rough estimates about the comparative value of slaves can be made.

In fact, among those planters giving both land and slaves to sons
and daughters, over 75 percent—twenty-two of twenty-nine men—
did not specifically assign all slaves but left apportionment to com-
missioners designated by the will or by the county court. In com-
missioners' divisions, choice was by lots equalized in value. Only
when a planter devised slaves by name could he ensure that a certain
child would receive that slave. Less than 25 percent followed that
method, and evidence does not indicate that even they gave daughters less valuable slaves. A lawsuit between Thomas Speller, Jr., and
his half sister Sarah Eliza Thompson over the settlement of their
father's estate is revealing on that issue. The elder Speller on his
deathbed had given his son some slaves by deed. Thompson argued
that her half brother had obtained the deed under false pretenses by
misrepresenting the slaves willed to her as more valuable than those
he would receive. According to Speller, his father had freely given the
deed because the division of slaves was biased in Thompson's favor.

25. Fifty-six of eighty wills were egalitarian: twenty-five divided property among
all children and thirty-one gave land and slaves in relatively equal-appearing amounts
to both sons and daughters. Will of John Waddell, in Brunswick County Wills.
26. Wyatt-Brown, "The Ideal Typology," 1–29.

Neither litigant disputed that Thomas Speller, Sr.—a planter who devised slaves by name—would wish to give slaves equal in value to each of his children. Such an interest in equality of inheritance among even those making special disposition of slaves makes it seem highly unlikely that daughters often received inferior or less productive slaves.[27]

Thus, over two-thirds of the North Carolina planters conveyed both landed and slave property in equal-appearing amounts to sons and daughters. Sons often received gifts of land; daughters were more apt to inherit it. But by the final settlement of the estate, the great majority of planters had divided their property fairly equally.

In the second main category, six men—only about 7 percent of the planters—believed that both sexes should receive land and slaves, but that males' portions should be more generous. For example, Stark Armistead gave his son Stark, Jr., eight thousand dollars more than either daughter received. William M. Clark directed that his extensive holdings in North Carolina and Louisiana be divided among his children "in such proportion that each of my Sons shall have one third more than each of my Daughters." The remaining eighteen planters of this second category, approximately 25 percent of the larger group, gave sons a different kind of property than daughters received. These elite Carolinians reserved land only for males and gave females personal property such as slaves, household furnishings, and money, stocks, or bonds. For example, Joseph J. Alston bequeathed equal shares of land to his sons and provided that the balance of the slaves, after twenty were allotted to each daughter, would be divided among the men. Alston also aimed at equality but of a more limited sort among offspring of the same sex, not between the sexes. John Brodie willed land and slaves to his three sons but money, slaves, and furniture to his daughters. In these cases, men received more valuable legacies than did their sisters.[28]

The practice of giving land to daughters (often a share equal to sons')

27. "Wills and Testaments," *Revised Statutes*, 619–25. Two of thirty-one planters giving property in relatively equal amounts wrote their wills after the abolition of slavery. Estate of Thomas Speller, in Bertie County Estates.

28. Will of Stark Armistead, Will of William M. Clark, both in Bertie County Wills; Will of Joseph J. Alston, in Chatham County Wills; Will of John Brodie, in Warren County Wills.

appears to have gained headway as the nineteenth century proceeded. Although planters favoring males in inheritance tended to be older and not Episcopalian, their most important difference seems to have been date of death (see Table 5). Slightly more than 60 percent of those who died before 1850 gave their daughters relatively equal shares; 80 percent of those who died after 1850 were evenhanded between the sexes.[29]

Only two exceptions to this rule of equality can be identified. Both instances illustrate the unusual and tentative nature of attempts to convey much property to one individual. Thomas P. Devereux inherited most of the vast Pollok-Devereux plantations mainly by de-

Table 5. Relation Between Bequests to Children
and Death Date of Testator

| | Planter's Death Date | | | |
| | Before 1840 | 1840–1849 | 1850–1859 | 1860 or Later |
Bequest	No. %	No. %	No. %	No. %
Equal property to both sexes (N = 25)	10 40.0	3 12.0	9 36.0	3 12.0
Land and slaves to both sexes (N = 31)	11 35.5	8 25.8	5 16.1	7 22.6
Favored males in amount (N = 6)	5 83.3	— —	1 16.7	— —
Differentiated kind of property between the sexes (N = 18)	10 55.6	3 16.7	3 16.7	2 11.1
TOTAL	36	14	18	12

29. Religious affiliations are identifiable for almost one-half (twelve of twenty-five) planters who differentiated between sons and daughters in inheritance; only three were Episcopalian and nine belonged to other denominations. Over 40 percent of those favoring males were aged sixty or older in 1830; slightly more than 20 percent of all planters belonged in that age group.

fault. Certainly, elderly John Devereux had earlier shown no propensity to treat his children unequally. Although he bequeathed no North Carolina lands to his daughter Frances, a letter written in 1832 reveals that he was then interested in giving her and her husband Leonidas Polk a North Carolina plantation valued at $75,000. Most likely the Polks' move to the Southwest where Leonidas owned extensive landholdings and the death of a third Devereux offspring, George, who was survived by a widow and two small daughters who preferred to live in Connecticut, left Thomas the only child available to manage and live upon the North Carolina lands. Although Josiah Collins, Jr., showed a stronger desire to maintain his plantation Somerset Place as a unit, he was indecisive over whether he should bequeath it to his oldest son. Collins' will, made in 1849, transferred all property to his wife to dispose of as she deemed fit. But should she not convey the property by will or deed, Collins gave his eldest son, Josiah, an option to take the plantation, its slaves, livestock, and implements. The younger Josiah would pay his siblings one-half of Somerset Place's worth only if it constituted over one-half of the estate's value. Since the elder Collins then had four children, all males, the eldest could receive as much as one-half and the younger sons as little as one-sixth each of the total. Collins further stipulated that should his son decide not to receive the plantation, "and it is not my desire or purpose to impose upon him any duty or obligation to accept the same," then all children would share equally in the estate. Although he chose to favor his eldest son greatly, Collins gave both his wife and eldest son the right to reject that settlement. The "escape clauses" and the tone of the will indicate that his commitment to inequality among his sons was uncertain and tenuous.[30]

Not only were portions relatively equal among children, planters, unlike their eighteenth-century Virginian counterparts, did not attempt to give their eldest son the manor house or home plantation as part of his share (see Table 6). Most often a younger son inherited the manor house; frequently two or more children shared it. Practical considerations about adequately settling their entire family probably

30. Crabtree and Patton (eds.), "Journal of a Secesh Lady," xix–xxvi; John Devereux to William Polk, November 27, 1832, in Leonidas Polk Papers; Will of Josiah Collins, Jr., in Collins Papers, NCDAH.

Table 6. Disposition of the Manor House

Disposition	Number Receiving	Percentage Receiving
Uncertain or none	37	46.8
To be sold	2	2.5
Daughter or grand- daughter	7	8.9
Two or more children	9	11.4
Oldest son	2	2.5
Only son	5	6.3
Younger son	14	17.7
Grandson	3	3.8
TOTAL	79	99.9

NOTE:
Excluded are cases in which the planter's home was a town house, in which an only child received the property, or the widow received it in fee simple.

governed planters' disposal of their home plantations. Often they were elderly men whose older sons had long ago established households and had little need for the dwelling. Furthermore, the widow by law could demand lifetime possession of the manor and one-third of its land. Since planter families preferred nuclear to extended households, the home plantation could be most conveniently received by a younger, perhaps the youngest, son who had not yet come of age and would not immediately need it.[31]

All these inheritance practices illustrate the value North Carolina planters placed upon helping all children. The majority wished to divide their property relatively equally among sons and daughters. Even those who planned that only males would receive land expected sons to share and share alike. This regard for all children, which dictated that each receive a substantial share of the estate, also demanded that eldest sons receive neither larger portions nor special parts of the estate such as the manor house or home plantation. Once again parents weighed the needs of all offspring.

31. "Widows," *Revised Statutes*, 612–18; C. Ray Keim, "Primogeniture and Entail in Colonial Virginia," *William and Mary Quarterly*, 3rd ser. XXV (1968), 562–66.

Wealthy North Carolinians not only espoused egalitarianism in the division of their estates but also rarely threatened recalcitrant offspring with disinheritance. In fact, the only case of disinheritance illustrates how shattered the parent-child relationship had to be before a child was cut out of a will. William Eaton, one of the richest planters on the Roanoke River, lived to the ripe old age of eighty-six. In his will, commissioned in 1862, he completely omitted Seigniora Lockhart, the only child of his deceased son Nathaniel; and she contested the will. Although William had disinherited a grandchild, almost all of those involved in the subsequent trial believed that his intent lay in punishing his son. The jury upheld the will after hearing testimony about the rift between father and son. William Eaton, Jr., testified that his father and brother quarreled in 1832 about the elder Eaton's third wife: "I heard him [William Eaton, Sr.] say that my Brother Nat came to his house, insulted and abused him and spoke very disrespectfully of his wife to him and threatened the both of them. He also said that he considered it necessary to bind him over to the peace and that he intended to do so." Another witness recounted the threats that William Eaton, Sr., declared that his son had uttered against him. In Eaton's case the act precipitating disinheritance was not the son's disregard of paternal wishes but animosity so severe that violence threatened to erupt.[32]

Other planters' treatment of wayward or disobedient sons indicates how little consideration they gave to property as a means to control such "black sheep." Peter Evans exasperatedly described the conduct of his eldest son, George: "He was the cause of my buying the McBryde land and then refused to take it and treated me in the most contemptuous manner. . . . George deserves less of favour from his parents than any human being I ever knew—he has always from the time he was knee high gone contrary to my advice and done everything that he thought would be disagreeable to me—I have now washed my hands of him." Although George had spent his share of the estate, his father "washed his hands" by bequeathing him the interest accruing upon ten thousand dollars.[33]

32. Estate of William Eaton, in Warren County Estates; Will of William Eaton, in Warren County Wills.

33. Peter Evans to William R. Smith, October, 1847, in P. E. Smith Papers; Will of Peter Evans, in Halifax County Wills, Vol. 4, pp. 334–35.

A man could be thoroughly disgusted with his son's behavior, yet not disinherit him. Unhappy in a second marriage, Benjamin F. Hawkins became heavily indebted, began drinking to excess, and finally committed suicide. His father, Philemon Hawkins, censoriously remarked that "the shock is not so Great owing to the manner that he has conducted himself for sometime past—a man that keeps himself drunk had better be dead unless there were a probability of a change for the better." Despite such disapproval of Benjamin's conduct, Philemon in his will, drawn up three years before the suicide and never superseded, gave Benjamin a share of the estate similar to other sons' portions. Philemon's extreme displeasure does not appear ever to have led him to consider disinheritance as a remedy.[34]

This failure to contemplate or (so far as we know) to threaten disinheritance shows how rarely planters considered the property they could bestow upon their children as a means of control. Of course most did not need such an economic weapon—their carefully reared children measured up to parental expectations. But even offspring whose behavior annoyed, embarrassed, or dismayed their elders were rarely harassed by parental withholding of property.

In fact, the North Carolina elite sometimes went to great lengths to secure a share of the family property to each legal heir. Since giving property directly to indebted sons or sons-in-law meant the younger men's creditors could seize it, planters in such cases used the trust deed designating a person to hold, administer, and pay the legatee all profits for his use and maintenance during the latter's lifetime. Benjamin Edmunds set up such a fund for his indebted son, Benjamin C. Edmunds, and even provided the younger man some power over its investment: "Nevertheless, if at any time it may be desired at the request of Benjn C. Edmunds[,] the Said Trustees may make sale of Such property as may be desired[,] a part or the whole thereof[,] and invest the proceeds thereof in such Manner and at such place as the Said Benjn C Edmunds shall request." John J. Gause decreed that property given to his son Julius be held in trust by the latter's brothers John P.

34. Philemon Hawkins to Joseph W. Hawkins, November 14, 1828, in Hawkins Family Papers; Will of Philemon Hawkins, in Warren County Wills. Although this will was probated in 1833, it had been drawn up in 1825.

and George Whitfield Gause. Trusts sprang from a desire to protect property from creditors rather than from the legatee.[35]

A similar desire to fend off creditors also appears in gifts and legacies given to daughters with indebted husbands. Under common law, a woman's legal existence and property merged into her husband's at marriage. The law of equity, however, recognized agreements holding a woman's property separate from her husband's. Most commonly used were trusts, but some women received only a life interest in property with title vesting in their children so that it could not be seized by creditors or sold. Over one-third (twenty-one of sixty-one) of the planters bequeathing property to married daughters or granddaughters used the trust or life estate. Most who put property in trust for one married daughter gave legacies in fee simple to others. Samuel Frink put all his gifts to both married and single daughters and granddaughters in trust, but his course was rare. Only four of fourteen planters who both used the trust or life estate and had more than one married daughter gave property in trust to all their married female legatees. Although some planters disliked or distrusted their sons-in-law, trust deeds generally arose from a desire to protect property against debts and creditors. In his will, Alexander Gray vividly described earlier dealings with a son-in-law over property Gray wished to give his daughter. The older man, soon after the wedding, gave his son-in-law Stephen Moore thirteen slaves and later increased their number:

> When Moore and his family started to the West I met them . . . to take my leave of the family and make Mr Moore a title to fifteen other negroes which I had sometime before put into his possession; when I was about to write a title to him for those Negroes, Stephen Moore told me not to do so, but make the title to his wife Mary M Moore and her children so the Negroes could not be taken for the payment of any debts due by him, for there was at that time a suit depending against him as Executor or administrator of his fathers Estate for a large amount which if recovered against him might take the property which I was giving for the benefit of my Daughter and Children to pay it; or other debts he might owe. . . . I accordingly wrote a deed of gift for the benefit of my said daughter and her children without giving Stephen Moore any right to the negroes except to manage them for

35. Will of Benjamin Edmunds, in Halifax County Wills, Vol. 5, pp. 37–41; Will of John Julius Gause, in Brunswick County Wills. See also Will of John Brodie, in Warren County Wills; Will of John Waddell, in Brunswick County Wills.

the benefit of his wife and children and see that the slaves should be equally divided among them when it might be thought best.

Obviously that trust deed resulted from close cooperation between planter and son-in-law. Others' concern also lay in thwarting creditors. Even when parents placed their gifts in trust, they showed no interest in punishing sons-in-law.[36]

In short, planters seem to have viewed a share of their estate—relatively equal in value to those given to others of the same sex—more as a child's right than as a special privilege. Fathers sought to establish offspring early and firmly in possession of property. Rather than tight-fistedly hoarding their possessions and the power derived from them, wealthy North Carolinians attempted to enter sons and daughters into adult society. Parental desires lay more in aiding than confining.

Planters' inheritance practices also closely resembled those of wealthy, middle-class nineteenth-century western Europeans and other Americans. Like rich English industrialists and businessmen and the well-to-do Parisian bourgeoisie, elite North Carolinians provided amply for each child. In their disposal of property, planters also radically differed from those traditional landed western European elites to whom Genovese has compared them. Among these European groups, primogeniture still held sway. Even the wealthiest English peers rarely gave landed property to more than two sons. Instead of adopting the practices of European aristocrats, planters preferred to disperse their wealth among their children.[37]

Both in their gifts and in their division of property, planters es-

36. For married women's property rights, see Mary R. Beard, *Woman as Force in History: A Study in Traditions and Realities* (New York, 1946), 131–33; Suzanne D. Lebsock, "Radical Reconstruction and the Property Rights of Southern Women," *Journal of Southern History*, XLIII (1977), 198–200. Will of Samuel Frink, in New Hanover County Wills; Will of Alexander Gray, in Randolph County Wills.

37. William D. Rubenstein, "Men of Property: The Wealthy in Britain, 1809–1939" (Ph.D. dissertation, Johns Hopkins University, 1975), 221; Daumard, *La Bourgeoisie parisienne*, 342–47; Genovese, *The Political Economy of Slavery*, 31; David Spring (ed.), *European Landed Elites in the Nineteenth Century* (Baltimore, 1977), 1–21; Ralph E. Giesey, "Rules of Inheritance and Strategies of Mobility in Prerevolutionary France," *American Historical Review*, LXXXII (1977), 271–89; Forster, *The Nobility of Toulouse*, 120–51; Mingay, *English Landed Society*, 176–77; F. M. L. Thompson, *English Landed Society in the Nineteenth Century* (London, 1963), 66–69; Eileen Spring, "The Settlement of Land in Nineteenth Century England," *American Journal of Legal History*, VIII (1964), 209–223.

chewed coerciveness—probably because they believed offspring should share in the parental estate regardless of all but the most unforgivable actions. Instead of securing their sons' and daughters' dependence upon them, parents sought to establish their children's autonomy. The interpersonal relationships between parents and adult offspring also illustrate mutual acceptance of young people's independence. Parents did not enforce deference but instead enjoyed warm, friendly companionship. By gifts and the division of their estates, planters sought to have a family of prosperous offspring. Part of their confidence in their wealth probably arose from the promise and lure of the expanding Southwest.

SIX

The Younger Generation as Adults
Economic Persistence and Migration

While examining child rearing and the evolving relationship be-tween parents and children, this study has thus far shown that North Carolina planter families resembled those of other well-to-do Amer-icans. Like the latter, elite Carolinians emphasized education, achievement, material success, and independence and desired affec-tionate family relations. But to explore further to what extent sons and daughters accepted parental values and what was the general outcome of their socialization, let us consider two important aspects of the second generation's adult lives: their economic position and their values and beliefs, as revealed in decision making about mi-gration.

The federal census is the best tool available for measuring the eco-nomic position of planters' offspring. To be sure, its information about landholding and slaveholding carries more import for farmers—about two-thirds (189 of 286) of planters' nonmigrant offspring—than for those in nonagricultural occupations. Obviously businessmen and professionals had other unlisted resources. Like tax lists, another fre-quently used source for wealth estimates, census returns cannot tell us about individual indebtedness or the community's debt structure. Finally, outmigrants are not easily traceable on the census and can-not be systematically located. The crudeness of its information means that the census best illustrates broad outlines rather than detailed analyses of group wealth; but despite those limitations, the census remains the best guide to aggregate wealth holding.[1]

1. See, for example, Lee Soltow, *Men and Wealth in the United States, 1850–1870* (New Haven, 1975); Yasuko Shinoda, "Land and Slaves in North Carolina in 1860" (Ph.D. dissertation, University of North Carolina, 1971); Randolph B. Campbell and

The amount of real estate owned in 1850 by North Carolina planters' sons and sons-in-law, over age twenty-one, indicates their general prosperity (see Table 7). Over one-half of the younger generation in the state then possessed over $5,000 in landed property. For example, William Dula's five living children each held land valued at over $6,000, and three of James Downey's five children estimated that their real property exceeded $7,000 each. Approximately one-third of the group owned real estate worth $10,000 or more, a handsome holding anywhere. In the Dancy family, William F. and John S. each valued their plantations in excess of $10,000, and Elizabeth Dancy Battle and her husband's landed property was worth over $20,000. A fourth sibling, widowed Delha Dancy Foreman, reported almost $5,000 in real estate. Thomas Speller Jr.'s plantations totaled $20,000; land worth over $10,000 belonged to his half sister Sarah Eliza Thompson and her husband.[2]

Even the number of landless offspring reported by the census is deceptively large. Although almost one-fifth of planters' sons and daughters appeared to hold no real estate, much of that group either

Table 7. Value of Real Estate Owned
by the Great Planters' Offspring, 1850

Value	Number of Offspring	Percentage of Offspring
None	65	19.7
Less than $1,000	11	3.3
$1,000–$4,999	66	20.0
$5,000–$9,999	82	24.9
$10,000–$19,999	65	19.7
$20,000–$49,999	33	10.0
$50,000 or more	8	2.4
TOTAL	330	100.0

Richard G. Lowe, *Wealth and Power in Antebellum Texas* (College Station, Tex., 1977); Joseph K. Menn, "The Large Slaveholders of the Deep South, 1860" (Ph.D. dissertation, University of Texas, 1964). Similar studies utilizing tax rolls include: Jackson T. Main, *The Social Structure of Revolutionary America* (Princeton, 1965); Edward Pessen, *Riches, Class and Power Before the Civil War* (Lexington, Mass., 1973).

2. MS Census of 1850, N.C., Caldwell County, Sch. I, pp. 35, 36, Wilkes County, Sch. I, p. 340, Granville County, Sch. I, pp. 201, 202, Edgecombe County, Sch. I, pp. 96, 103, Bertie County, Sch. I, pp. 36, 66.

Table 8. Value of Real Estate Owned
by Offspring Age Forty or Older, 1850

Value	Number of Offspring	Percentage of Offspring
None	11	7.7
Less than $1,000	5	3.5
$1,000–$4,999	29	20.3
$5,000–$9,999	44	30.8
$10,000–$19,999	33	23.1
$20,000–$49,999	15	10.5
$50,000 or more	6	4.2
TOTAL	143	100.1

owned or would soon own land. Errors of the census takers probably account for some listed as landless. The Bertie County enumerator mistakenly included no real estate value for Stephen A. Norfleet, who owned and operated large plantations.[3] According to the returns, brothers Philip, Nathaniel, and Gideon Alston possessed no real estate but each owned over sixty slaves and likely a large farm as well.

One-half of the landless group was aged less than thirty, and most would soon obtain land either as gifts, through inheritance, or by their own efforts. For example, William E. Hill in 1850 was a young attorney residing with his parents. According to the census taker, he owned no realty or slaves. In 1860, Hill was a wealthy farmer with land worth over $10,000 and personal property in excess of $30,000. Philemon B. Hawkins owned no land in 1850, but received a gift of over 1,000 acres from his father in 1855.[4] In fact, if one excludes those who received legacies, gifts of land, or otherwise obtained land during the 1850s, only eighteen of the sixty-five were actually landless and apt to remain so. Moreover, a survey of the real estate holdings of offspring over age forty confirms that by mature adulthood, most owned considerable realty (see Table 8). Although the proportion of very large holdings is similar to that for all children, the percentage of landless is considerably smaller among the older group—approximately 8

3. Consult Norfleet Family Papers, SHC, which includes some plantation diaries.
4. MS Census of 1850, N.C., Duplin County, Sch. I, p. 47; MS Census of 1860, N.C., Duplin County, Sch. I, p. 189; John D. Hawkins to Philemon B. Hawkins, 1855, in Franklin County Deeds, Vol. 32, p. 389.

percent. Even this figure includes several people who owned many slaves, and their inclusion was probably an error on the part of the census taker. This percentage likely represents the upper limit of the truly landless among all offspring.

Landlessness held less importance for some professional men. Other sources indicate that some landless lawyers and doctors among the planters' offspring were not necessarily perceived as being "down-and-out." In 1850, physician Charles E. Johnson, Jr., listed as landless, still moved in genteel society as marriage to a former governor's daughter indicated. Among others holding no real estate, lawyer Bartholomew F. Moore then served as state attorney general. Superior court judge John W. Ellis was only eight years away from the gubernatorial office.[5]

Still a few planters' children, having lost their wealth through misfortune or mismanagement, had to struggle to survive. The Waddell family had suffered a series of financial losses, and Haynes Waddell and his widowed sister Sarah DeRosset attempted to live on small incomes. Some, like James T. Downey, who resided with a wealthy brother, were completely dependent upon relatives' generosity. Debts had forced James to mortgage even an annuity.[6]

Slightly more than 3 percent of the great planters' progeny held real estate valued at less than one thousand dollars. Most of this small group, like the truly landless, had lost property through mercantile or speculative ventures. Early in his career as a merchant, James Monroe Forney was bankrupted; by 1850 he owned land valued at four hundred dollars and two slaves who helped him farm. Protheus E. A. Jones and William J. Andrews, brothers-in-law from Granville County, had suffered setbacks in their business and farming enterprises, and only the aid of the Hawkins family, their wives' relatives, had saved them from complete loss of property.[7]

But, in general, this survey of planters' children shows that almost all by age forty owned valuable land. Some notion of their prosperity can be gained by a comparison of their holdings to those of other

5. *North Carolina Standard*, April 18, 1849; W. C. Allen, *History of Halifax County* (Boston, 1918), 99; *Cyclopedia of Eminent Men*, II, 187.

6. MS Census of 1850, N.C., Orange County, Sch. I, p. 177, New Hanover County, Sch. I, p. 403, Chowan County, Sch. I, p. 111, Granville County, Sch. I, p. 202.

7. Estate of Peter Forney, in Lincoln County Estates; Frank Hawkins to John D. Hawkins, January 26, February 20, 1843, both in Hawkins Family Papers; MS Census of 1850, N.C., Cleveland County, Sch. I, p. 219, Sch. II, p. 563.

southerners. Unfortunately, wealth data have been tabulated for only one southern state, Texas, in this period, but the distribution of landed property there should provide a helpful, though crude, benchmark of the standing of North Carolina planters' offspring. Only 7 percent of household heads in Texas owned real estate valued at $5,000 or more; 57 percent of planters' children and almost 70 percent of those over forty possessed that amount. Slightly over 3 percent of Texans held lands worth $10,000 or more; 32 percent of the Carolinians belonged to that category. A sample of slaveholders drawn by James Oakes from selected upper and lower South counties similarly highlights the North Carolinians' economic well-being. He discovered that only about 16 percent of the slaveowners in his sample held $5,000 or more in real estate. Such findings make it quite likely that this second generation in North Carolina held a disproportionate share of its own state's real estate.[8]

Moreover, most great planters' offspring owned sizable slaveholdings. Over two-thirds of all children in 1850 and approximately three-fourths in 1860 held slaves numbering over twenty, the total most often used to designate a planter (see Table 9). Almost 31 percent in

Table 9. Slaveholdings of
the Great Planters' Offspring, 1850, 1860

Number of Slaves	Offspring 1850		Offspring 1860	
	No.	%	No.	%
None	42	12.4	25	7.5
1–19	69	20.3	60	18.1
20–49	125	36.8	94	28.3
50–69	47	13.8	72	21.7
70 or more	57	16.8	81	24.4
TOTAL	340	100.1	332	100.0

NOTE:
The number holding no slaves in 1860 is estimated from those children found in the 1850 census but not located on the 1860 slaveholding schedule and not known to have either died or migrated. Although it does not take into account offspring reaching maturity between 1850 and 1860, it probably still is an overestimation.

8. Campbell and Lowe, *Wealth and Power*, 39–43, 128–29; Oakes, *The Ruling Race*, 248.

1850, and over 45 percent in 1860, owned fifty or more slaves, a large holding anywhere in the South. Most sons and daughters remaining in North Carolina (155 of the 214 traced in both censuses) possessed either the same number of or more slaves in the later census, and many with diminished holdings had either given slaves to their children or sent blacks to work upon southwestern plantations.

The distribution of these slaveholdings probably is skewed downward by the presence of young people who had not yet received legacies or established themselves in life. A closer examination of the 1850 "nonslaveholders" reveals that twenty-three, at least 60 percent of those alive and in North Carolina in 1860, owned slaves. Four others—and probably more—either died or left the state. The size of slaveholdings among mature offspring (aged forty or older in 1850) further bolsters this conclusion (see Table 10). Less than 25 percent of the older group owned fewer than twenty slaves, and only 7 percent held no slaves. In fact, the percentage of nonslaveholders is actually halved (to 3 percent) if one subtracts the obvious mistakes: people who owned over $3,000 in real estate in 1850 and over twenty slaves in 1860 and thus probably owned slaves in 1850. Finally, the ownership of few or no slaves, as of land, would hold less significance for men in nonagricultural occupations.

A lack of data makes it impossible to measure the landholdings of parents against those of their children, and numerous methodological problems make a comparison of slaveholdings only suggestive. For example, although scholars such as Lee Soltow, Randolph Campbell, and Richard Lowe have found a relationship between advancing age

Table 10. Slaveholdings of
Offspring Age Forty or Older, 1850

Number of Slaves	Number of Offspring	Percentage of Offspring
None	10	7.0
1–19	23	16.1
20–49	53	37.1
50–69	22	15.4
70 or more	35	24.5
TOTAL	143	100.1

and increased wealth, parents' and children's property usually cannot be evaluated at similar ages. Multiple holdings and migrant children add further difficulties. Moreover, the planter often advanced slaves to his adult sons and daughters, making the older man's total at death not an accurate indicator of his full worth. Other problems include the early deaths of some offspring that further subdivided holdings so that they cannot be reconstituted. Slaves belonging to planters' sons and daughters also usually came in part from their spouses' families. Thus, any comparison can be only rough.[9]

Although individual children generally held fewer slaves than had their parents, total family holdings increased among the second generation. In 1860, approximately one-fourth of great planters' offspring owned 70 or more slaves, the number held by their parents in 1830. But brothers and sisters collectively almost always possessed more slaves than had their parents. For example, William Williams in 1830 owned 168 slaves; by 1860 two of his three children held 289. Ralph Outlaw's four offspring with a total of 101 slaves in 1850 had surpassed their father's 1830 holding of 79. Some family holdings had soared. William R. Smith owned 138 slaves in 1830, but in 1860 three of his four children possessed 527. The Hilliard family's bondsmen rose from the 125 belonging to paterfamilias James in 1830 to the 367 owned by his six heirs in 1850. In all but one of the fifty-two families in which the slaveholdings of most children could be combined, the total was higher than the parental holding of 1830. Although natural increase among the slaves originally owned could account for this growth, it does indicate that the younger generation was keeping much of the property handed down to it.[10]

Still another way of measuring the affluence of planters' offspring is to investigate their position among the state's wealthiest slaveholders in 1860. Such an examination can also provide insight into

9. Lee Soltow, *Patterns of Wealthholding in Wisconsin Since 1850* (Madison, 1971), 45–55; Campbell and Lowe, *Wealth and Power*, 57–58; Robert Doherty, *Society and Power: Five New England Towns, 1800–1860* (Amherst, Mass., 1977), 48–75.

10. MS Census of 1830, N.C., Warren County, p. 603, Bertie County, p. 79, Halifax County, p. 341, Nash County, p. 178; MS Census of 1860, N.C., Warren County, Sch. II, p. 397, Northampton County, Sch. II, p. 333, Halifax County, Sch. II, pp. 416, 418, 420; MS Census of 1850, N.C., Bertie County, Sch. II, pp. 421, 485, 581, Nash County, Sch. II, pp. 429, 433, 445, Edgecombe County, Sch. II, p. 339, Halifax County, Sch. II, p. 210, Franklin County, Sch. II, p. 633, Warren County, Sch. II, p. 817.

the group's staying power and social mobility. Studies of intergenerational mobility have tended to focus upon lower classes. An exception is Jonathan Wiener's survey of the richest citizens of five Alabama black belt counties from 1850 to 1870. But Wiener kept constant over time the size of his elite (while varying his wealth criterion for membership in it) and counted an entire family as persistent if one member remained in the elite.[11] Given the egalitarian inheritance practices of North Carolina planters and the emphasis they placed upon the economic well-being of each child, a focus upon individuals rather than families seemed to me more appropriate.

By 1860, surviving great planters of 1830 and their children did not monopolize the elite of large slaveholders. Then North Carolina encompassed 328 holdings of seventy or more slaves, over 140 more than had existed in 1830. Great planters of 1830 and their direct descendants (children, grandchildren, and even great-grandchildren) owned 101 such holdings, almost one-third. Fifty-one, almost 40 percent of the 132 wealthiest planters who possessed one hundred or more slaves in 1860 came from the 1830 planter elite, and this total reaches 62 if nieces and nephews, heirs of childless planters, are included. This decline in the proportion they formed of the largest slaveholders should not, however, be exaggerated. Naturally, the division of the estates of the many deceased great planters (87 percent of the 1830 elite had died by 1860) ensured that most descendants would not have an opportunity to hold as many as seventy slaves. Nonetheless, offspring maintained a close economic proximity to the wealthiest slaveholders of 1860. In addition to those children with over seventy slaves, one-half of the group owned between twenty and seventy. This latter economic stratum does not appear much removed from the elite since many new great planters' origins were in that layer of society. Although a careful tracing of these parvenus' background lies outside this study's scope, likely many great planters of 1860 had been well-to-do in 1830 and had gradually increased their holdings. For exam-

11. Examples of studies focusing upon lower classes include Stephan Thernstrom, *Poverty and Progress: Social Mobility in a Nineteenth Century City* (Cambridge, Mass., 1964), and *The Other Bostonians: Poverty and Progress in the American Metropolis, 1880–1970* (Cambridge, Mass., 1973). Jonathan M. Wiener, "Planter Persistence and Social Change: Alabama, 1850–1870," *Journal of Interdisciplinary History*, VII (1976), 235–60.

ple, Weldon N. Edwards' slave force gained in number from 59 in 1830 to 73 in 1860. Similarly, William B. Meares possessed 51 slaves in 1830; by 1860 a descendant controlled over 100. A combination of inheritance, financially advantageous marriage, and profit-making techniques of farming probably helped many middling and some smaller planters to vault into positions as the state's largest slaveholders. Furthermore, other newcomers had direct links with the 1830 elite. B. L. Hill, the owner of 133 slaves in 1860, was the brother of great planter William L. Hill and had married Anna Maria Ward, the childless widow of another wealthy planter. Joseph B. Skinner's brothers and nephews in Perquimans County formed part of the 1860 elite there. In sum, the fragmentation of the great planters' estates through inheritance had resulted in a reshuffling of positions among the well-to-do slaveowners rather than in any precipitous decline in status of the planters' children.[12]

Economic prosperity also appears to have prevailed for North Carolina planters' offspring living outside the state. Over 29 percent of 664 children known to have lived to adulthood (age twenty-one or marriage) emigrated from North Carolina, and most—23 percent of the total—chose the old Southwest. Deaths and problems of tracing the moves preclude a systematic analysis of migrants' economic status, but scattered information, though biased toward prosperity, indicates affluence, or at least comfort, for most who can be located. For example, Hugh Torrence, formerly of Mecklenburg County, owned 57 slaves in Yalobusha County, Mississippi, and valued his real estate at thirty thousand dollars. Joseph J. Williams, a migrant to Leon County, Florida, there held 7,000 acres and 245 slaves in 1860. That year at least three of the migrant Boddie brothers each owned over 60 slaves and twenty-five thousand dollars in land. Even William P. Little, who thought of himself as an utter failure, still possessed three working hands as well as considerable real estate near Memphis, Tennessee.[13]

12. MS Census of 1830, N.C., Warren County, p. 584, Brunswick County, p. 333; MS Census of 1860, N.C., Warren County, Sch. II, p. 368, Brunswick County, Sch. II, p . 107, Duplin County, Sch. II, p. 64.
13. Menn, "The Large Slaveholders," 364, 974, 1077, 1202; J. F. Smith, *Slavery and Plantation Growth*, 220; William P. Little to Sally Watkins, May 4, 1849, in Bullock and Hamilton Papers.

Sons' and daughters' continued high economic standing would have pleased their parents, who had attempted to prepare their children for success and achievement. As well as emphasizing education, parents also tried to instill values of hard work, thrift, self-control, and an appreciation of competition—all of which could aid in later life, as could the judicious marriages the young people contracted.

The relative influence of upbringing, education, marriage, class, and inheritance in assuring this prosperity cannot be determined. Still it is worth noting that the values transmitted and education given the young in planter families would encourage and aid them in retention of property and position. Certainly their share of parental wealth gave most an enormous advantage over poorer social groups. But surely training further bolstered that head start. Whatever the basis of their economic persistence, most adult children would measure up to parental desires about continued financial ease.

The sort of individual reared in North Carolina planter families can be viewed from yet another revealing angle: decision making about migration. In their evaluation of whether to leave or remain in North Carolina, nonmigrant and migrant alike carefully balanced the potentially conflicting values of financial incentives and familial feeling, both admired by parents.

North Carolinians, like other Americans, looked to the West in the early nineteenth century. Constantly expanding settlement—first Tennessee, Kentucky, and parts of Georgia, later Alabama, Mississippi, Arkansas, and Louisiana, finally Florida and Texas—drained much of North Carolina's population between 1830 and 1860. Like their fellows, members of the planter elite also contemplated the West. The Ohio River, however, bounded their visions since they desired a frontier where they could retain their slaves.[14]

Reared by parents who had stressed achievement and advancement, planters' sons and daughters considered the economic factors in migration. They never discussed the excitement of opening the

14. On southwestern migration, see William O. Lynch, "The Westward Flow of Southern Colonists Before 1861," *Journal of Southern History*, IX (1943), 303–327; Frank L. Owsley, "The Pattern of Migration and Settlement on the Southern Frontier," *Journal of Southern History*, XI (1945), 147–76; James W. Williams, "Emigration from North Carolina, 1789–1860" (M.A. thesis, University of North Carolina, 1939); Oakes, *The Ruling Race*, 69–95.

Southwest as a reason to move. Edgar M. Alston assured his mother that he planned to remain in Texas, "but in what part I cannot say untill I commence doing business for myself, then I shall live in that portion which [*sic*] I can make the most money." Lucius J. Polk, already living in Tennessee, linked his proposed removal to Florida to the possibility of greater financial reward.[15]

Sons and daughters sometimes favorably contrasted potential profits to be made in the Southwest with those offered by North Carolina. Ann Eliza Toole Robards justified her wish to sell inherited lands and invoked her deceased father's blessing: "I feel that could my Father know it, he would approve and smile upon me. . . . he did not think there was, or ever could be better land than his, and it was quite natural he should think so, but I know in this age of improvement, that neither of the children ever think of returning to NC to settle . . . if it was converted into money, and *that* . . . invested in property [near Memphis] that would be daily increasing in value." A gentleman described his niece's home in Alabama: "it is in the woods (last years clearing excepted) but is a Garden of plenty, compar'd to old-fields and empty cornhouses." Thomas Cain advised a brother against remaining in Hillsborough, North Carolina, because "the poverty[,] indolence and indifference of the citizens forbids one ever anticipating success."[16]

Planters' children, however, also showed prudence in reaching their decisions. To them, moving family and possessions to the Southwest was a course not lightly embarked upon. As sober businessmen, they attempted to learn about southwestern areas before buying land or settling there. William Cain asked his brother-in-law, then a U.S. senator, to send whatever information was available upon the "agricultural advantages" of the Southwest, especially Mississippi, and enclosed a list of questions. Others, like Memnucan Hunt and Patrick Hamilton, sought letters of introduction to prominent men in

15. Edgar M. Alston to Sarah M. Alston, August 25, 1847, in Alston Papers; Lucius J. Polk to William Polk, December 23, 1829, in Polk, Brown, and Ewell Family Papers.
16. Ann Eliza Robards to Daniel S. Hill, October, 23, 1850, in D. S. Hill Papers; John G. Smith to Jane Downey, February 9, 1827, in Downey Papers; Thomas Cain to Minerva Caldwell, April 22, 1852, in Caldwell Papers, SHC. See also the advertisement quoted in Alfred G. Smith, *Economic Readjustment of an Old Cotton State: South Carolina, 1820–1860* (Columbia, S.C., 1958), 91 n.

western areas they wished to investigate. Those considering migration saw exploratory trips as necessary before buying land and settling slaves.[17]

Although migrants and nonmigrants alike might agree about the potential attractiveness of the Southwest for moneymaking, their caution showed itself in consideration of other problems. Moving large numbers of slaves to the Southwest by the common overland route or by sea could be a troublesome, costly task, especially if they became ill. Planter families also owned much land in North Carolina; disposing of it in a market depressed by migration could be difficult. Some, like Henry Seawell and John R. Hicks, offered plantations for sale only to withdraw them, probably because amounts offered did not meet their expectations. James L. G. Baker complained that a potential purchaser bid less than Baker's father-in-law had paid for a tract. Adult sons also pondered high prices that rich southwestern lands could command. They attempted to ascertain how much they could reasonably invest. Frank Hawkins decided that the expensiveness of improved land in Mississippi meant he should buy no more than his slave force could cultivate. Paul C. Cameron voiced fears about too great indebtedness when he pronounced some Louisiana plantations "too *deep* sailing" for him. This prudence and careful consideration of migration's financial implications can be found in both those who moved and those who remained.[18]

Migration was more common among families already possessing southwestern lands. In over one-third (twenty-two of fifty-five) of planter families containing a migrant, parents had owned southwestern land. In fact, four-fifths of the North Carolina elite planters

17. William Cain to Willie P. Mangum, February 2, 1833, Memnucan Hunt to Willie P. Mangum, December 2, 1834, both in Shanks (ed.), *The Papers of Willie Person Mangum*, II, 18–19, 226–27; William H. Bowers to D. T. Witte, n.d., in Bullock and Hamilton Papers; H. H. Biddle to Sarah F. Norcott, November 22, 1852, in Bryan Scrapbook; Bethell Diary, August 2, 1855; J. W. Williams, "Emigration from North Carolina," 58–60; R. H. Taylor, *Slaveholding*, 57–64.

18. Raleigh *Register*, June 26, 1844, August 30, 1854; James L. G. Baker to William R. Smith, December 10, 1845, in P. E. Smith Papers. See also Frank Hawkins to William J. Hawkins, August 29, 1849, in Hawkins Family Papers; Edgar M. Alston to Sarah M. Alston, August 25, 1847, in Alston Papers; Leonidas Polk to Kenneth Rayner, February 25, 1852, in Rayner Papers; Frank Hawkins to John D. Hawkins, December 6, 1847, in Hawkins Family Papers; Paul C. Cameron to Duncan Cameron, January 23, 1851, in Cameron Family Papers.

known to possess absentee holdings (sixteen of twenty) had one or more migrant children. Such holdings, acquired cheaply before the great boom in values, provided a nest egg to allow purchase of lands elsewhere in the Southwest or themselves offered a financial incentive to migration. Kenneth M. Clark disliked moving from North Carolina but believed it necessary to live upon his inherited Rapides Parish plantation: "although I have never seen how I could leave Louisiana without great sacrafice of property and feel duty bound to remain here, I feel well assurd that I shall never have the same admiration for her people and customs as for the frank manners and generous impulses of the people of Carolina." In families owning western property, legacies provided a solution to the problem of buying expensive plantations and made emigration a more tempting financial prospect.[19]

Both migrants and nonmigrants mulled over possible consequences for their families in leaving North Carolina. Migration to the Southwest could not be strictly an economic decision since it held great import for all areas of their lives. A major topic of interest to those contemplating migration was their families' continued physical well-being. Common opinion held much of the Southwest to be more malarial and less wholesome than North Carolina. Mary Bethell rejoiced at her husband's decision not to move to their Arkansas property: "I don't think we could have health in that sickly country." William Plummer discarded his plans for migration because of the insalubrity of the climate. Those who left for the Southwest also kept the question of health before them. Frank Hawkins generally approved of his new home in Mississippi, but resolved that, should illness strike, he would take his family back to North Carolina. For Franklin L. Smith, describing his toddler daughter, the decision to stay in Mississippi hinged upon family health: "if she and her mother only continue to look as well as they now do & enjoy the same health I am willing to put up with all the other disadvantages of Mississippi of which there are not a few."[20]

19. Kenneth M. Clark to Lewis Thompson, December 15, 1856, in Thompson Papers. See also M. H. Pettway to Charles J. Gee, February 19, 1847, in Sterling, Nevill, and Joseph Gee Papers, Duke.

20. Bethell Diary, July 23, 1860; Lucy Battle to William H. Battle, February 23, 1847, in Battle Family Papers; James Hamilton to Robert Hamilton, July 31, 1854, in Bullock

Planters considered their families' happiness as well as health. Some women disliked the idea of settling in a rough, new country with fewer churches and schools; others did not want to leave friends and family. North Carolina husbands, like their contemporaries elsewhere in the United States making such decisions, often had to cope with their wives' opposition. Faced with such disapproval, some of the wealthiest Carolinians abandoned plans to migrate. Lewis Thompson never resided on his large Louisiana plantation because his wife was unwilling to stay there; their daughter-in-law similarly convinced her husband to keep it only an absentee unit. Susan Biddle Cobb's growing reluctance to settle on their Alabama holdings helped to persuade her husband to stay in North Carolina.[21]

Still other sorts of family ties significantly influenced decisions to remain or leave. William L. Tarry, a great planter's grandson, contemplated seeking his fortune in Texas but doubted that he could bear leaving relatives: "It would be almost impossible to wean myself from them, the longer I stay away from them the more I want to see them." Others were willing to migrate only if some kinfolks accompanied them. Robert Hamilton discussed his position with his brother Charles: "If you move out and carry Sister Jenny I feel but little hesitation in saying that I shall be desirous of going to Mississippi. I could not without overruling reasons, consent to carry my wife out without Sister Jenny or some other lady of our family." Neither Robert nor Charles ever moved to Mississippi although the latter owned a plantation there. In 1815, Peter Evans had explored the possibilities of the Mississippi Territory; twenty-five years later he was willing to move with at least three of his six children. When a daughter and son-in-law decided to remain in North Carolina, Evans abandoned the plan: "I have all the time told them it was primarily on their account

---

and Hamilton Papers; A. Henderson to William Gaston, January 15, 1836, in Gaston Papers; Frank Hawkins to John D. Hawkins, November 14, 1848, in Hawkins Family Papers; Franklin L. Smith to Mary Smith, May 21, 1837, in Reid Papers (similarly Ann Eliza Robards to Elizabeth Toole, July 3, 1846, in D. S. Hill Papers).

21. Degler, *At Odds*, 42–51; Kenneth M. Clark to Lewis Thompson, December 23, 1851, in Thompson Papers; Sitterson, "Lewis Thompson," in Green (ed.), *Essays in Southern History*, 18, 26; B. Franklin Biddle to Sarah F. Carraway, August 22, 1854, in Bryan Scrapbook; Bethell Diary, July 23, 1860; Fletcher M. Green (ed.), *The Lides Go South . . . and West: The Record of a Planter Migration in 1835* (Columbia, S.C., 1952), 9, 15, 19, 35.

I consented to go—I am perfectly satisfied where I am—for as regards farming I can not be much bettered."[22]

This desire to maintain close family ties likely influenced those who made migration a cooperative family venture. At least five and probably seven of the eleven Forney siblings settled in Alabama. After Jeremiah Perry's death in 1846, seven of his eight children moved to Harrison County, Texas. Three or four of the Waddell brothers migrated to Louisiana in the early 1830s. An old classmate from the University of North Carolina remarked about Hugh, a fifth Waddell, who "still lives in this place, tho' strongly persuaded by his Brothers to remove to the S. West."[23]

Other sons and daughters who had made their own decisions to leave sought to persuade siblings to join them. Ann Eliza Toole Robards pictured a warm reunion should her brothers-in-law, sisters, and widowed mother join her family near Memphis: "Could you be persuaded to move to this country, I would be so glad, if you and bro Joe, would come out with your families, and bring Mama with you, and all settle together." Ann Eliza also knew the attraction of greater profits and she added it to family considerations: "I know you could coin money here, There are more ways to make it than any place I ever saw." Such exhortations sometimes led siblings to reconsider decisions. William Bethell's migrant brother and sisters influenced him to weigh seriously leaving North Carolina. Even unsuccessful calls for togetherness emphasized ties of kinship and amity.[24]

Some sons and daughters compromised between migration's lure and a resolve to remain in North Carolina by purchasing and running absentee plantations. In twenty-eight families (23 percent of all non-migrants with direct descendants), the younger generation held

22. William L. Tarry to Sarah A. Watkins, January 25, 1845, in Tarry Papers; Robert Hamilton to Charles E. Hamilton, January 15, 1845, in Bullock and Hamilton Papers; Peter Evans to William R. Smith, Jr., December 22, 1839, in W. R. Smith Papers.

23. John H. Wheeler, *Reminiscences and Memoirs of North Carolina and Eminent North Carolinians* (Columbus, Ohio, 1884), 244–45; Estate of Peter Forney, in Lincoln County Estates; Estate of Jeremiah (Fork) Perry, in Franklin County Estates; Teacher's General Report, March-July, 1855, Levin Perry to Theophilus Perry, February 19, 1851, both in Person Papers; William M. Green to James K. Polk, June 6, 1836, in McPherson (ed.), "Unpublished Letters," 196.

24. Ann Eliza Robards to Daniel S. Hill, October 23, 1850, in D. S. Hill Papers; Bethell Diary, August 2, 1855, July 23, 1860. See also J. H. D. Jelks to Louisa M. Sills, February 9, 1852, in Sills Papers.

southwestern lands on which they did not reside. Such investments offered the Southwest's riches without the disadvantages of leaving North Carolina.

The way that planters' offspring reached their verdicts about migration would have pleased many of their parents. The elders had attempted to point their children toward achievement, respectability, and continued prosperity. Old Philemon Hawkins bluntly summed up such aspirations in his advice to "keep out of difficulties and always be on the gaining hand." Charles E. Johnson closed his will with: "Now May God bless you all my Dear Children & make you prosperous, virtuous, & happy in life & in death is the humble but sincere prayer of your father who has ever loved you with a father's love." Johnson's last benediction also points up how much planters treasured loving families and harmonious interaction among relatives. In his will, Philemon Hawkins beseeched his children to be "at all times . . . in perfect friendship and Union with each other." The younger generation's choices about where to live attempted to balance the values so often stressed to them.[25]

Among planters' offspring can be found many who lived up to their parents' expectations. Sons' and daughters' economic achievement in retaining many slaves and much real estate surely would have pleased the elders. The way that the young people carefully weighed the benefits and disadvantages of migration, taking into account both financial and familial considerations, also would have been in accord with the wishes of parents who were sentimental as well as shrewd. Thus, great planters' adult offspring had matured and were much like their parents wanted them to be. On the eve of the Civil War, wealthy North Carolinians' descendants formed a prosperous group looking to the present and future.

25. As quoted in Mary B. Polk to Lucius J. Polk, June 3, 1826, in Polk, Badger, and McGehee Family Papers; Will of Charles E. Johnson, in Chowan County Wills; Will of Philemon Hawkins, March 5, 1810 (never probated), in Hawkins Family Papers.

SEVEN

The White Family and
Its Slaves

The changing relationship between parents and children over time is a means to understanding the domestic lives of wealthy North Carolinians. Yet to comprehend fully the values and beliefs guiding planters' lives, one must examine their relations with one remaining component of their households, their slaves. Planters sometimes called their bondsmen their "black family," but historians should not allow that term to mask the stark contrast that existed between the treatment of slaves and of children. Despite the demands elite Carolinians sometimes made of their offspring and the concern they sometimes manifested toward slaves, their treatment of slaves was far harsher. Unlike their loving fascination with white sons and daughters, planters tended to place much psychological and social distance between themselves and bondsmen. Racism and harsh punishments increased that gulf. Moreover, a careful examination of the white youngsters' actions shows that they too acted upon the oppressive racial rule that characterized the planter household.[1]

Planters' care of children and slaves differed greatly. Wealthy North Carolinians invariably provided good physical care for their white progeny: no cases of neglect or abuse have been discovered. For slaves the record was much more complicated. To be sure, many great planters adequately saw to their bondsmen's physical needs. John C.

---

1. On racism North and South, see David M. Potter, *The Impending Crisis, 1848–1861* (New York, 1976), 458–61; George M. Fredrickson, *The Black Image in the White Mind: The Debate on Afro-American Character and Destiny, 1817–1914* (New York, 1971), 90–96, 130–59, and "Masters and Mudsills," 34–48; Carl N. Degler, *Place Over Time: The Continuity of Southern Distinctiveness* (Baton Rouge, 1977), 88–92; Leon F. Litwack, *North of Slavery: The Negro in the Free States, 1790–1860* (Chicago, 1961), 156–69, 204–207.

Lea and Simmons J. Baker added provisions to their wills for the maintenance of superannuated slaves. Others, like Paul C. Cameron, took pains to see that slaves were properly clothed and fed. Mary Anderson, a former slave born on Samuel Brodie's plantation, remembered that her owners provided good food, warm clothes, and two-room cabins.[2]

Yet other elite North Carolinians were negligent or cruel to slaves to the point of brutality. A Warren County black woman who disliked her wealthy master reported that three slaves belonging to a neighboring planter family died from exposure during cold weather. Her cynical comment was, "Dey said de more slaves a man had[,] de wusser he wus to slaves." A small slaveholder in central North Carolina similarly reminisced to his son about how poorly his very wealthy neighbors—correctly identified by name and plantation—treated their slaves. After many years, Louisa Adams, whose family had belonged to a great planter's son, still held unpleasant memories of her old master: "I sho do 'member my Marster Tom Covington and his wife too, Emma. De old man wuz the very Nick. He would take what we made and lowance us, dat is lowance it out to daddy after he had made it."[3]

Whether they provided well or indifferently for their slaves, planters erected a barrier between themselves and their servants by focusing upon blacks as property. Sentimental whites who would have been horrified to think of their own children as possessions could discuss slaves and slavery as dispassionately and calculatedly as they would cattle weights or tobacco prices. Ezekiel E. Lane's letter to his brother, then studying medicine abroad, mentioned only female slaves who were pregnant or had recently given birth. Moorhead Wright, who had deeply mourned his newborn child's death, reported births and deaths among his slaves in terms of profits and losses: "that makes several

2. Will of John C. Lea, in Caswell County Wills; Will of Simmons J. Baker, in Halifax County Wills, Vol. 4, p. 345; Paul C. Cameron to Mildred and Margaret Cameron, February 8, 1844, in Cameron Family Papers; George P. Rawick (ed.), *The American Slave: A Composite Autobiography* (Westport, Conn., 1972), Vol. XIV, Pt. 1, pp. 20–21.

3. Rawick (ed.), *The American Slave,* Vol. XV, Pt. 2, pp. 102–103, Vol. XIV, Pt. 1, pp. 2–6; Clarence Poe, "Wherein I Set a Good Example: Recording Traditions of an Average Southern Family, 1675–1865," *South Atlantic Quarterly,* XXXV (1936), 36–37.

[deaths] in the last year or so, however I should not complain for I have had a great deal of luck[,] take it all round[.] I have a very goodly number of negro children coming and have paid a great deal of attention to that part of business[.] my rule is first a plenty of corn and meat to be raised[,] negro children taken care of and cotton afterwards." Planters also talked about slaves in market terms such as "valuable," "prime," and "superannuated." Even when slaves' conduct became infuriating and made consideration of them as people unavoidable, slaveholders still stressed the profit motive. Thomas P. Devereux sought to calm a daughter angered by two slaves he had given her and emphasized how punishment should not be allowed to decrease property values: "we must not let them so vex us as to impare their value. . . . if I was to do as you wish we might both loose money and have something to blame ourselves about when our 'backs were not up.' "[4]

Slaves' chattel status could subject them to sale. Like other slaveholding southerners, North Carolina planters trafficked in slaves. Elizabeth Pearson vacillated over whether to exercise a buy-back clause covering some slaves belonging to her deceased husband's estate. Her doubts sprang not from sentimental attachment or qualms of guilt but from uncertainty that the price obtained reflected the slaves' actual value. "I did not want these Negroes sold," Pearson fretted, "but Jack sold better than I expected, the others not so well as they ought to have sold. I do not know whether I ought to take them or not, if I could hire [out] Jack for $126, which would be the interest of the purchase money, I would feel safe to take them, & as he is a pretty good carpenter I think he ought to bring that much." Leaving aside those planters burdened by heavy debts or facing possible financial disaster, one can still find an interest in selling slaves. In some cases, wealthy North Carolinians considered selling slaves as a way of dispatching a bothersome, though not urgent, debt. Others, un-

4. Ezekiel E. Lane to Walter W. Lane, April 7, 1856, in Lane Papers; Moorhead Wright to Isaac Wright, August 10, 1850, in Gillespie and Wright Family Papers; M. M. Harrison to Alexander Cuningham, December 17, 1845, in Cuningham Papers; Kenneth M. Clark to Lewis Thompson, January 14, 1853, in Thompson Papers; Josiah Collins, Jr., to Thomas S. Hathaway, July 29, 1859, in Collins Papers, NCDAH; Thomas P. Devereux to Sophia Turner, December 27, 1859, in Turner Papers. See Nathan I. Huggins, *Black Odyssey: The Afro-American Ordeal in Slavery* (New York, 1977), 126–28.

prompted by any pressing financial worries, were willing to part with at least some slaves if the price were right. Lewis A. Boyd recommended to a potential buyer Negro boys and girls that Boyd's uncle, John D. Hawkins, might be persuaded to sell. Leonidas Polk, although avowing his intention to be satisfied with a "moderate" income, also considered selling his slaves: "Land & slaves is all I have & I want to make the most of them. I don't know wheather it would be more profitable to sell the negroes & land I have, & live on what they could bring me, or rather the interest of it, or to farm under all the inconveniences attending it in the West." To be sure, Leonidas, a future Episcopal minister and bishop, expressed an interest in determining the suitability of the purchaser of slaves that he designated as "family Negroes," but the number of his slaves included in that category is unclear.[5]

Treating slaves as property also entailed separations of parent and child that planters would have found unacceptable for their own families. To be sure, genteel parents did send children—usually ten years of age or older—away to school. Although these temporary partings were not easy, elite children spent vacations at home and also received visits at school from parents. Moreover, some planters emphasized that only the importance of education made their offspring's absences bearable. On the other hand, planters, while not indifferent to slaves' family relations, could rather easily sever them. Even those North Carolinians who prided themselves on rarely selling slaves allowed the events within their own families to dictate the organization of the slave family.

For slaves as property were, as Herbert Gutman has posited, subject to the changes within the planter family's life cycle. Two events in the "big house"—marriage and death—posed the greatest threats to the slave family's security. As described earlier, a wedding called

5. Elizabeth Ellis Pearson to John W. Ellis, June 18, 1858, in Tolbert (ed.), *The Papers of John Willis Ellis*, I, 196–97. Hugh Waddell to Duncan Cameron, March 24, 1850, in Cameron Family Papers; Lunsford Lane, *The Narrative of Lunsford Lane, Formerly of Raleigh, N.C. . . .* (3rd ed.; Boston, 1845), 19–20; Lewis A. Boyd to John D. Hawkins, January 16, 1824, in Hawkins Family Papers; Leonidas Polk to Lucius J. Polk, August 22, 1828, in Leonidas Polk Papers, and September 22, 1828, in Polk and Yeatman Family Papers. See also James Hamilton to Charles E. Hamilton, November 26, 1849, in Bullock and Hamilton Papers; John Garner to Alexander Cuningham, February 1, 1830, in Cuningham Papers.

for gifts to the new couple. Planters' presents of slaves to newly married children, especially those who lived elsewhere in North Carolina or even outside the state, could wrench blacks from close relations and their kinship network. Even a planter who recognized a
black's unwillingness to leave gave precedence to his own arrangements. William Cain told his daughter Minerva that widespread illness among his slaves prevented him from sending Becky, who wished
to nurse a sick sister. Cain's own interpretation—that Becky's reluctance arose from a suspicion that she would not return—does not appear to have lessened his resolve to give this servant to his recently
married daughter.[6]

The planter's death marked the most threatening time for slave
families. Wealthy North Carolinians' main interest lay in securing
their children's financial well-being, and that could menace the black
family's stability. Although many planters showed at least some regard for black family ties, that concern had easily reached limits. A
survey of planters' wills mentioning slaves by name indicates that at
least some were grouped in families or mother-headed groups. But a
closer scrutiny reveals numerous cases of separation. At first glance,
Philemon Hawkins' will seems unexceptional, but his son John D.
coolly analyzed its disposition of slave families. Armed with numerous examples, he firmly disputed a brother-in-law's contention that
the elder Hawkins meant slave children to accompany their parents:

> Burton the husband is given to Dr Hawkins and Siller his wife is given to
> Mrs Little. That Sillers daughter Lucinda who was only 4 years old is given
> to Mary Jane Hawkins. That Edy the mother is given to Dr Hawkins and
> Edys small Daughters Martha and Phillis one 6 and the other 7 years old
> are given to Lucy Coleman & Matilda Hawkins. That Great Ben the only
> surviving Parent is given to Mrs S. Haywood & his youngest child Sarah
> to Mrs D. Haywood, That Jesse and Penny are given to me and their small
> Daughter Penny is given to Celestia Hawkins.

Legacies given by planters such as Samuel Ashe, William Bethell, and
John Brodie also separated close relatives. Joseph J. Alston's will gave
each daughter a specific number of slaves, and his sons divided the

6. Gutman, *The Black Family*, 129–37, 284–91, 310–17; Edward W. Phifer, Jr.,
"Slavery in Microcosm: Burke County, North Carolina," *Journal of Southern History*,
XXVIII (1962), 153–57; William Cain to Minerva Caldwell, June 5, 1842, in Caldwell
Papers, SHC.

remainder. A delay in settling the estate meant the Alston brothers shared the recently born offspring of slaves their sisters had inherited. The courts awarded the Alston women financial compensation for their brothers' dilatory actions; there is no indication that slave families thus broken were reunited.[7]

In fact, planters, as doting grandparents, further added to the disruption of the slave family by giving Negro youngsters to grandsons and granddaughters. Thirteen of ninety-two North Carolina male planters with wills, approximately 15 percent, bequeathed young servants to their grandchildren, and a few others presented slaves in deeds of gift. Although the family status of the youngsters bequeathed is uncertain, it seems unlikely that most were orphans. Four planters who gave an unspecified slave boy or girl to a grandchild obviously cared little whether that child was separated from parents and siblings. Even if the Negro child had relatives belonging to the white child's parents, the seeds of future separation had been early sown. Gifts of slaves to grandchildren pampered the white children at the blacks' expense.

Perhaps the most telling testimony about planters' attitudes toward the slave family came from those who made special efforts to protect it. Only eight planters out of the ninety-two, approximately 9 percent, urged the executors of their wills to respect slave family relationships. One of them, Dr. Stephen Davis, apparently saw division by families primarily as a way to equalize his own children's legacies, for he ordered that one son receive fifty slaves "in families or of a fair average value of my other negroes." Even the others could not escape seeing slaves in terms of property and thus hedged their instructions. While Duncan Cameron told his executors to divide his slaves with "respect being had to families as far as practicable," William Baird phrased his injunction as "due regard for keeping families togeather as much as may be." Isaac Wright was more blunt: "families should be broken as little as practicable and also the relation of man and wife shall be respected as far as can be done without undue

7. John D. Hawkins to William Polk, March 13, 1833, in Polk and Yeatman Family Papers; Will of Samuel Ashe, in Cumberland County Wills; Will of William Bethell, in Rockingham County Estates; Will of John Brodie, in Warren County Wills; Will of Joseph J. Alston, in Chatham County Wills; Estate of Joseph J. Alston, in Chatham County Estates. See also Phifer, "Slavery in Microcosm," 156–57.

sacrifice of interest." Moreover, planters defined "family" rather narrowly. Richard Hines specified that it meant "the husband and Wife (or mother of the children) and their or her children under ten years of age together." Alexander Gray's interpretation was similar: "no seperation shall be made between husband and wife or young children from their mother." Although these planters recognized a two-parent household, they would allow youngsters and adolescents to be permanently separated from parents and siblings.[8]

Not only slaves' status as property but their skin color affected planters' views. Thoroughly racist, wealthy North Carolinians held doubts about Negroes' capabilities that did not at all resemble their faith in white children's abilities. Peter W. Hairston commented upon the "fine" article he had read in the *Times* of London: "He says the abolition of slavery in St Domingo and the British colonies has not elevated the black race; but lowered the white and treats them as an inferior race. He ascribes the superiority of the Anglo Saxon race in countries where slavery has been introduced to their keeping themselves separated from them [*i.e.,* blacks] while the Spanish nations have mixed with them." Thomas Bennehan too found Negroes inferior and commented about a free black he had employed as a groom: "I had thought him a smart man of his colour, & that I might trust him, but I have no doubt I have been deceived in his character." Others in jokes or stories poked fun at Negroes as lesser beings.[9]

Planters' racism and slaves' chattel status combined to encourage emotional distance between master and slave. Elite North Carolinians' continued concern about each of their children's development and activities had little parallel in their relations with slaves. On the

8. Will of Stephen Davis, in Warren County Wills; Will of Duncan Cameron, in Wake County Wills; Will of William Baird, in Person County Wills, Vol. 17, pp. 474–77; Will of Isaac Wright, in Bladen County Wills, Bk. 2, pp. 4–19; Will of Richard Hines, in Wake County Wills; Will of Alexander Gray, in Randolph County Wills. See also Will of Ezekiel E. Lane, in New Hanover County Wills. Compare my interpretation to that in Genovese, *Roll, Jordan, Roll,* 450–58.

9. P. W. Hairston Diary, December 3, 1859, November 22, n.d., in Hairston Papers; Thomas Bennehan to Samuel S. Downey, August 1, 1830, in Downey Papers; John W. Ellis to Mary D. Ellis, March 6, 1859, in Tolbert (ed.), *The Papers of John Willis Ellis,* I, 226–27; E. Jones Erwin to George Phifer Erwin, December 17, 1857, in Erwin Papers. Consult also S. E. Devereux to Thomas P. Devereux, December 4, [1840], in Devereux Family Papers; Bartlett Yancey to Willie P. Mangum, January 25, 1826, in Shanks (ed.), *The Papers of Willie Person Mangum,* I, 240; Crabtree and Patton (eds.), *"Journal of a Secesh Lady, "* 20.

large plantation, black and white coexisted, but physical closeness did not necessarily bring psychological intimacy. Paul Escott and Thomas Webber have richly documented both a feeling of community among blacks in the slave quarters and a lack of identification of slaves with their white owners. These authors point out the slaves' belief that they formed an oppressed group set apart from whites. Escott and Webber similarly emphasize slaves' awareness of condescension—an awareness that led many to conceal their actual feelings and beliefs from their masters. Thus few slaves, according to Webber, were able to establish a relationship of trust with their "white family." And these generalizations indeed have much validity for North Carolina large planters. Most slaves lacked individual importance for their masters. Illustrative of common attitudes was an anecdote often repeated by former slaves concerning a white man and his own slave who met in the road. Neither recognized the other until the slaveowner asked the black his owner's name. Although this story emphasized the size of the plantation's work force, it also correctly shows the gulf existing between master and most slaves on large holdings. Doc Edwards, a former slave of Paul C. Cameron, recited one variant of that folktale when he asserted that Cameron owned so many slaves that he couldn't recognize them all. Edwards continued: "When we opened de gate for him or met him in the road[,] he would say, 'Who is you? Whare you belong?' We would say 'We belong to Marse Paul.' 'Alright run along' he'd say den, an' he would trow us a nickel or so."[10]

To be sure, some slaves stood out among the numerous blacks. Some house servants and artisans held privileged status—a special importance to their masters and mistresses—and such relationships at times transcended the strictures of the slave system. But planters' reactions to favored servants usually differed from their appreciation of white children. Far from valuing initiative and achievement in slaves, most planters emphasized loyalty and blind service, the servile nature of slaves. These planters believed that natural affection bound them to their white children; they were most likely to express

10. Paul D. Escott, *Slavery Remembered: A Record of Twentieth-Century Slave Narratives* (Chapel Hill, 1979), 20–30, 50–67; Thomas L. Webber, *Deep Like the Rivers: Education in the Slave Quarter Community, 1831–1865* (New York, 1978), 61–93; Rawick (ed.), *The American Slave*, Vol. XIV, Pt. 1, pp. 296, 248, Vol. XV, Pt. 2, p. 35.

a special tie to slaves who "deserved" it. Showing great anxiety over the illness of her children's nurse, Anne Cameron revealingly commented that this slave's "faithfulness" had attached all the family to her. Even so humane and upright a man as William Gaston described his feeling for a deceased slave as prompted by the man's good conduct. Josiah Collins, Jr., wrote about an aged slave who had been sold (when the business of Collins' brother failed) but had returned to the Collins plantation "to die": "She was a daughter of a favorite and faithful negro of my grandfather and I am willing on that account to gratify her and permit her to spend the rest of her days with her kindred—and of course bear the expense of maintaining her." The special position of that slave's family had not saved her from sale, but her parent's past devotion to a planter family had won her a concession.[11]

Even among house servants, only a favored few actually appear to have had close ties with the white family. Planter families such as the Averys, Simpson-Biddles, and Hamiltons seldom mentioned their household retainers in correspondence. The Skinner family, to all appearances conscientious in its dealings with slaves, referred frequently only to one slave, Annie, the head housekeeper. Eliza Skinner described her arrival as a bride at the Skinner plantation: "Annie and Harriet—the two principal members of the household met me at the door—with a 'howdye do mistress'—'welcome home'—'we have been looking for you a long time.' After a while the washer woman was presented—Aunt Eliza—I have not seen her since. Nor have I become acquainted with the others. Annie and Harriet are always in attendance." Eliza Skinner's apparent isolation from most Skinner slaves, even house servants, may have been engineered by Annie as a way of maintaining her power and position. But whether by Annie's design or not, Eliza made little mention of other servants in her letters. After the first months, such distance from slaves in the big house was obviously more emotional than physical. Margaret Devereux in long, frank letters to her beloved sister occasionally mentioned house

11. Anne Cameron to Paul C. Cameron, April 22, 1844, in Cameron Family Papers; William Gaston to Susan Gaston, February 14, 1823, in Gaston Papers; Josiah Collins, Jr., to Thomas S. Hathaway, July 29, 1859, in Collins Papers, NCDAH. See also Genovese, Roll, Jordan, Roll, 327–65; Blake, "Ties of Intimacy," 137–44, 147.

servants Clara, Adelaide, and Minerva but had little to say about any of them.[12]

Blacks, however, could not always be ignored, and slaveholders feared that a more frightening aspect of their slaves' personalities existed. Insurrection and murder were subjects that planter families preferred to avoid but could not completely dismiss. Duncan Cameron's sister became almost hysterical over what she believed to be attempts to murder their father through arson and poison. Josiah Collins, Jr., in 1848 suspected slaves of attempting to poison his overseer. Isaac T. Avery discussed the rumors of insurrection that plagued his neighborhood after a Negro preacher visited that area. Although Avery believed that "the great number of slaves employed about the mines would make vigilance among Managers and Patrollers proper at all times," he discounted the current suspicions since "the Negroes of the County are as orderly and submissive, as I ever knew them."[13]

These fears about violent actions, together with a belief in Negro inferiority, influenced the conduct expected of and punishment levied upon disobedient slaves. The compulsion inherent in slavery pushed planters to rely upon severe chastisement. North Carolina large slaveholders differentiated between the correction of slaves and the discipline of children. Parents tried to mold their erring white children's conduct by example and exhortation but did not expect such mild measures to subdue bondsmen. In State v. Mann (1829), North Carolina jurist Thomas Ruffin summed up such attitudes when he described the "impassable gulf" between the correction of white children and of slaves. To him, the discipline involved in rearing children necessarily differed from that of slavery because the aims of each varied. The punishment of children looked toward their future

12. Eliza Skinner to Mrs. Galt, February 23, 1849, in Skinner Family Papers. See also Eliza Skinner to Tristrim L. Skinner, November 12, 1851, Tristrim L. Skinner to Eliza Skinner, August 7, 1850, both in Skinner Family Papers; Huggins, Black Odyssey, 103–107; Leslie Howard Owens, This Species of Property: Slave Life and Culture in the Old South (New York, 1976), 109–116; Margaret Devereux to Ellen Mordecai, n.d. [ca. 1841], November 7, 1846, April 16, 1847, January 11, 1841, March 17, 1854, all in M. M. Devereux Papers.

13. M. Anderson to Duncan Cameron, March 28, April 10, 1807, both in Cameron Family Papers; Blake, "Ties of Intimacy," 135–46; Isaac T. Avery to Selina L. Lenoir, September 26, 1821, in Lenoir Family Papers. Consult G. G. Johnson, Ante-bellum North Carolina, 514–15.

as citizens and equals of their parents. Not so with that of the slave, Ruffin noted: "The end is the profit of the master, his security and public safety."

Among North Carolina planters, indulgent parents could be severe slaveholders. Samuel S. Downey wrote affectionate letters to his children away at school. Yet this fond parent, also a pious Presbyterian, would brook no insubordination from slaves under his management. When one escaped during a whipping Downey was administering, the planter asked a friend to recapture the man and "take him immediately to some negro traders of your county & make immediate sale of him for what price he will command but if he can not be sold have him sent to the jail of your county." Josiah Collins, Jr., a loving parent and devout Episcopalian, wished a troublesome slave sold if his full value could be obtained and further stipulated that "If sold he must not be *resold* to live in the Albemarle district of the state," Collins' own area. The chastisement ordered, though not corporal punishment, would tear the young man away from family and friends. Collins' desire that his slave be sent to another area also increased the possibility of sale to someone in the lower South.[14]

Whether planters used or threatened physical punishment or sale, a prominent theme in their discussion of slave discipline involved setting an example. Planters felt compelled to levy punishments to keep order among their other slaves. Paul C. Cameron advised his sisters that he believed it worth the trouble and expense to try to retrieve a runaway slave the women had inherited. Paul revealed his reasoning: "But as a slaveholder[,] as the representative of the estate and of my sisters I think it my Duty to have the effort made. *His* flight has had a very bad *effect here* and to bring him back would render others better contented and improve the spirit of subordination." Samuel S. Downey's decision to sell a runaway slave was based upon similar premises: "if he is not made an example of[,] it will greatly injure the others." Sarah Elizabeth Devereux too believed in the ef-

14. Samuel S. Downey to Jane E. S. Downey, August 5, 1840, Samuel S. Downey to R. J. Smith, October 20, 1828, both in Downey Papers; Josiah Collins, Jr., to T. W. Hudgins, n.d., in Collins Papers, NCDAH; Ulrich B. Phillips, *Life and Labor in the Old South* (Boston, 1929), 253. See also Eleanor Haywood to John D. Hawkins, April 1, 1830, in Hawkins Family Papers; William Tyree to Alexander Cuningham, November 13, 1844, in Cuningham Papers.

ficacy of example and told her brother-in-law about a recalcitrant slave: "she has given us trouble enough ever since she was grown, and if you think it best to make her an example, sell her."[15]

The need for obedient slaves led planters to inflict hard and sometimes unmerited punishment. Elijah B. Hilliard detailed the latest attempts to catch his brother Isaac's runaway slave Prince. Although two members of the chase accidentally shot another slave belonging to Isaac, Elijah reported that his brother "takes it very calmly." Furthermore, the mistaken identity meant that no one, according to Elijah, "thought hard of" the incident. During the division of his deceased father's estate, James N. McPherson contemptuously remarked about the slaves' preference for his brother-in-law: "All of the negroes want to belong to Willoughby—they say he is so very good and easey—I should not be surprized however if he made some of their backs feel sore before the end of next year." James clearly believed that Willoughby would eventually be forced to use coercion to achieve his ends.[16]

Even the white children joined in the oppression of slaves. Youngsters early learned the etiquette of race relations and the hierarchy that the household contained. From their earliest years, planters' children encountered blacks. Youngsters with slave nurses or child tenders often liked them, but white mothers jealously guarded their own favored position. White children also met black children. Two extreme opinions have been recorded about these relationships. Thomas Jefferson's beliefs that slavery taught tyranny in the nursery are as well known as the southern apologists' stories of black and white children happily at play together. Both versions actually reflected reality, but Jefferson's views better describe the guiding principle of such relationships.[17]

15. Paul C. Cameron to Margaret and Mildred Cameron, n.d. [ca. 1852–53], in Cameron Family Papers; Samuel S. Downey to R. J. Smith, October 20, 1828, in Downey Papers; Sarah E. Devereux to Thomas P. Devereux, December 4, 1840, in Devereux Family Papers. See similar rationales in Stampp, The Peculiar Institution, 114–15.

16. Elijah B. Hilliard to John B. Williams, May 6, 1851, in J. B. Williams Papers; James N. McPherson to Elizabeth McPherson, December 22, 1836, in Ferebee, Gregory, and McPherson Family Papers.

17. Thomas Jefferson, Notes on the State of Virginia, ed. Thomas P. Abernethy (New York, 1964), Query 28, p. 155; Thomas Nelson Page, Social Life in Old Virginia (New

Both black and white learned early in life that the household contained a racial hierarchy and that slaves were lowly subjects. White children could make slave youngsters miserable by petty tyrannies, and such relationships were sometimes fraught with tension. Joshua Swift, after three years in the lower Cape Fear region, had observed unhappy black-white relations among children there: "the worst consequence of slavery was its influence upon the minds and habits of the white children. The natural disposition to rule, that is inherent in the human mind, is nourished in the 'young master' and mistress. They become impatient and domineering, and vent their angry passions upon the negro children."[18]

Even when planters' sons and daughters did not test their dominance over slave children, parents sometimes were eager to enforce it for them. Mary Henderson was more than willing to intervene on her children's behalf and she rigidly drew the color line: "I had to slap Phillis well last night for striking Johnie—I cannot bear such impertinence from little negroes, she fights her own color but must not raise her hand to my children." Sarah Alston, a great planter's widow, wrote her grandson about the carriage her carpenter had built for him and indicated that she was not averse to seeing it drawn by slave youngsters: "[the carpenter] put two seats in your carriage, so little brother might ride with you, I reckon it will take all your little waiting men to pull it, unless you *hitch* the *old grey*." Growing up as a slave in the household of Sherwood and Eleanor Hawkins Haywood, Lunsford Lane found himself and the white children socialized into proper racial behavior as he reached age ten. Lane described his experience: "When I began to work, I discovered the difference between myself and the master's white children. They began to order me about, and were told to do so by my master and mistress."[19]

York, 1897), 22; Ulrich B. Phillips, *American Negro Slavery: A Survey of the Supply, Employment and Control of Negro Labor as Determined by the Plantation Regime* (New York, 1918), 313–14.

18. Kemp P. Battle (ed.), *Letters and Documents Relating to the Early History of the Lower Cape Fear* (Chapel Hill, 1903), 104. See John Hope Franklin, *The Militant South, 1800–1861* (Cambridge, Mass., 1956), 66–68, and compare to Owens, *This Species of Property*, 204.

19. M. S. Henderson Diary, October 29, 1855, in Henderson Papers; Sarah M. Alston to Willis Alston, February 10, 1854, in Alston Papers; Lane, *Narrative*, 7. Consult also Huggins, *Black Odyssey*, 170–71.

Parents also discouraged relationships with slaves that did not sufficiently recognize the white child's superior position. Mary Henderson sent her five-year-old son to school each day, in part to prevent him from participating in the fun of the Negro youngsters. Anne Cameron worried that her ten-year-old daughter enjoyed the camaraderie of the kitchen help and advised her sister-in-law not to allow the girl during a visit to spend time with them.[20]

Some white youngsters early realized the prerogatives of race. Ann C. Hawkins laughingly recounted her toddler daughter's threats against a servant: "she says to Peggy some times when she displeases her[:] I will make my Papa whip you, her Papa pets her a good [d]eal and she has all confidence in him." Other white children clearly understood the distinction between their own position and that of the blacks. Joshua McPherson complained bitterly that he had been ordered around "like a slave."[21]

In addition, planters' children accepted slaves' status as property, and adults further reinforced that concept. When Peter Evans gave his granddaughter two slaves as a reward for her scholastic achievements, he impressed upon her their financial value: "You will recollect I told you if you learned well and stood well in the school I would make you a present & I have been as good as my word—I gave your father a deed of gift for Jane and Patience in your name; so they are your property—& at your uncle Hines's sale they would have sold for $1000 each—such negroes are now in great demand." Other less formal arrangements sometimes allotted slaves to adolescents, whose remarks also showed that they sometimes considered slaves primarily to be property. Seventeen-year-old Susan Capehart noted: "We had a death here this morning—one of the little servants and he belonged to me." Teen-aged Mary B. Polk flippantly underlined the chattel aspect of slavery: "I had forgot to inform you of a very great *mishap* I have met with lately in the death of my waiter man *Salvester*—one third of my estate."[22]

20. M. S. Henderson Diary, July 2, 1855, in Henderson Papers; Anne Cameron to Mildred Cameron, June 19, n.d. [ca. 1846], in Cameron Family Papers.
21. Ann C. Hawkins to Jane Hawkins, June 7, 1851, in Hawkins Family Papers; Joshua McPherson to Willie McPherson, May 4, 1822, in Ferebee, Gregory, and McPherson Family Papers.
22. Peter Evans to Louisa J. Hall, February 26, 1852, in S. H. Hill Papers, III, 270;

White children began to grasp their roles as masters and owners and to differentiate themselves from slaves. And so the older generation passed on its cultural as well as material possessions to the young. In spite of some consideration of slaves' needs, much of planters' interest in their servants remained bound up in property values. Even dealings with favored servants often reflected planters' preoccupation with their own needs—service and faithfulness from slaves. Relationships with their bondsmen usually varied widely from the closeness and emotional interchange common among planters and their white children. These genteel people refused to think of their progeny as property or to punish them like slaves. They made children a focal point of their lives but relegated most slaves to the periphery. Wealthy North Carolinians were child-centered in relations with offspring but remained self-centered in relations with their slaves. Slavery and the racism so closely tied to it dulled the sensibilities of people who in dealing with their kin could be very sensitive.

Susan M. Capehart to Robert Martin, March 6, 1859, in Scotch Hall Papers; Mary B. Polk to Lucius J. Polk, March 16, 1826, in Polk, Badger, and McGehee Family Papers.

Afterthoughts

This study, although focused upon parent-child relations among the wealthiest planters in one state, should hold further implications. The domestic lives of elite North Carolinians cast new light upon their social group, their society, and the nineteenth-century family. Students of the family have long questioned what relationship existed between the modern child-centered household and the forces of industrialization and urbanization. In recent years scholars have tended to modify—or even dismiss—earlier generalizations that the modern family was the direct outcome of the industrial revolution.[1] This study cannot, of course, determine what impact industrialization had upon the family. But that the family type of an agricultural southern elite also was child-centered further suggests that industrialization and urbanization were not necessary preconditions for such family practices.

Another historiographical battle has long raged about the nature of antebellum southern society. Some observers of the nineteenth-century South have argued that the region by the time of the Civil War had become a separate and distinct civilization. Historians as widely divergent on other questions as Eugene D. Genovese and Rollin Osterweis have posited that fundamental differences divided North and South.[2]

Among scholars who believe that deep cultural cleavages existed between the sections, some such as Frank Owsley and Charles Beard

1. For example, compare William J. Goode, *World Revolution and Family Patterns* (New York, 1963), to Tamara K. Hareven, "Themes in the History of the Family," in Hareven (ed.), *Themes*, 17–23.
2. Genovese, *The Political Economy of Slavery*, 3–39, 243–78; Rollin G. Osterweis, *Romanticism and Nationalism in the Old South* (New Haven, 1949).

have pointed primarily to the agrarian nature of the South, but others have seen the planter as a pivotal figure. Osterweis has emphasized how wealthy southerners espoused a peculiar romanticism (emphasizing the cult of chivalry) that distinguished their society. To Genovese, who has been among the foremost proponents of the planter's importance for southern distinctiveness, the large slaveholder has symbolized a prebourgeois orientation. Genovese's planter, a nineteenth-century seigneur, imposed his social vision upon southern society. Those values of leisure, conspicuous consumption, and a disdain for money seeking and achievement formed a distinctive ethos infusing much of southern civilization.[3]

Historians who have challenged these views have tended to stress features of life and mind shared by both sections. In a recent essay, Edward Pessen has surveyed the voluminous literature on politics, economic development, and social structure in North and South. He has concluded that the antebellum North and South were far more alike than the conventional scholarly wisdom would lead us to believe: "Without being replicas of one another, both sections were relatively rich, powerful, aggressive, and assertive communities, socially stratified and governed by equally—and disconcertingly—oligarchic internal arrangements." David Potter in his examination of southern nationalism has admitted differences between North and South but has emphasized common cultural factors such as shared language, evangelical Protestantism, and "the common system of values which exalted progress, material success, individual self-reliance, and distrust of authority."[4]

Some scholars who have rejected the notion of a radically different

3. Frank L. Owsley, *Plain Folk of the Old South* (Baton Rouge, 1949); Charles Beard and Mary Beard, *The Rise of American Civilization* (2 vols.; New York, 1927); Osterweis, *Romanticism and Nationalism*, 8–22, 87–110, 118–31; Genovese, *The Political Economy of Slavery*, 3–39, 243–78, and *Roll, Jordan, Roll*. See also Barrington Moore, Jr., *Social Origins of Dictatorship and Democracy: Lord and Peasant in the Making of the Modern World* (Boston, 1966), 111–55; Eric J. Hobsbawm, *The Age of Capital* (New York, 1975).

4. Edward Pessen, "How Different from Each Other Were the Ante-bellum North and South?" *American Historical Review*, LXXXV (1980), 1147–48; David M. Potter, *The South and the Sectional Conflict* (Baton Rouge, 1968), 70. See also Potter, *The Impending Crisis*, 9–16, 32–43, 456–63; Grady McWhiney, *Southerners and Other Americans* (New York, 1973); Charles G. Sellers, Jr. (ed.), *The Southerner as American* (Chapel Hill, 1960).

South have posited planters' similarity to other Americans. Robert Fogel and Stanley Engerman have cast the planter as a capitalistic businessman who, in his careful calculation of profit and loss, implicitly resembled his northern contemporary. Although Carl N. Degler believes southern life possessed distinctive features, he has viewed planters as similar to other Americans in beliefs and actions.[5]

Elite North Carolinians' family practices provide a new perspective on this issue. In attitudes and behavior toward children, planters markedly resemble northerners of similar social status. Scholars such as Anne Firor Scott and Bertram Wyatt-Brown have at least implicitly differentiated southern from northern families. To them, the institution of slavery encouraged a patriarchy that dominated family life as well.[6] But close scrutiny reveals a more complicated interaction among parents and children in North Carolina's slaveholding elite. Like well-to-do northerners, planters applauded the conjugal family held together by bonds of affection. As fond, anxious parents in the nineteenth-century mold, wealthy Carolinians sought to shape their children's characters and to cultivate the youngsters' self-reliance and self-discipline. Parents wished to be friends and confidants as well as figures of authority to their children.

Similarities exist between elite North Carolinians and northerners not only in their view and manner of rearing children but also in their values. Planters sought to transmit not the values of leisure and disdain for work and material success that Genovese has imputed to them, but the importance of education, hard work, thrift, self-control, and achievement. Here they closely resembled genteel northerners.[7]

Democratic ideals also played a part in North Carolina planters' family life. Like other Americans of their day, they sought to advance all their children by education and inheritance. The great majority of planters who drew up wills divided property relatively equally among all offspring, including daughters.

5. Fogel and Engerman, *Time on the Cross*, 73–78, 129, 232–57; Degler, *Place Over Time*, 51–62.

6. Consult, for example, Anne Firor Scott, "Woman's Perspective on the Patriarchy in the 1850s," *Journal of American History*, LXI (1974), 52–64, and *The Southern Lady*, 4–79; Wyatt-Brown, "The Ideal Typology," 1–29.

7. Genovese, *The Political Economy of Slavery*, 28–31.

Wealthy Carolinians, like their northern counterparts, set material success as a goal for their heirs. Inevitably some financial tragedies, whether caused by personal incapacity or larger economic forces, occurred. But also like the genteel northerners, planters remained well-to-do across generations. Firmly entrenched within the planting and professional elites, the younger generation was a prosperous group. Despite a huge advantage in inherited wealth, they must be credited with the desire and ability to hold tenaciously to high position.[8]

Such similarities in both domestic arrangements and values cast much doubt upon the existence not only of a distinctive family type among planters but also of a separate southern culture established by that social group. Instead one must examine other aspects of antebellum life to find the important differences dividing North and South.

Despite the similarities between the domestic lives of elite northerners and southerners, one enormous difference existed: the northerners had servants, the southerners held slaves. Children in both sections learned to differentiate themselves from their "inferiors," though the southerners perhaps expressed their position with greater vehemence. But slavery was not only a set of labor and caste relations within the South, it increasingly became a point of difference between North and South. Certainly, most whites in both sections agreed upon black inferiority. But slavery for assorted reasons became distasteful to many northerners. Some opposed it as inhumane, others as uneconomical, still others disliked blacks even as slaves.[9] Tied to slavery by economic interests and racist philosophies, white southerners would not easily relinquish their "peculiar" institution. To be sure, they shared in the heightened sensibilities that led some northerners to oppose slavery. The sensitivity and sentimentality that infused planters' relations with their close relatives could not be completely stifled. But such emotions most often found their outlet in generally improved physical conditions for bondsmen. Southerners still maintained an extremely coercive labor system.

8. See Pessen, *Riches, Class and Power*; Frederic C. Jaher, "Nineteenth Century Elites in Boston and New York," *Journal of Social History*, VI (1972), 32–77.

9. See Fredrickson, *The Black Image in the White Mind*, 1–42, 97–164; Eric Foner, *Free Soil, Free Labor, Free Men: The Ideology of the Republican Party Before the Civil War* (New York, 1970).

North Carolina planters—and likely their counterparts elsewhere in the South—psychologically separated their black and white households. As slavery bifurcated planters' lives, it similarly drove a wedge between sections which otherwise shared many values.

The North Carolina
Great Planters of 1830

Name	County of Slaveholding
Alston, John J.	Chatham
Alston, Joseph John	Chatham
** Alston, Thomas	Wake
Alston, Willis	Halifax
* Amis, John D.	Northampton
Armistead, Stark	Bertie
Ashe, Colonel Samuel	New Hanover
Atkinson, Ben Ashly	Pitt
Atkinson, John, Sr.	Johnston
Avery, Isaac T.	Burke
Baird, William	Person
* Baker, John C.	Brunswick
Baker, Simmons J.	Halifax
Baskerville, George D.	Warren
Battle, James S.	Edgecombe
Benbury, Thomas	Chowan
** Bennehan, Thomas	Orange
Bethell, William	Rockingham
** Blackmore, Herrold	Duplin
Boddie, George, Sr.	Nash
Bond, Lewis	Bertie
Boyd, Richard	Warren

*Took up permanent residence outside North Carolina
**Had no legitimate direct descendants

Name	County of Slaveholding
* Boylan, Alexander	Wake
Branch, Thomas	Northampton
Brodie, John	Warren
** Brodnax, Edward T.	Rockingham
Brodnax, Robert	Rockingham
Bullock, Nancy	Warren
Bullock, Richard	Warren
Bunn, Bennett	Nash
** Burges, Thomas	Halifax
Cain, William	Orange
Cameron, Duncan	Orange
* Campbell, Marsden	Brunswick
Capehart, Cullen	Bertie
** Chambers, William	Rowan
** Clark, Colin and William	Halifax
Clark, Samuel	Beaufort
Clark, William M.	Bertie
Coffield, James	Chowan
** Coffield, Josiah	Chowan
Collins, Josiah	Chowan
Collins, Josiah, Jr.	Washington
Covington, Jane	Richmond
Cowan, Thomas	Brunswick
Cox, Thomas	Halifax
Cuningham, Alexander	Person
Dancy, Francis L.	Edgecombe
Davidson, Captain William	Mecklenburg
** Davis, Peter R.	Warren
Davis, Stephen	Warren
Davis, Thomas I.	New Hanover
Devereux, John	Bertie
** Doggett, Henry	Halifax
Downey, James, Sr.	Granville
Dudley, Edward B.	Onslow

Name	County of Slaveholding
Dula, William	Wilkes
Eaton, Susan	Granville
Eaton, William	Warren
Edmunds, Benjamin	Halifax
Ellis, Anderson	Rowan
* Ely, Horace	Washington
Erwin, William W.	Burke
Evans, Peter	Edgecombe
Foreman, Ivey	Pitt
Forney, Peter	Lincoln
Frink, Samuel	Brunswick
Gaston, Alexander	Craven
Gause, John Julius	Brunswick
* Govan, Andrew R.	Northampton
Gray, Alexander, Sr.	Randolph
Green, James S.	New Hanover
Hairston, Peter	Stokes
Hamilton, Patrick	Granville
** Harrison, Richard	Edgecombe
* Hatch, Alfred	Craven
* Hatch, Durant	Jones
* Hatch, Lemuel D.	Duplin
Haughton, Jonathan H.	Chowan
Hawkins, John D.	Franklin
Hawkins, Micajah T.	Warren
Hawkins, Philemon	Warren
Henderson, Sarah	Rowan
Herring, Rachel	Lenoir
Hill, Nathaniel M.	New Hanover
Hill, Whitmell J.	Halifax
Hill, William L.	Duplin
Hilliard, James	Nash
Hines, Richard	Edgecombe
* Hinton, Noah B.	Bertie

Name	County of Slaveholding
Hogan, William	Randolph
** Holley, Josiah	Bertie
** Huggins, Luke	Onslow
* Huie, G. L.	Rowan
Hunt, William	Granville
Johnson, Charles E.	Chowan
** Johnston, James C.	Chowan, Halifax, and Pasquotank
* Jones, Edward S.	Onslow
** Jones, Robert A.	Bertie and Halifax
* Jones, William Watts	Brunswick
Kearney, William K.	Warren
Lane, Ezekiel	New Hanover
Lea, John C.	Caswell
Little, Ann	Warren
Lockhart, William B.	Northampton
Long, Nicholas M.	Halifax
** Lord, William	Cumberland
Macay, William S.	Rowan
** McKay, James I.	Bladen
McPherson, Willie	Camden
Moody, William	Northampton
Murphy, James	Burke
Norfleet, Thomas	Bertie
Outlaw, Ralph	Bertie
Owen, John	Bladen
* Pearson, Joseph	Rowan
Perry, Colonel Jeremiah	Franklin
Perry, Jeremiah (Fork)	Franklin
Perry, John	Franklin
* Pettway, Mark H.	Halifax
Pickett, Flora	Anson
* Polk, Thomas G.	Rowan
** Pollok, George	Halifax and Northampton

Name	County of Slaveholding
Potter, Samuel, Sr.	Brunswick
Proctor, Samuel	Camden
Pugh, William	Bertie
Purnell, John, Jr.	Halifax
Rascoe, Peter	Bertie
Righton, William	Chowan
Sanders, John	Johnston
Seawell, Henry	Wake
Sills, David	Nash
Simpson, Samuel	Craven
Skinner, Joseph B.	Chowan
Slade, Henry	Martin
* Smith, Nathaniel	Craven
Smith, William R., Sr.	Halifax
Somervell, James	Warren
** Spaight, Richard D.	Craven
Speller, Thomas	Bertie
Spruill, George E.	Halifax
* Stanly, Alfred	Jones
* Taylor, John	Granville
Telfair, Hugh	Pitt
Thompson, William T.	Bertie
Toole, Geraldus	Edgecombe
Torrence, James G.	Mecklenburg
Turner, Betsy	Warren
Turner, Daniel	Warren
Turner, Thomas	Granville
Waddell, Francis N.	Brunswick
Waddell, John	Brunswick
** Ward, Edward	Onslow
* Whitfield, Nathan B.	Lenoir
Wilcox, Littlebury	Halifax
Wilkins, William W.	Northampton
Williams, Henry G.	Warren

Name	County of Slaveholding
Williams, Joseph J.	Halifax
Williams, Lewis	Bertie
* Williams, Nathaniel T.	Northampton
Williams, Robert F. J. H.	Pitt
Williams, General William	Warren
* Wilson, Robert H.	Northampton
** Wood, John E.	Bertie
Wortham, James L.	Granville
Wright, Isaac	Bladen
Yancey, Nancy	Caswell

Selected Bibliography

I. PRIMARY SOURCES

A. Manuscript Collections

Duke University Library, Durham, N.C.
  Biddle, Samuel Simpson. Papers.
  Brodnax, John G. Papers.
  Bullock, John. Papers.
  Caldwell, Tod R. Papers.
  Collins, Josiah. Papers.
  Cuningham, Alexander. Papers.
  Devereux Family Papers.
  Downey, Samuel Smith. Papers.
  Gee, Sterling, Nevill, and Joseph. Papers.
  Hill, Daniel S. Papers.
  Johnson, Charles Earl. Papers.
  Jones, Kimbrough. Papers.
  Louisburg Female and Male Academy Papers.
  Mangum, Willie P. Papers.
  Perry, Algernon S. Papers.
  Perry, Allen C. Papers.
  Person, Presly C. Papers.
  Saunders, William L. Papers.
  Sills, Louisa M. (Jelks). Papers.
  Tarry, William. Papers.
  Williams, John Buxton. Papers.

North Carolina Collection, University of North Carolina Library, Chapel Hill
  Simpson and Bryan Family Papers.

North Carolina Division of Archives and History, Raleigh
  Baker, Simmons J. Papers.
  Collins, Josiah. Papers.
  Edmondston, Catherine A. Diary.
  Pollock-Devereux Papers.

Pollock Papers.
Simpson, Samuel. Papers.

North Carolina Division of State Library, Raleigh
Hill, Stuart Hall. Papers.

Southern Historical Collection, Library of the University of North Carolina
at Chapel Hill
Alston, Archibald D. Papers.
Armistead, Stark. Papers.
Avery, Alphonso C. Papers.
Avery, Waightstill. Papers.
Badger, George E. Papers.
Badger Family Papers.
Bailey, John L. Papers.
Baker, Simmons J. Papers.
Battle Family Papers.
Benbury and Haywood Family Papers.
Bethell, Mary Jeffreys. Diary.
Brodnax, John G. Papers.
Brodnax, John Wilkins. Papers.
Bryan, Mary N. Scrapbook.
Bullock, John, and Charles E. Hamilton. Papers.
Caldwell, Tod R. Papers.
Cameron Family Papers.
Capehart, Meeta A. Papers.
Capehart, William R. Papers.
Chambers Family Papers.
Clarke, William J. Papers.
Covington, Edmund D. Book.
Covington, H. W. Papers.
Cowan, Thomas. Papers.
DeRosset Family Papers.
Devereux, Margaret M. Papers.
Donnell Family Papers.
Drane, Robert B. Papers.
Eaton, John R. Papers.
Eaton, William. Papers.
Ellis, John W. Papers.
Erwin, George Phifer. Papers.
Ferebee, Gregory, and McPherson Family Papers.
Gale and Polk Family Papers.
Gaston, William. Papers.
Gillespie and Wright Family Papers.
Hairston, Peter W. Papers.
Hamblen, Mary F. Recollections.

Hawkins Family Papers.
Henderson, John S. Papers.
Hill, John H. Papers.
Jones, Robert A. Account Book.
Lane, Levin. Papers.
Lenoir Family Papers.
Macay and McNeely Family Papers.
Mangum Family Papers.
Martin, Robert C. Papers.
Mebane, Giles. Papers.
Moore, Stephen. Papers.
Norfleet Family Papers.
Outlaw, David. Papers.
Owen, John. Papers.
Paine, Robert T. Papers.
Patton, James W. Papers.
Pearson, Richmond W. Papers.
Polk, Badger, and McGehee Family Papers.
Polk, Brown, and Ewell Family Papers.
Polk, George W. Papers.
Polk, Leonidas. Papers.
Polk and Yeatman Family Papers.
Potter and Platt Family Papers.
Rayner, Kenneth. Papers.
Recollections of Woodville.
Reid, Rufus. Papers.
Saunders, Joseph H. Papers.
Saunders, William L. Papers.
Scotch Hall Papers.
Skinner Family Papers.
Smith, Peter E. Papers.
Smith, William R. Papers.
Swann Family Papers.
Thompson, Lewis. Papers.
Turner, Josiah. Papers.
Waddell, Alfred Moore. Papers.
Walton, Thomas G. Papers.
Wilkins, Edmonia C. Papers.
Williams, Henry G. Papers.
Williamson, William B. Papers.

B. Public Records

I extensively used the excellent records of the North Carolina Division of Archives and History. Aided by their catalog, *Guide to Research Materials in the North Carolina State Archives, Section B: County Records* (3rd ed.;

Raleigh, 1975), I examined marriage bonds, estates records, wills, deeds, tax lists, and other local records, mainly from the counties where great planters resided.

I also utilized the federal manuscript censuses of population in North Carolina for 1830, 1840, 1850, and 1860. Original manuscript copies of schedules I and II for each county in 1850 and 1860 are deposited at the North Carolina Division of Archives and History; microfilm copies of all can be obtained from the National Archives and Records Service, Washington, D.C.

C. NEWSPAPERS

Cape Fear *Recorder*
North Carolina Standard
Raleigh *Register*

D. PUBLISHED MATERIALS

Barnard, Henry. "The South Atlantic States in 1833, as Seen by a New Englander." Edited by Bernard C. Steiner. *Maryland Historical Magazine*, XIII (1918), 267–386.
Bassett, John S., ed. "The Westover Journal of John A. Selden, Esqr., 1858–1862." *Smith College Studies in History*, VI (1921), 253–330.
Battle, Kemp P. *Memories of an Old Time Tar Heel*. Chapel Hill, 1945.
——, ed. *Letters and Documents Relating to the Early History of the Lower Cape Fear*. Chapel Hill, 1903.
Bonner, James C., ed. "Plantation Experiences of a New York Woman." *North Carolina Historical Review*, XXXIII (1956), 384–412, 529–46.
Bryan, Mary Norcott. *Echoes from the Past*. New Bern, N.C., 1921.
——. *A Grandmother's Recollection of Dixie*. New Bern, N.C., n.d.
Coon, Charles L., ed. *North Carolina Schools and Academies, 1790–1840: A Documentary History*. Raleigh, 1915.
Crabtree, Beth G., and James W. Patton, eds. *"Journal of a Secesh Lady": The Diary of Catherine Ann Devereux Edmondston, 1860–1866*. Raleigh, 1979.
Devereux, Margaret. *Plantation Sketches*. Cambridge, Mass., 1946.
Fitzhugh, George. *Cannibals All! or Slaves Without Masters*. Edited by C. Vann Woodward. Cambridge, Mass., 1960.
Green, Fletcher M., ed. *The Lides Go South . . . and West: The Record of a Planter Migration in 1835*. Columbia, S.C., 1952.
Hairston, Peter W., ed. "J. E. B. Stuart's Letters to His Hairston Kin, 1850–1855." *North Carolina Historical Review*, LI (1974), 261–333.
Hamilton, J. G. de Roulhac, ed. *The Papers of Thomas Ruffin*. 4 vols. Raleigh, 1918.
Hundley, Daniel R. *Social Relations in Our Southern States*. New York, 1860.
Jefferson, Thomas. *Notes on the State of Virginia*. Edited by Thomas P. Abernethy. New York, 1964.
Knight, Edgar W., ed. *A Documentary History of Education in the South Before 1860*. 5 vols. Chapel Hill, 1949.

Lane, Lunsford. *The Narrative of Lunsford Lane, Formerly of Raleigh, N.C. . . .* 3rd ed. Boston, 1845.

Lathrop, Barnes A., ed. "A Southern Girl at Saratoga Springs, 1834." *North Carolina Historical Review*, XV (1938), 159–60.

McLean, Robert C., ed. "A Yankee Tutor in the Old South." *North Carolina Historical Review*, XLVII (1970), 41–85.

McPherson, Elizabeth G., ed. "Unpublished Letters from North Carolinians to Polk." *North Carolina Historical Review*, XVI (1939), 174–200; XVII (1940), 37–66, 139–66, 249–66.

Miller, Stephen F. *Recollections of Newbern Fifty Years Ago.* Raleigh, 1874.

Montgomery, Lizzie W. *Sketches of Old Warrenton, North Carolina.* Raleigh, 1924.

Olmsted, Frederick Law. *A Journey in the Seaboard Slave States, with Remarks on Their Economy.* New York, 1856.

Page, Thomas Nelson. *Social Life in Old Virginia.* New York, 1897.

Parker, Robert J., ed. "A Yankee in North Carolina: Observations of Thomas Oliver Larkin, 1821–26." *North Carolina Historical Review*, XIV (1937), 325–42.

Poe, Clarence. "Wherein I Set a Good Example: Recording Traditions of an Average Southern Family, 1675–1865." *South Atlantic Quarterly*, XXXV (1936), 27–41.

Rawick, George P., ed. *The American Slave: A Composite Autobiography.* 17 vols. Westport, Conn., 1972.

Revised Statutes of the State of North Carolina. Raleigh, 1837.

Rose, Willie Lee, ed. *A Documentary History of Slavery in North America.* New York, 1976.

Sanders, John L., ed. "Diary of Ruffin Wirt Tomlinson." *North Carolina Historical Review*, XXX (1953), 86–114, 233–60.

Shanks, Henry T., ed. *The Papers of Willie Person Mangum.* 5 vols. Raleigh, 1952–56.

Tolbert, Noble J., ed. *The Papers of John Willis Ellis.* 2 vols. Raleigh, 1964.

Watters, Fanny C. *Plantation Memories of the Cape Fear River Country.* Asheville, N.C., 1944.

Wheeler, John H. *Historical Sketches of North Carolina from 1584 to 1851.* Baltimore, 1964.

———. *Reminiscences and Memoirs of North Carolina and Eminent North Carolinians.* Columbus, Ohio, 1884.

Wills, William Henry. "A Southern Sulky Ride in 1837, from North Carolina to Alabama." *Publications of the Southern History Association*, VI (1902), 471–83; VII (1903), 7–16, 79–84, 187–92.

II. SECONDARY SOURCES

Aldrich, C. Anderson. "The Advisability of Breast Feeding." *Journal of the American Medical Association*, CXXXV (1947), 915–16.

Allcott, John V. "Robert Donaldson: The First North Carolinian to Become

Prominent in the Arts." *North Carolina Historical Review*, LII (1975), 333–66.

Allen, Madeline May. "A Historical Study of Moravian Education in North Carolina: The Evolution and Practice of the Moravian Concept of Education as It Applied to Women." Ph.D. dissertation, Florida State University, 1971.

Allen, W. C. *History of Halifax County*. Boston, 1918.

Alterman, Hyman. *Counting People: The Census in History*. New York, 1969.

Anderson, Michael. *Family Structure in Nineteenth Century Lancashire*. London, 1971.

Ariès, Philippe. *Centuries of Childhood: A Social History of Family Life*. Translated by Robert Baldick. New York, 1962.

———. *Western Attitudes Toward Death from the Middle Ages to the Present*. Translated by Patricia M. Ranum. Baltimore, 1974.

Arthur, John P. *Western North Carolina: A History*. Raleigh, 1914.

Ashe, Samuel A., Stephen B. Weeks, and Charles L. Van Noppen, eds. *Biographical History of North Carolina from Colonial Times to the Present*. 8 vols. Greensboro, N.C., 1905–1917.

Auwers, Linda. "Fathers, Sons, and Wealth in Colonial Windsor, Connecticut." *Journal of Family History*, III (1978), 136–49.

———. "From One Generation to Another: Mobility in Seventeenth Century Windsor, Connecticut." *William and Mary Quarterly*, 3rd ser., XXXI (1974), 79–95.

Baltzell, E. Digby. *Philadelphia Gentlemen: The Making of a National Upper Class*. Glencoe, Ill., 1958.

Bancroft, Frederic. *Slave-Trading in the Old South*. Baltimore, 1931.

Barney, William. *The Road to Secession: A New Perspective on the Old South*. New York, 1972.

Baskervill, Patrick H. *The Hamiltons of Burnside, North Carolina and Their Ancestors and Descendants*. Richmond, 1916.

Bassett, John S. *Slavery in the State of North Carolina*. Baltimore, 1899.

Bateman, Fred, James Foust, and Thomas Weiss. "The Participation of Planters in Manufacturing in the Ante Bellum South." *Agricultural History*, XLVIII (1974), 277–97.

Bates, Alan. "Parental Roles in Courtship." *Social Forces*, XX (1942), 483–86.

Battle, Kemp P. *The Early History of Raleigh. . . .* Raleigh, 1893.

———. *History of the University of North Carolina. . . .* 2 vols. Raleigh, 1907–1912.

Beard, Charles, and Mary Beard. *The Rise of American Civilization*. 2 vols. New York, 1927.

Beard, Mary R. *Woman as Force in History: A Study in Traditions and Realities*. New York, 1946.

Beigel, Hugo G. "Romantic Love." *American Sociological Review*, XVI (1951), 326–34.

Bell, Robert R. *Marriage and Family Interaction*. 4th ed. Homewood, Ill., 1975.

Benedek, Therese. "Psychological Aspects of Mothering." *American Journal of Orthopsychiatry*, XXVI (1956), 272–78.

Berkner, Lutz. "Recent Research on the History of the Family in Western Europe." *Journal of Marriage and the Family*, XXXV (1973), 395–405.

———. "The Use and Misuse of Census Data for the Historical Analysis of Family Structure." *Journal of Interdisciplinary History*, V (1975), 721–38.

Berlin, Ira. *Slaves Without Masters: The Free Negro in the Antebellum South*. New York, 1974.

Bertelson, David. *The Lazy South*. New York, 1967.

Bieder, Robert E. "Kinship as a Factor in Migration." *Journal of Marriage and the Family*, XXXV (1973), 429–39.

Billings, Dwight B., Jr. *Planters and the Making of a "New South": Class, Politics, and Development in North Carolina, 1865–1900*. Chapel Hill, 1979.

Bishir, Catherine W. "The 'Unpainted Aristocracy': The Beach Cottages of Old Nags Head." *North Carolina Historical Review*, LIV (1977), 367–92.

Blair, Marian H. "Contemporary Evidence—Salem Boarding School, 1834–1944." *North Carolina Historical Review*, XXVII (1950), 142–61.

Blake, Russell L. "Ties of Intimacy: Social Values and Personal Relationships of Ante-bellum Slaveholders." Ph.D. dissertation, University of Michigan, 1978.

Blassingame, John W. *The Slave Community: Plantation Life in the Antebellum South*. New York, 1972.

Bluche, François. *La Vie quotidienne de la noblesse française au XVIIIe siècle*. Paris, 1973.

Blumin, Stuart M. *The Urban Threshold: Growth and Change in a Nineteenth Century American Community*. Chicago, 1976.

Boddie, John Thomas, and John Bennett Boddie. *Boddie and Allied Families*. Chicago[?], 1918.

Bonner, James C. "Profile of a Late Antebellum Community." *American Historical Review*, XLIX (1944), 663–80.

Boucher, Ann Williams. "Wealthy Planter Families in Nineteenth-Century Alabama." Ph.D. dissertation, University of Connecticut, 1978.

Boyd, W. K. "Currency and Banking in North Carolina, 1790–1836." *Trinity College Historical Society Papers*, X (1914), 52–86.

Branca, Patricia. *Silent Sisterhood: Middle Class Women in the Victorian Home*. Pittsburgh, 1975.

Breen, T. H. "Horses and Gentlemen: The Cultural Significance of Gambling Among the Gentry of Virginia." *William and Mary Quarterly*, 3rd ser., XXXIV (1977), 239–57.

Brewster, Lawrence Fay. *Summer Migrations and Resorts of South Carolina Low Country Planters*. Durham, N.C., 1947.

Bridgers, Henry C. *The Story of Banking in Tarboro*. Tarboro, N.C., 1969.

Bridges, William E. "Family Patterns and Social Values in America, 1825–1875." *American Quarterly*, XVII (1965), 3–11.

Brown, C. K. "A History of the Piedmont Railroad Company." *North Carolina Historical Review*, III (1926), 198–222.

Brown, James Stephen. "Social Class, Intermarriage and Church Membership in a Kentucky Community." *American Journal of Sociology*, LVII (1951), 232–42.

Brown, Joseph P. *The Commonwealth of Onslow: A History*. New Bern, N.C., 1960.

Brown, Norman D. *Edward Stanly: Whiggery's Tarheel "Conqueror."* University, Ala., 1974.

Bruce, Dickson D., Jr. "Hunting: Dimensions of Antebellum Southern Culture." *Mississippi Quarterly*, XXX (1977), 259–81.

———. "Religion, Society and Culture in the Old South: A Comparative View." *American Quarterly*, XXVI (1974), 399–416.

Burgess, Fred. *Randolph County: Economic and Social*. Chapel Hill, 1924.

Burnham, John C. "American Historians and the Subject of Sex." *Societas*, II (1972), 307–316.

Calhoun, Arthur W. *A Social History of the American Family: From Colonial Times to the Present*. 3 vols. Cleveland, 1917–19.

Camp, Cornelia. *Sketches of Burke County*. Morganton, N.C., 1934.

Campbell, Randolph B. "Planters and Plain Folk: Harrison County, Texas, as a Test Case, 1850–1860." *Journal of Southern History*, XL (1974), 369–98.

Campbell, Randolph B., and Richard G. Lowe. *Wealth and Power in Antebellum Texas*. College Station, Tex., 1977.

Cappon, Lester J. "Iron-Making—A Forgotten Industry of North Carolina." *North Carolina Historical Review*, IX (1932), 331–48.

Cardwell, Guy A. "The Duel in the Old South: Crux of a Concept." *South Atlantic Quarterly*, LXVI (1967), 50–69.

Cash, W. J. *The Mind of the South*. New York, 1941.

Cathey, C. O. *Agricultural Developments in North Carolina, 1783–1860*. Chapel Hill, 1956.

Cavan, Ruth S. *The American Family*. 3rd ed. New York, 1963.

———, ed. *Marriage and Family in the Modern World: A Book of Readings*. 3rd ed. New York, 1969.

Clinton, Catherine. "The Plantation Mistress: Another Side of Southern Slavery, 1780–1835." Ph.D. dissertation, Princeton University, 1980.

Coale, Ansley J., and Melvin Zelnik. *New Estimates of Fertility and Population in the United States: A Study of Annual White Births. . . .* Princeton, 1963.

Conner, Paul. "Patriarchy: Old World and New." *American Quarterly*, XVII (1965), 48–62.

Corbitt, David. *The Formation of the North Carolina Counties, 1663–1943*. Raleigh, 1969.

Coser, Rose Laub, ed. *The Family: Its Structure and Functions.* 2nd ed. New York, 1974.

Coulter, E. Merton. *College Life in the Old South.* Athens, Ga., 1951.

Counihan, Harold J. "North Carolina, 1815–1836: State and Local Perspectives on the Age of Jackson." Ph.D. dissertation, University of North Carolina, 1971.

————. "The North Carolina Constitutional Convention of 1835: A Study in Jacksonian Democracy." *North Carolina Historical Review,* XLVI (1969), 335–64.

Cumming, Elaine, and David M. Schneider. "Sibling Solidarity: A Property of American Kinship." *American Anthropologist,* LXIII (1961), 498–505

Cyclopedia of Eminent and Representative Men of the Carolinas of the Nineteenth Century. 2 vols. Madison, 1892.

Daumard, Adeline. *La Bourgeoisie parisienne de 1815 à 1848.* Paris, 1963.

Davidson, Chalmers G. "Catawba Springs—Carolina's Spa." *North Carolina Historical Review,* XXVIII (1951), 414–20.

————. *The Last Foray: The South Carolina Planters of 1860.* Columbia, S.C., 1971.

————. *The Plantation World Around Davidson: The Story of North Mecklenburg "Before the War."* Davidson, N.C., 1970.

Davis, Edward H. *Historical Sketches of Franklin County.* Raleigh, 1948.

Davis, Richard Beale. *Intellectual Life in Jefferson's Virginia, 1790–1830.* Chapel Hill, 1964.

Degler, Carl N. *At Odds: Women and the Family in America from the Revolution to the Present.* New York, 1980.

————. *The Other South: Southern Dissenters in the Nineteenth Century.* New York, 1974.

————. *Place Over Time: The Continuity of Southern Distinctiveness.* Baton Rouge, 1977.

de Mause, Lloyd, ed. *The History of Childhood.* New York, 1975.

Demos, John. *A Little Commonwealth: Family Life in Plymouth Colony.* New York, 1970.

Dew, Charles B. "Disciplining Slave Ironworkers in the Antebellum South: Coercion, Conciliation and Accommodation." *American Historial Review,* LXXIX (1974), 393–418.

Dick, Everett N. *The Dixie Frontier: A Social History of the Southern Frontier. . . .* New York, 1948.

Doherty, Robert. *Society and Power: Five New England Towns, 1800–1860.* Amherst, Mass., 1977.

Douglas, Ann. *The Feminization of American Culture.* New York, 1977.

Drake, William E. *Higher Education in North Carolina Before 1860.* New York, 1964.

Eaton, Clement. *The Growth of Southern Civilization, 1790–1860.* New York, 1961.

———. "Slave-Hiring in the Upper South: A Step Toward Freedom." *Mississippi Valley Historical Review,* XLVI (1960), 663–78.

Elkins, Stanley. *Slavery: A Problem in American Institutional and Intellectual Life.* Chicago, 1959.

Ellis, James A. *History of the Bunn Family in America.* Chicago, 1928.

Engerman, Stanley L. "Studying the Black Family." *Journal of Family History,* III (1978), 78–101.

Escott, Paul D. *Slavery Remembered: A Record of Twentieth-Century Slave Narratives.* Chapel Hill, 1979.

Eshleman, J. Ross, ed. *Perspectives in Marriage and the Family: Text and Readings.* Boston, 1969.

Ezell, John S. "A Southern Education for Southrons." *Journal of Southern History,* XVII (1951), 303–327.

Falk, Stanley L. "The Warrenton Female Academy of Jacob Mordecai, 1809–1818." *North Carolina Historical Review,* XXXV (1958), 281–98.

Farber, Bernard, ed. *Kinship and Family Organization.* New York, 1966.

Firth, Raymond, ed. *Two Studies of Kinship in London.* London, 1956.

Fischer, David Hackett. *Growing Old in America.* New York, 1977.

Flandrin, Jean-Louis. *Families in Former Times: Kinship, Household and Sexuality in Early Modern France.* Translated by Richard Southern. Cambridge, 1979.

Fogel, Robert W., and Stanley L. Engerman. *Time on the Cross: The Economics of American Negro Slavery.* Boston, 1974.

Foner, Eric. *Free Soil, Free Labor, Free Men: The Ideology of the Republican Party Before the Civil War.* New York, 1970.

Forster, Robert. *The House of Saulx-Tavanes: Versailles and Burgundy, 1700–1830.* Baltimore, 1971.

———. *The Nobility of Toulouse in the Eighteenth Century: A Social and Economic Study.* Baltimore, 1960.

Forster, Robert, and Orest Ranum, eds. *Family and Society: Selections from the Annales, Economies, Sociétés, Civilisations.* Translated by Elborg Forster and Patricia Ranum. Baltimore, 1976.

———, eds. *Rural Society in France: Selections from the Annales, Economies, Sociétés, Civilisations.* Translated by Elborg Forster and Patricia Ranum. Baltimore, 1977.

Fox, Claire E. "Pregnancy, Childbirth, and Early Infancy in Anglo-American Culture, 1675–1830." Ph.D. dissertation, University of Pennsylvania, 1966.

Fox, Robin. *Kinship and Marriage: An Anthropological Perspective.* Harmondsworth, 1967.

Franklin, John Hope. *The Free Negro in North Carolina, 1790–1860.* Chapel Hill, 1943.

———. *The Militant South, 1800–1861.* Cambridge, Mass., 1956.

———. *A Southern Odyssey: Travelers in the Antebellum North.* Baton Rouge, 1976.

————. "Masters and Mudsills: The Role of Race in the Planter Ideology of
Fredrickson, George M. *The Black Image in the White Mind: The Debate on
Afro-American Character and Destiny, 1817–1914.* New York, 1971.
South Carolina." In Jack R. Censer and N. Steven Steinert, eds. *South Atlantic Urban Studies,* II (1978), 34–48.

Freehling, William W. *Prelude to Civil War: The Nullification Controversy in South Carolina, 1816–1836.* New York, 1966.

Friedman, Lawrence M. "Patterns of Testation in the Nineteenth Century: A Study of Essex County (New Jersey) Wills." *American Journal of Legal History,* VIII (1964), 34–53.

Frisch, John R. "Youth Culture in America, 1790–1865." Ph.D. dissertation, University of Missouri, 1970.

Furstenberg, Frank E., Jr. "Industrialization and the American Family: A Look Backward." *American Sociological Review,* XXXI (1966), 326–37.

Galloway, L. E., and R. K. Vedder. "Mobility of Native Americans." *Journal of Economic History,* XXXI (1971), 613–49.

Gass, W. Conrad. "A Felicitous Life: Lucy Martin Battle, 1805–1874." *North Carolina Historical Review,* LII (1975), 367–93.

Gates, Paul W. "Southern Investments in Northern Lands Before the Civil War." *Journal of Southern History,* V (1939), 155–85.

Gathorne-Hardy, Jonathan. *The Rise and Fall of the Victorian Nanny.* London, 1972.

Gay, Dorothy Ann. "The Tangled Skein of Romanticism and Violence in the Old South: The Southern Response to Abolitionism and Feminism." Ph.D. dissertation, University of North Carolina, 1975.

Gehrke, William Herman. "The German Element in Rowan and Cabarrus Counties, North Carolina." M.A. thesis, University of North Carolina, 1934.

Gélis, Jacques, Mireille Laget, and Marie-France Morel. *Entrer dans la vie: Naissances et enfances dans la France traditionelle.* Paris, 1978.

Genovese, Eugene D. *In Red and Black: Marxian Explorations in Southern and Afro-American History.* New York, 1971.

————. *The Political Economy of Slavery: Studies in the Economy and Society of the Slave South.* New York, 1965.

————. *Roll, Jordan, Roll: The World the Slaves Made.* New York, 1974.

————. *The World the Slaveholders Made: Two Essays in Interpretation.* New York, 1969.

————. "Yeomen Farmers in a Slaveholders' Democracy." *Agricultural History,* XLIX (1975), 331–43.

George, Carol V. R., ed. *"Remember the Ladies": New Perspectives on Women in American History.* Syracuse, 1975.

Giesey, Ralph E. "Rules of Inheritance and Strategies of Mobility in Prerevolutionary France." *American Historical Review,* LXXXII (1977), 271–89.

Gillis, John R. *Youth and History: Tradition in European Age Relations, 1770–Present.* New York, 1974.

Glass, D. V., and D. E. C. Eversley, eds. *Population in History: Essays in Historical Demography.* London, 1965.

Goode, William J. "Force and Violence in the Family." *Journal of Marriage and the Family,* XXXIII (1971), 624–36.

———. "The Theoretical Importance of Love." *American Sociological Review,* XXIV (1959), 38–47.

———. *World Revolution and Family Patterns.* New York, 1963.

Goody, John R. "Strategies of Heirship." *Comparative Studies in Society and History,* XV (1973), 3–20.

———, comp. *Kinship: Selected Readings.* London, 1971.

Goody, John R., et al., eds. *Family and Inheritance: Rural Society in Western Europe, 1200–1800.* New York, 1976.

Gordon, Michael, and M. Charles Bernstein. "Mate Choice and Domestic Life in the Nineteenth Century Marriage Manual." *Journal of Marriage and the Family,* XXXII (1970), 665–73.

Goubert, Pierre. "Historical Demography and the Reinterpretation of Early Modern French History: A Research Review." *Journal of Interdisciplinary History,* I (1970), 37–48.

Grant, Daniel Lindsay, ed. *Alumni History of the University of North Carolina.* 2nd ed. Durham, N.C., 1924.

Gray, Lewis Cecil. *History of Agriculture in the Southern United States to 1860.* 2 vols. Washington, D.C., 1933.

Green, Fletcher M. "Gold Mining: A Forgotten Industry of Ante-bellum North Carolina." *North Carolina Historical Review,* XIV (1937), 133–55.

———, ed. *Essays in Southern History.* Chapel Hill, 1949.

Greenberg, Michael S. "Gentlemen Slaveholders: The Social Outlook of the Virginia Planter Class." Ph.D. dissertation, Rutgers University, 1972.

Greenfield, Sidney M. "Industrialization and the Family in Sociological Theory." *American Journal of Sociology,* LXVII (1961), 312–22.

Greven, Philip J., Jr. *Four Generations: Population, Land, and Family in Colonial Massachusetts.* Ithaca, N.Y., 1970.

———. *The Protestant Temperament: Patterns of Child-Rearing, Religious Experience, and the Self in Early America.* New York, 1977.

Grimmelmann, Jan Lewis. "This World and the Next: Religion, Death, Success, and Love in Jefferson's Virginia." Ph.D. dissertation, University of Michigan, 1977.

Griswold, Robert Lawrence. "The Character of the Family in Rural California, 1850–1890." Ph.D. dissertation, Stanford University, 1979.

Grossberg, Michael C. "Law and the Family in Nineteenth Century America." Ph.D. dissertation, Brandeis University, 1979.

Groves, Joseph A. *The Alstons and Allstons of North and South Carolina.* . . . Atlanta, 1901.

Gutman, Herbert G. *The Black Family in Slavery and Freedom, 1750–1925*. New York, 1976.

Guttsman, W. L., ed. *The English Ruling Class*. London, 1969.

Hagstrom, Warren O., and Jeffrey K. Hadden. "Sentiment and Kinship Terminology in American Society." *Journal of Marriage and the Family*, XXVII (1965), 324–32.

Hall, Peter Dobkin. "Family Structure and Class Consolidation Among the Boston Brahmins." Ph.D. dissertation, State University of New York at Stony Brook, 1973.

Handlin, Oscar, and Mary Handlin. *Facing Life: Youth and the Family in American History*. Boston, 1971.

Hareven, Tamara K. "Cycles, Courses and Cohorts: Reflections on Theoretical and Methodological Approaches to the Historical Study of Family Development." *Journal of Social History*, XII (1978), 97–109.

———, ed. *Family and Kin in Urban Communities, 1700–1930*. New York, 1977.

———, ed. *Themes in the History of the Family*. Worcester, Mass., 1978.

———, ed. *Transitions: The Family and the Life Course in Historical Perspective*. New York, 1978.

Hareven, Tamara K., and Maris A. Vinovskis, eds. *Family and Population in Nineteenth-Century America*. Princeton, 1978.

Henretta, James A. *The Evolution of American Society, 1700–1815: An Interdisciplinary Analysis*. Lexington, Mass., 1973.

Henry, Louis, and Claude Lévy. "Ducs et pairs sous l'Ancien Régime: Caractéristiques démographiques d'une caste." *Population* (1960), 807–830.

Hill, John Hampden. *Stories of the Old Plantations*. Baltimore, 1933.

Hinshaw, Clifford R., Jr. "North Carolina Canals Before 1860." *North Carolina Historical Review*, XXV (1948), 1–56.

Hixson, Ivy M. "Academic Requirements of Salem College, 1854–1909." *North Carolina Historical Review*, XXVII, (1950), 419–29.

Hobsbawm, Eric J. *The Age of Capital*. New York, 1975.

Hollingsworth, T. H. "The Demography of the British Peerage." Supplement to *Population Studies*, XVIII (1964), i–108.

Houghton, Walter E. *The Victorian Frame of Mind, 1830–1870*. New Haven, 1957.

Howe, Daniel Walker. *The Unitarian Conscience: Harvard Moral Philosophy, 1805–1861*. Cambridge, Mass., 1970.

———, ed. *Victorian America*. Philadelphia, 1976.

Huggins, Nathan I. *Black Odyssey: The Afro-American Ordeal in Slavery*. New York, 1977.

Huneycutt, James E., and Ida C. Huneycutt. *A History of Richmond County*. . . . Raleigh, 1976.

Hunter, C. L. *Sketches of Western North Carolina: Historical and Biographical*. Baltimore, 1970.

Jaher, Frederic C. "Nineteenth Century Elites in Boston and New York." *Journal of Social History*, VI (1972), 32–77.

Jeffrey, Kirk. "The Family as Utopian Retreat from the City: The Nineteenth Century Contribution." *Soundings*, LV (1972), 21–41.

Johnson, Guion G. *Ante-bellum North Carolina: A Social History*. Chapel Hill, 1937.

———. "Courtship and Marriage Customs in Antebellum North Carolina." *North Carolina Historical Review*, VIII (1931), 384–402.

Johnson, Michael P. "Planters and Patriarchy: Charleston, 1800–1860." *Journal of Southern History*, XLVI (1980), 45–72.

Johnson, Paul E. *A Shopkeeper's Millennium: Society and Revivals in Rochester, New York, 1815–1837*. New York, 1978.

Jordan, Weymouth T. *Antebellum Alabama: Town and Country*. Tallahassee, Fla., 1957.

———. *Hugh Davis and His Alabama Plantation*. University, Ala., 1948.

Keim, C. Ray. "Primogeniture and Entail in Colonial Virginia." *William and Mary Quarterly*, 3rd ser., XXV (1968), 545–86.

Kett, Joseph F. "Adolescence and Youth in Nineteenth Century America." *Journal of Interdisciplinary History*, II (1971), 283–98.

———. *Rites of Passage: Adolescence in America, 1790 to the Present*. New York, 1977.

Kiefer, Monica. *American Children Through Their Books, 1700–1835*. Philadelphia, 1948.

King, Henry T. *Sketches of Pitt County*. Raleigh, 1911.

Knight, Edgar W. *Public School Education in North Carolina*. New York, 1969.

Knights, Peter W. "Accuracy of Age Reporting in the Manuscript Federal Censuses of 1850 and 1860." *Historical Methods Newsletter*, IV (1971), 79–83.

———. *The Plain People of Boston, 1830–1860: A Study in City Growth*. New York, 1971.

Konkle, Burton A. *John Motley Morehead and the Development of North Carolina, 1796–1866*. Philadelphia, 1922.

Kuhn, Anne L. *The Mother's Role in Childhood Education: New England Concepts, 1830–1860*. New Haven, 1947.

Kulikoff, Allan. "Tobacco and Slaves: Population, Economy, and Society in Eighteenth Century Prince George's County, Maryland." Ph.D. dissertation, Brandeis University, 1976.

Land, Aubrey C., comp. *Bases of the Plantation Society*. New York, 1969.

Lantz, Herman R., *et al.* "Pre-Industrial Patterns in the Colonial Family in America: A Content Analysis of Colonial Magazines." *American Sociological Review*, XXXIII (1968), 413–26.

Laslett, Barbara. "The Family as a Public and Private Institution: An Historical Perspective." *Journal of Marriage and the Family*, XXXV (1973), 480–94.

Laslett, Peter. *Family Life and Illicit Love in Earlier Generations*. Cambridge, 1977.
———. *The World We Have Lost: England Before the Industrial Age*. 2nd ed. New York, 1971.
Lebergott, Stanley. "Migration Within the United States, 1800–1960: Some New Estimates." *Journal of Economic History*, XXX (1970), 839–47.
Le Brun, François. *La Vie conjugale sous l'Ancien Régime*. Paris, 1975.
Lebsock, Suzanne D. "Radical Reconstruction and the Property Rights of Southern Women." *Journal of Southern History*, XLIII (1977), 195–216.
Lee, Lawrence. *The Lower Cape Fear in Colonial Days*. Chapel Hill, 1965.
———. *New Hanover County: A Brief History*. 2nd ed. Raleigh, 1977.
Lefler, Hugh T., and Albert Newsome. *North Carolina: The History of a Southern State*. 3rd ed. Chapel Hill, 1973.
Levine, Lawrence W. *Black Culture and Black Consciousness: Afro-American Folk Thought from Slavery to Freedom*. New York, 1977.
Lewis, Henry W. "Horses and Horsemen in Northampton Before 1900." *North Carolina Historical Review*, LI (1974), 126–48.
———. *Northampton Parishes*. Jackson, N.C., 1951.
Lichtman, Allan J., and Joan R. Challinor, eds. *Kin and Communities: Families in America*. Washington, D.C., 1979.
Lidz, Theodore. *The Person: His or Her Development Throughout the Life Cycle*. 2nd ed. New York, 1976.
Litwack, Leon F. *Been in the Storm So Long: The Aftermath of Slavery*. New York, 1979.
———. *North of Slavery: The Negro in the Free States, 1790–1860*. Chicago, 1961.
Litwak, Eugene. "Geographical Mobility and Extended Family Cohesion." *American Sociological Review*, XXV (1960), 385–94.
Longton, William Henry. "Banking and Bankers in North Carolina, 1819–1843." M.A. thesis, University of North Carolina, 1965.
Lynch, William O. "The Westward Flow of Southern Colonists Before 1861." *Journal of Southern History*, IX (1943), 303–327.
McColley, Robert. *Slavery and Jeffersonian Virginia*. 2nd ed. Urbana, Ill., 1973.
McCormick, John G. *Personnel of the Convention of 1861*. Chapel Hill, 1900.
McDonald, Forrest, and Grady McWhiney. "The Ante-bellum Southern Herdsman: A Reinterpretation." *Journal of Southern History*, XLI (1975), 147–66.
———. "The South from Self-Sufficiency to Peonage: An Interpretation." *American Historical Review*, LXXXV (1980), 1095–1118.
Macfarlane, Alan. *The Family Life of Ralph Josselin, a Seventeenth Century Clergyman: An Essay in Historical Anthropology*. Cambridge, 1970.
McGlone, Robert Elno. "Suffer the Children: The Emergence of Modern Middle Class Family Life in America, 1820–1870." Ph.D. dissertation, University of California at Los Angeles, 1971.

McGowen, Faison W. *Flashes of Duplin's History and Government*. Kenansville, N.C., 1971.

McIver, George W. "North Carolinians at West Point Before the Civil War." *North Carolina Historical Review*, VII (1930), 15–45.

McLachlan, James. *American Boarding Schools: A Historical Study*. New York, 1970.

McLoughlin, William G. "Evangelical Childrearing in the Age of Jackson: Francis Wayland's Views on When and How to Subdue the Willfulness of Children." *Journal of Social History*, IX (1975), 20–43.

———. *The Meaning of Henry Ward Beecher: An Essay on the Shifting Values of Mid-Victorian America*. New York, 1970.

McMillen, Sally. "Mother or Mammy? Infant Feeding in the Antebellum South." Paper, Duke University, 1981.

McReynolds, James Michael. "Family Life in a Borderland Community: Nacogdoches, Texas, 1779–1861." Ph.D. dissertation, Texas Tech. University, 1978.

McWhiney, Grady. *Southerners and Other Americans*. New York, 1973.

Main, Jackson T. "The One Hundred." *William and Mary Quarterly*, 3rd ser., XI (1954), 354–84.

———. *The Social Structure of Revolutionary America*. Princeton, 1965.

Malone, Michael T. "The Episcopal School of North Carolina, 1832–1842." *North Carolina Historical Review*, XLIX (1972), 178–94.

Mandle, Jay R. "The Plantation Economy: An Essay in Definition." *Science and Society*, XXXVI (1972), 49–62.

Martinez-Alier, Verena. *Marriage, Class and Colour in Nineteenth Century Cuba: A Study of Racial Attitudes and Sexual Values in a Slave Society*. Cambridge, 1974.

Mathews, Donald G. *Religion in the Old South*. Chicago, 1977.

———. *Slavery and Methodism: A Chapter in American Morality*. Princeton, 1965.

Mead, Margaret, and Martha Wolfenstein, eds. *Childhood in Contemporary Cultures*. Chicago, 1955.

Mechling, Jay E. "Advice to Historians on Advice to Mothers." *Journal of Social History*, IX (1975), 44–63.

Medley, Mary Louise. *History of Anson County, North Carolina, 1750–1976*. Wadesboro, N.C., 1976.

Menn, Joseph K. "The Large Slaveholders of the Deep South, 1860." Ph.D. dissertation, University of Texas, 1964.

———. *The Large Slaveholders of Louisiana—1860*. New Orleans, 1964.

Merrens, Harry R. *Colonial North Carolina in the Eighteenth Century: A Study in Historical Geography*. Chapel Hill, 1964.

Milden, James W. "The Sacred Sanctuary: Family Life in Nineteenth Century America." Ph.D. dissertation, University of Maryland, 1974.

Miles, Edwin A. "The Old South and the Classical World." *North Carolina Historical Review*, XLVIII (1971), 258–75.

Miller, Elinor, and Eugene D. Genovese, eds. *Plantation, Town, and County: Essays on the Local History of American Slave Society.* Urbana, Ill., 1974.

Mingay, G. E. *English Landed Society in the Eighteenth Century.* London, 1963.

Mitchell, Memory F. "The Bar Examination and Beginning Years of Legal Practice in North Carolina, 1820–1860." *North Carolina Historical Review,* XXIX (1952), 159–70.

———. "The Legal Profession in North Carolina, 1820–1860." M.A. thesis, University of North Carolina, 1949.

———. "Off to Africa—with Judicial Blessing." *North Carolina Historical Review,* LIII (1976), 265–87.

Modell, John. "Family and Fertility on the Indiana Frontier, 1820." *American Quarterly,* XXIII (1971), 615–34.

———. "The Peopling of a Working Class Ward: Reading, Pennsylvania, 1850." *Journal of Social History,* V (1971), 71–95.

Mohr, James C. *Abortion in America: The Origins and Evolution of National Policy, 1800–1900.* New York, 1978.

Moore, Barrington, Jr. *Social Origins of Dictatorship and Democracy: Lord and Peasant in the Making of the Modern World.* Boston, 1966.

Morgan, Edmund S. *The Puritan Family: Religion and Domestic Relations in Seventeenth Century New England.* New York, 1966.

———. *Virginians at Home: Family Life in the Eighteenth Century.* Williamsburg, Va., 1952.

Mullin, Gerald W. *Flight and Rebellion: Slave Resistance in Eighteenth Century Virginia.* New York, 1972.

Nash, Gary, B., ed. *Class and Society in Early America.* Englewood Cliffs, N.J., 1970.

Newsome, Albert R. "Twelve North Carolina Counties in 1810–1811." *North Carolina Historical Review,* V (1928), 419–46; VI (1929), 171–79, 281–309.

Niemi, Albert W., Jr. "Inequality in the Distribution of Slave Wealth: The Cotton South and Other Southern Agricultural Regions." *Journal of Economic History,* XXXVII (1977), 747–53.

Norton, Clarence C. *The Democratic Party in Ante-bellum North Carolina, 1835–1861.* Chapel Hill, 1930.

Norton, Susan L. "Marital Migration in Essex County, Massachusetts, in the Colonial and Early Federal Periods." *Journal of Marriage and the Family,* XXXV (1973), 406–418.

Nye, F. Ivan, *et al. Role Structure and Analysis of the Family.* Beverly Hills, Calif., 1976.

Oakes, James. *The Ruling Race: A History of American Slaveholders.* New York, 1982.

O'Brien, Gail W. "Power and Influence in Mecklenburg County, 1850–1880." *North Carolina Historical Review,* LIV (1977), 120–44.

Olsen, Otto. "Historians and the Extent of Slave Ownership in the Southern United States." *Civil War History,* XVIII (1972), 101–116.

Osterweis, Rollin G. *Romanticism and Nationalism in the Old South*. New Haven, 1949.

Owens, Leslie Howard. *This Species of Property: Slave Life and Culture in the Old South*. New York, 1976.

Owsley, Frank L. "The Pattern of Migration and Settlement on the Southern Frontier." *Journal of Southern History*, XI (1945), 147–76.

———. *Plain Folk of the Old South*. Baton Rouge, 1949.

Owsley, Frank L., and Harriet Owsley. "Economic Basis of Society in the Late Antebellum South." *Journal of Southern History*, VI (1940), 24–45.

Parkhurst, Jessie. "The Role of the Black Mammy in the Plantation Household." *Journal of Negro History*, XXIII (1938), 349–69.

Parks, Joseph H. *General Leonidas Polk, C.S.A.: The Fighting Bishop*. Baton Rouge, 1962.

Paschal, George W. *History of Wake Forest College*. Wake Forest, N.C., 1935.

Patton, James W. "Glimpses of North Carolina in the Writings of Northern and Foreign Travelers, 1783–1860." *North Carolina Historical Review*, XLV (1968), 298–323.

———. "New England Tutors in Granville County, North Carolina, 1845–1850." *North Carolina Historical Review*, XXXVII (1960), 544–67.

———. "Serious Reading in Halifax County, 1860–1865." *North Carolina Historical Review*, XLII (1965), 169–79.

Peace, Samuel T. *"Zeb's Black Baby": Vance County, North Carolina: A Short History*. Henderson, N.C., 1955.

Pearce, T. H. *Franklin County, 1779–1979*. Freeman, S.D., 1979.

Pease, Jane H. "A Note on Patterns of Conspicuous Consumption Among Seaboard Planters." *Journal of Southern History*, XXXV (1969), 381–93.

Pegg, Herbert D. *The Whig Party in North Carolina*. Chapel Hill, 1969.

Pessen, Edward. "How Different from Each Other Were the Ante-bellum North and South?" *American Historical Review*, LXXXV (1980), 1119–48.

———. *Riches, Class and Power Before the Civil War*. Lexington, Mass., 1973.

Peterson, Owen M. "W. W. Avery in the Democratic National Convention of 1860." *North Carolina Historical Review*, XXXI (1954), 463–78.

Phifer, Edward W., Jr. *Burke: The History of a North Carolina County 1777–1920 with a Glimpse Beyond*. Morganton, N.C., 1977.

———. "Certain Aspects of Medical Practice in Ante-bellum Burke County." *North Carolina Historical Review*, XXXVI (1959), 28–46.

———. "Champagne at Brindletown: The Story of the Burke County Gold Rush, 1829–1833." *North Carolina Historical Review*, XL (1963), 489–500.

———. "Money, Banking, and Burke County in the Ante-bellum Era." *North Carolina Historical Review*, XXXVII (1960), 22–37.

———. "Saga of a Burke County Family." *North Carolina Historical Review*, XXXIX (1962), 1–17, 140–47, 305–39.

———. "Slavery in Microcosm: Burke County, North Carolina." *Journal of Southern History*, XXVIII (1962), 137–65.

Phillips, Ulrich B. *American Negro Slavery: A Survey of the Supply, Em-*

ployment and Control of Negro Labor as Determined by the Plantation Regime. New York, 1918.

———. *A History of Transportation in the Eastern Cotton Belt to 1860.* New York, 1908.

———. *Life and Labor in the Old South.* Boston, 1929.

Pinchbeck, Ivy,and Margaret Hewitt. *Children in English Society.* Vol. I of 2 vols. London, 1969.

Pope, Christie Farnum. "Preparation for Pedestals: North Carolina Antebellum Female Seminaries." Ph.D. dissertation, University of Chicago, 1977.

Potter, David M. *The Impending Crisis, 1848–1861.* New York, 1976.

———. *The South and the Sectional Conflict.* Baton Rouge, 1968.

Powell, William S. "Patrons of the Press: Subscription Book Purchases in North Carolina, 1733–1850." *North Carolina Historical Review,* XXXIX (1962), 423–99.

Prince, B. Otis. *Southern Frinks.* N.p., n.d.

Prost, Antoine. *Histoire de l'enseignement en France, 1800–1967.* Paris, 1968.

Pugh, Jesse F. *Three Hundred Years Along the Pasquotank: A Biographical History of Camden County.* Durham, N.C., 1957.

Pugh, Jesse F., and Frank T. Williams. *The Hotel in the Great Dismal Swamp and Contemporary Events Thereabouts.* Richmond, 1964.

Rabb, Theodore K., and Robert I. Rotberg, eds. *The Family in History: Interdisciplinary Essays.* New York, 1971.

Ramsey, Robert W. *Carolina Cradle: Settlement of the Northwest Carolina Frontier, 1747–1762.* Chapel Hill, 1964.

Rapson, Richard L. "The American Child as Seen by British Travelers, 1845–1935." *American Quarterly,* XVIII (1965), 520-34.

Reed, C. Wingate. *Beaufort County: Two Centuries of Its History.* Raleigh, 1962.

Reinier, Jacqueline Reusser. "Attitudes Toward and Practices of Childrearing: Philadelphia, 1790 to 1830." Ph.D. dissertation, University of California at Berkeley, 1977.

Reniers, Perceval. *The Springs of Virginia: Life, Love, and Death at the Waters, 1775–1900.* Chapel Hill, 1941.

Rich, Robert. " 'A Wilderness of Whigs': The Wealthy Men of Boston." *Journal of Social History,* IV (1971), 263–76.

Rives, Ralph H. "Panacea Springs: Fashionable Spa." *North Carolina Historical Review,* XLII (1965), 430–39.

Roark, James L. *Masters Without Slaves: Southern Planters in the Civil War and Reconstruction.* New York, 1977.

Roberts, B. W. C. "Cockfighting: An Early Entertainment in North Carolina." *North Carolina Historical Review,* XLII (1965), 306–374.

Roberts, David. *Paternalism in Early Victorian England.* New Brunswick, N.J., 1979.

Robinson, Blackwell P. "Willie Jones of Halifax." *North Carolina Historical Review*, XVIII (1941), 1–26.

Rogers, Lou. *Tar Heel Women*. Raleigh, 1949.

Rogers, Tommy W. "The Great Population Exodus from South Carolina, 1850–1860." *South Carolina Historical Magazine*, LXVIII (1967), 14–21.

Rosenberg, Charles E., ed. *The Family in History*. Philadelphia, 1975.

Rossi, Alice S. "Naming Children in Middle Class Families." *American Sociological Review*, XXX (1965), 499–513.

Rossi, Alice S., Jerome Kagan, and Tamara K. Hareven, eds. *The Family*. New York, 1978.

Rothstein, Morton. "The Antebellum South as Dual Economy: A Tentative Hypothesis." *Agricultural History*, XLI (1967), 373–84.

Rubenstein, William D. "Men of Property: The Wealthy in Britain, 1809–1939." Ph.D. dissertation, Johns Hopkins University, 1975.

Rubin, Julius. "Limits of Agricultural Progress in the Nineteenth Century South." *Agricultural History*, XLIX (1975), 362–73.

Rulfs, Donald J. "The Ante-Bellum Professional Theater in Raleigh." *North Carolina Historical Review*, XXIX (1952), 344–58.

Salley, Katherine B., ed. *Life at St. Mary's*. Chapel Hill, 1942.

Sanders, Charles Richard. *The Cameron Plantation in Central North Carolina (1776–1973) and Its Founder, Richard Bennehan*. Durham, N.C., 1974.

Saum, Lewis O. "Death in the Popular Mind of Pre–Civil War America." *American Quarterly*, XXVI (1974), 477–95.

Scarborough, William K. *The Overseer: Plantation Management in the Old South*. Baton Rouge, 1966.

Scholten, Catherine M. " 'On the Importance of the Obstetrick Art': Changing Customs of Childbirth in America, 1760 to 1825." *William and Mary Quarterly*, 3rd ser., XXXIV (1977), 426–45.

Scott, Anne Firor. *The Southern Lady: From Pedestal to Politics, 1830–1930*. Chicago, 1970.

———. "Woman's Perspective on the Patriarchy in the 1850s." *Journal of American History*, LXI (1974), 52–64.

Scott, Joan W., and Louise A. Tilly. "Women's Work and the Family in Nineteenth Century Europe." *Comparative Studies in Society and History*, XVII (1975), 36–64.

Segalen, Martine. *Nuptialité et alliance: Le Choix du conjoint dans une commune de l'Eure*. Paris, 1972.

Sellers, Charles G., Jr. "Old Mecklenburg and the Meaning of the American Experience." *North Carolina Historical Review*, XLVI (1969), 142–56.

———, ed. *The Southerner as American*. Chapel Hill, 1960.

Seward, Rudy Ray. *The American Family: A Demographic History*. Beverly Hills, Calif., 1978.

Shalhope, Robert E. "Race, Class, Slavery and the Antebellum Southern Mind." *Journal of Southern History*, XXXVII (1971), 557–74.

Shingleton, Roger G. "The Utility of Leisure: Game as a Source of Food in the Old South." *Mississippi Quarterly,* XXV (1972), 429–45.

Shinoda, Yasuko. "Land and Slaves in North Carolina in 1860." Ph.D. dissertation, University of North Carolina, 1971.

Shorter, Edward. *The Making of the Modern Family.* New York, 1975.

Shugg, Roger. "Survival of the Plantation System in Louisiana." *Journal of Southern History,* III (1937), 311–25.

Sides, Sudie Duncan. "Southern Women and Slavery." *History Today,* XX (1970), 54–60, 124–30.

———. "Women and Slaves: An Interpretation Based on the Writings of Southern Women." Ph.D. dissertation, University of North Carolina, 1969.

Siegel, Fred Fein. "A New South in the Old: Sotweed and Soil in the Development of Danville, Virginia." Ph.D. dissertation, University of Pittsburgh, 1978.

Sitterson, J. Carlyle. "Economic Sectionalism in Antebellum North Carolina." *North Carolina Historical Review,* XVI (1939), 134–46.

———. *The Secession Movement in North Carolina.* Chapel Hill, 1939.

Sklar, Kathryn Kish. *Catherine Beecher: A Study in American Domesticity.* New Haven, 1973.

Skolnik, Arlene. "The Family Revisited: Themes in Recent Social Science Research." *Journal of Interdisciplinary History,* V (1975), 703–719.

Slater, Miriam. "The Weightiest Business: Marriage in an Upper-Gentry Family in Seventeeth Century England." *Past and Present,* LXXII (1976), 25–54.

Smith, Alfred G. *Economic Readjustment of an Old Cotton State: South Carolina, 1820–1860.* Columbia, S.C., 1958.

Smith, Bonnie G. *Ladies of the Leisure Class: The Bourgeoises of Northern France in the Nineteenth Century.* Princeton, 1981.

Smith, Daniel Blake. *Inside the Great House: Planter Family Life in Eighteenth-Century Chesapeake Society.* Ithaca, N.Y., 1980.

Smith, Daniel Scott. "Child Naming Patterns and Family Structure Change: Hingham, Massachusetts, 1640–1860." *Newberry Papers in Family and Community History,* No. 76–5.

———. "Family Limitation, Sexual Control, and Domestic Feminism in Victorian America." *Feminist Studies,* I (1973), 40–57.

———. "Parental Power and Marriage Patterns: An Analysis of Historical Trends in Hingham, Massachusetts." *Journal of Marriage and the Family,* XXXV (1973), 419–28.

Smith, Daniel Scott, and Michael Hindus. "Premarital Pregnancy in America, 1640–1971: An Overview and Interpretation." *Journal of Interdisciplinary History,* V (1975), 537–70.

Smith, Julia Floyd. *Slavery and Plantation Growth in Ante-bellum Florida, 1821–1860.* Gainesville, Fla., 1973.

Smith, Stuart, and Claiborne T. Smith. *The History of Trinity Parish, Scotland Neck and Edgecombe Parish, Halifax County.* Durham, N.C., 1955.

Smith-Rosenberg, Carroll. "The Female World of Love and Ritual: Relations Between Women in Nineteenth Century America." *Signs*, I (1975), 1–29.

Soltow, Lee. "Economic Inequality in the United States in the Period from 1790 to 1860." *Journal of Economic History*, XXXI (1971), 822–39.

———. *Men and Wealth in the United States, 1850–1870.* New Haven, 1975.

———. *Patterns of Wealthholding in Wisconsin Since 1850.* Madison, 1971.

Spring, David. "Aristocracy, Social Structure and Religion in the Early Victorian Period." *Victorian Studies*, VI (1963), 261–80.

———. *The English Landed Estate in the Nineteenth Century: Its Administration.* Baltimore, 1963.

———, ed. *European Landed Elites in the Nineteenth Century.* Baltimore, 1977.

Spring, Eileen. "The Settlement of Land in Nineteenth Century England." *American Journal of Legal History*, VIII (1964), 209–223.

Sprunt, James. *Chronicles of the Cape Fear River.* Raleigh, 1914.

———. *Tales and Traditions of the Lower Cape Fear, 1661–1896.* Wilmington, N.C., 1896.

Stampp, Kenneth M. *The Peculiar Institution: Slavery in the Antebellum South.* New York, 1956.

Standard, Diffee W., and Richard W. Griffin. "The Cotton Textile Industry in Ante-Bellum North Carolina." *North Carolina Historical Review*, XXIV (1947), 15–35, 131–64.

Starling, Robert B. "The Plank Road Movement in North Carolina." *North Carolina Historical Review*, XVI (1939), 1–22, 147–73.

Starobin, Robert S. *Industrial Slavery in the Old South.* New York, 1970.

———. "Privileged Bondsmen and the Process of Accommodation: The Role of Houseservants and Drivers as Seen in Their Own Letters." *Journal of Social History*, V (1971), 46–70.

Steel, Edward M., Jr. *T. Butler King of Georgia.* Athens, Ga., 1964.

Stone, Lawrence. *The Family, Sex and Marriage in England, 1500–1800.* New York, 1977.

Stowe, Steven Mac. "All the Relations of Life: A Study in Sexuality, Family, and Social Values in the Southern Planter Class." Ph.D. dissertation, State University of New York at Stony Brook, 1979.

———. " 'The *Thing*, Not Its Vision': A Woman's Courtship and Her Sphere in the Southern Planter Class." *Feminist Studies*, IX (1983), 113–30.

Strong, Bryan. "Toward a History of the Experiential Family: Sex and Incest in the Nineteenth Century Family." *Journal of Marriage and the Family*, XXXV (1973), 457–66.

Sussman, Marvin B. "Parental Participation in Mate Selection and Its Effects upon Family Continuity." *Social Forces*, XXXII (1953), 76–81.

———, ed. *Sourcebook in Marriage and the Family.* Boston, 1974.

Takaki, Ronald T. *A Pro-Slavery Crusade: The Agitation to Reopen the African Slave Trade.* New York, 1971.

Taylor, Rosser H. *Antebellum South Carolina: A Social and Cultural History.* Chapel Hill, 1942.

————. "The Gentry of Antebellum South Carolina." *North Carolina Historical Review,* XVII (1940), 114–31.

————. "Humanizing the Slave Code of North Carolina." *North Carolina Historical Review,* II (1925), 323–31.

————. *Slaveholding in North Carolina: An Economic View.* Chapel Hill, 1926.

Taylor, William R. *Cavalier and Yankee: The Old South and American Character.* New York, 1961.

————. "Toward a Definition of Orthodoxy: The Patrician South and the Common Schools." *Harvard Educational Review,* XXXVI (1966), 412–26.

Thernstrom, Stephan. *The Other Bostonians: Poverty and Progress in the American Metropolis, 1880–1970.* Cambridge, Mass., 1973.

————. *Poverty and Progress: Social Mobility in a Nineteenth Century City.* Cambridge, Mass., 1964.

Thomas, David. "The Social Origins of Marriage Partners of the British Peerage in the Eighteenth and Nineteenth Centuries." *Population Studies,* XXVI (1972), 99–112.

Thompson, F. M. L. *English Landed Society in the Nineteenth Century.* London, 1963.

Thornton, J. Mills, III. *Politics and Power in a Slave Society: Alabama, 1800–1860.* Baton Rouge, 1978.

Tilly, Louise A., and Joan W. Scott. *Women, Work, and Family.* New York, 1978.

Touchstone, Donald Blake. "Planters and Slave Religion in the Deep South." Ph.D. dissertation, Tulane University, 1973.

Trumbach, Randolph. "The Aristocratic Family in England, 1690–1780: Studies in Childhood and Kinship." Ph.D. dissertation, Johns Hopkins University, 1972.

————. *The Rise of the Egalitarian Family: Aristocratic Kinship and Domestic Relations in Eighteenth-Century England.* New York, 1978.

Turner, Joseph K., and J. L. Bridgers. *History of Edgecombe County.* Raleigh, 1920.

Vinovskis, Maris A. "Marriage Patterns in Mid-Nineteenth Century New York State: A Multivariate Analysis." *Journal of Family History,* III (1978), 51–61.

————. "Mortality Rates and Trends in Massachusetts Before 1860." *Journal of Economic History,* XXXII (1972), 184–213.

Wall, Bennett H. "The Founding of the Pettigrew Plantations." *North Carolina Historical Review,* XXVII (1950), 395–418.

Wall, James W. *Davie County: A Brief History.* Raleigh, 1976.

Wallace, Anthony F. C. *Rockdale: The Growth of an American Village in the Early Industrial Revolution. . . .* New York, 1978.

Walser, Richard. "The Mysterious Case of George Higby Throop (1818–1896); or the Search for the Author of the Novels *Nag's Head, Bertie* and *Lynde Weiss*." *North Carolina Historical Review*, XXXIII (1956), 12–44.
———, ed. *The North Carolina Miscellany*. Chapel Hill, 1962.
Walters, Ronald G. *The Antislavery Appeal: American Abolitionism After 1830*. Baltimore, 1976.
———. "The Family and Antebellum Reform: An Interpretation." *Societas*, III (1973), 221–32.
Watson, Alan D. "Orphanage in Colonial North Carolina: Edgecombe County as a Case Study." *North Carolina Historical Review*, LII (1975), 105–19.
Watson, Elgiva Dundas. "The Pursuit of Pride: Cultural Attitudes in North Carolina, 1830–1861." Ph.D. dissertation, University of North Carolina, 1972.
Watson, Harry L. "Squire Oldway and His Friends: Opposition to Internal Improvements in Ante-bellum North Carolina." *North Carolina Historical Review*, LIV (1977), 105–119.
Webber, Thomas L. *Deep Like the Rivers: Education in the Slave Quarter Community, 1831–1865*. New York, 1978.
Wellman, Manly Wade. *The County of Warren, North Carolina, 1586–1917*. Chapel Hill, 1959.
Wells, Robert V. "Demographic Change and the Life Cycle of American Families." *Journal of Interdisciplinary History*, II (1971), 273–82.
Welter, Barbara. "The Cult of True Womanhood, 1820–1860." *American Quarterly*, XVIII (1966), 151–74.
———. *Dimity Convictions: The American Woman in the Nineteenth Century*. Athens, Ohio, 1976.
Welter, Rush. *The Mind of America, 1820–1860*. New York, 1975.
Wenhold, Lucy L. "The Salem Boarding School Between 1802 and 1822." *North Carolina Historical Review*, XXVII (1950), 32–45.
Wheaton, Robert. "Family and Kinship in Western Europe: The Problem of the Joint Family Household." *Journal of Interdisciplinary History*, V (1975), 601–628.
Wiener, Jonathan M. "Planter Persistence and Social Change: Alabama, 1850–1870." *Journal of Interdisciplinary History*, VII (1976), 235–60.
———. *Social Origins of the New South: Alabama, 1860–1885*. Baton Rouge, 1978.
Williams, James W. "Emigration from North Carolina, 1789–1860." M.A. thesis, University of North Carolina, 1939.
Williams, Max R. "The Foundations of the Whig Party in North Carolina: A Synthesis and a Modest Proposal." *North Carolina Historical Review*, XLVII (1970), 115–29.
Williams, William M. *The Sociology of an English Village: Gosforth*. London, 1956.
———. *A West Country Village, Ashworthy: Family, Kinship and Land*. London, 1963.

Willmott, Peter, and Michael Young. *Family and Kinship in East London.* Baltimore, 1962.

Winchester, Ian. "The Linkage of Historical Records by Man and Computer: Techniques and Problems." *Journal of Interdisciplinary History*, I (1970), 107–124.

Wishy, Bernard. *The Child and the Republic: The Dawn of Modern Child Nurture.* Philadelphia, 1972.

Wohl, Anthony S., ed. *The Victorian Family: Structure and Stresses.* New York, 1978.

Woody, Thomas. *A History of Women's Education in the United States .* 2 vols. New York, 1966.

Wooster, Ralph A. *The People in Power: Courthouse and Statehouse in the Lower South, 1850–1860.* Knoxville, 1969.

————. *Politicians, Planters and Plain Folk: Courthouse and Statehouse in the Upper South, 1850–1860.* Knoxville, 1975.

————. "Wealthy Texans, 1860." *Southwestern History Quarterly*, LXXI (1967), 163–80.

Wright, Carroll D., and William C. Hunt. *The History and Growth of the United States Census.* Washington, D.C., 1900.

Wright, Gavin. *The Political Economy of the Cotton South: Households, Markets and Wealth in the Nineteenth Century.* New York, 1978.

Wrigley, E. A. *Population and History.* New York, 1969.

Wyatt-Brown, Bertram. "The Ideal Typology and Antebellum Southern History: A Testing of a New Approach." *Societas*, V (1975), 1–29.

Yasuba, Yasukichi. *Birth Rates of the White Population in the United States, 1800–1860.* Baltimore, 1961.

Yoder, Paton. "Private Hospitality in the South, 1775–1850." *Mississippi Valley Historical Review*, XLVII (1960), 419–33.

Index

DATE DUE		